THE IMPACT AGENDA

Controversies, Consequences and Challenges

Katherine E. Smith, Justyna Bandola-Gill,
Nasar Meer, Ellen Stewart and Richard Watermeyer

P

First published in Great Britain in 2020 by

Policy Press
University of Bristol
1-9 Old Park Hill
Bristol
BS2 8BB
UK
t: +44 (0)117 954 5940
pp-info@bristol.ac.uk
www.policypress.co.uk

North America office:
Policy Press
c/o The University of Chicago Press
1427 East 60th Street
Chicago, IL 60637, USA
t: +1 773 702 7700
f: +1 773-702-9756
sales@press.uchicago.edu
www.press.uchicago.edu

British Library Cataloguing in Publication Data
A catalogue record for this book is available from the British Library

Library of Congress Cataloging-in-Publication Data
A catalog record for this book has been requested

ISBN 978-1-4473-3987-8 paperback
ISBN 978-1-4473-3985-4 hardcover
ISBN 978-1-4473-3988-5 ePub
ISBN 978-1-4473-3986-1 ePdf

Cover design by Clifford Hayes
Front cover image: Explosion of a filament light bulb
© Copperpipe / Freepik
Printed and bound in Great Britain by CPI Group (UK) Ltd,
Croydon, CR0 4YY
Policy Press uses environmentally responsible print partners

Contents

List of figures, tables and boxes   iv

List of abbreviations   v

Notes on authors   vi

Acknowledgements   viii

1   Introduction: critical reflections on research impact   1

2   The rise of research impact   13

3   Debating the UK impact agenda   27

4   Do experiences and perceptions of research impact vary by discipline?   63

5   Impact on whom? Contrasting research impact with public engagement   99

6   Public intellectualism and the impact agenda: international perspectives   115

7   Academic life in the impact vanguard: the view from knowledge exchange organisations   137

8   Looking back: evolving public health perspectives on research impact   161

9   Telling tales of impact: as seen through the eyes of user assessors   183

10   Conclusion: what would an evidence-informed impact agenda involve?   195

Index   231

List of figures, tables and boxes

Figures

2.1	Timeline of key developments in the emergence of research impact in the UK	18
3.1	Time, attribution, impact	32
3.2	'Impact ladder': significance versus demonstrability	32
4.1	Chubb's 'two-by-two' cultures of research impact	66
4.2	The 'upside-down' pyramid of impact	85
5.1	The main external audiences described by different disciplines	112

Tables

1.1	Summary of the disciplinary context of the twenty-four participants who contributed to the qualitative data employed in Chapters 4 and 5	9
3.1	Penfield et al's (2014) account of the strengths and limitations of four approaches to capturing research impact for assessment	37
4.1	A summary of Chowdhury and colleagues' (2016) account of the contrasting forms of impact preferred in different disciplines, based on REF2014 impact case studies	65
7.1	Stakeholder engagement in strategic priorities of the UK research councils	141
7.2	Knowledge brokers' perceived differences between impact in practice and impact as assessed in REF	155
8.1	Creative adapters' concerns with, and management of, the UK's research impact agenda	174

Box

8.1	Summary of participant suggestions for improving the use and impact of health inequalities research in the UK that are consistent across two studies (Petticrew et al, 2004; Smith, 2013)	163

List of abbreviations

AHRC	Arts and Humanities Research Council (UK)
BBSRC	Biotechnology and Biological Sciences Research Council (UK)
EPSRC	Engineering and Physical Sciences Research Council (UK)
ESRC	Economic and Social Research Council (UK)
HEFCE	Higher Education Funding Council for England
MRC	Medical Research Council (UK)
NCPPE	National Coordinating Centre for Public Engagement
NERC	Natural Environment Research Council
RAE	Research Assessment Exercise (a reviewing exercise undertaken approximately every five years, between 1986 and 2008, on behalf of the UK's higher education funding councils to evaluate the quality of research undertaken by British higher education institutions. The results informed the distribution of block research funding from the UK government)
RCUK	Research Councils UK (an umbrella organisation that coordinated the UK's seven research funding councils from 2002 until 2018)
REF	Research Excellence Framework (the successor to the RAE, introduced for the review in 2014 and upcoming again in 2021. The key difference between the RAE and the REF was the incorporation of impact case studies to assess the impact of research (as well as its quality)
STFC	Science and Technology Facilities Council
UKBA	UK Border Agency
UKRI	UK Research and Innovation (quasi-autonomous non-governmental organisation created in 2018, replacing the Research Councils UK, RCUK, and some functions of HEFCE, the Higher Education Funding Council for England)

Notes on authors

Justyna Bandola-Gill is a Postdoctoral Researcher in the School of Social and Political Science, University of Edinburgh. She is currently working on the ERC-funded grant METRO, examining international organisations and the rise of a global metrological field. Justyna works at the intersection of science and technology studies and public policy. Her research interests include knowledge politics and policies (including the research impact agenda), evidence-based policymaking, evidence use and the co-production of knowledge, and measurement and quantification in public policy. Recent publications include a 2019 *Science and Public Policy* article, 'Between Relevance and Excellence? Research Impact Agenda and the Production of Policy Knowledge'.

Nasar Meer is a Professor of Race, Identity and Citizenship in the School of Social and Political Sciences at the University of Edinburgh, a Royal Society of Edinburgh Research Fellow, and Principal Investigator of the H2020 funded Governance and Local Integration of Migrants and Europe's Refugees (GLIMER). His principal research interests are questions of unity and diversity (specifically in relation to race, migration, nationhood and citizenship), public intellectuals and academic-media dynamics. Nasar is Editor-in-Chief of the interdisciplinary journal, *Identities: Global Studies in Culture and Power*. His recent publications include *Whiteness and Nationalism* (an edited collection with Routledge, forthcoming in 2020).

Katherine E. Smith is Professor of Public Health Policy at the University of Strathclyde's School of Social Work and Social Policy. Her principal research interests are the dynamics of, and influences on, policy change, the interplay between evidence, expertise, policy and practice, and public health (especially health inequalities). Her publications include the monograph *Beyond Evidence-Based Public Health Policy: The Interplay of Ideas* (Palgrave Macmillan, 2013) and a British Medical Association award-winning edited collection, *Health Inequalities: Critical Perspectives* (Oxford University Press, 2016). She is Co-Editor-in-Chief of *Evidence & Policy* and Co-Editor of the book series *Palgrave Studies in Science, Knowledge & Policy*.

Ellen Stewart is a Chancellor's Fellow in Social Studies of Health and Medicine at the University of Edinburgh, where she works at the intersection of medical sociology, social policy and public administration. Ellen is an Associate Director of SKAPE (the Centre for Science Knowledge and Policy at Edinburgh) and Associate Lead for Beyond Engagement in the Centre for Biomedicine, Self and Society. Ellen's principal research interests concern how health systems accommodate and negotiate different forms of 'lay' and 'expert' knowledge, including demands for public engagement and evidence-based policy. Her publications include the monograph *Publics and Their Health Systems* (Palgrave Macmillan, 2016).

Richard Watermeyer is Professor of Higher Education in the School of Education at the University of Bristol and is a sociologist of educational policy, practice and pedagogy. His research is predominantly concerned with a sociological analysis of change in higher education as motivated and framed by currents of, and challenges to, global capitalism and (the weakening of) its policy incantations. He is especially well known for his internationally comparative and critical analyses of public engagement and societal impact generation as valorised academic functions. He is the author of *Competitive Accountability in Academic Life: The Struggle for Social Impact and Public Legitimacy* (Edward Elgar, 2019); co-editor of *Pedagogical Peculiarities: Conversations at the Edges of Teaching and Learning in Higher Education* (Sense Publishers, 2018); and is principal editor of the *Handbook on Academic Freedom* (Edward Elgar, 2020).

Acknowledgements

First and foremost, we want to thank and acknowledge the huge number of interviewees and focus group participants who contributed to the research reported in this book. We would also like to acknowledge the research funding support that underpinned the various research projects from which this book draws. This includes research supported by the following sources: the British Sociological Association (Meer), the ESRC (PTA-037-27-0181 and ES/K001728/1, Smith), the UK Society for Research into Higher Education (Watermeyer) and the University of Edinburgh (Bandola-Gill and Smith).

1

Introduction: critical reflections on research impact

One of the most significant changes to have taken place during our collective time working at UK universities has been the rise of the 'impact agenda'. Fifteen years ago, few academics had heard of, or were using, the term 'research impact'. Back then, the contribution of academic work beyond universities was often only of concern to applied disciplines or to individual academics with an inclination towards achieving external engagement and influence. Institutional support for undertaking externally facing work was variable and funding opportunities generally limited. In that context, external engagement and impact were rarely core to academic job descriptions or promotion criteria.

All of this has changed. Working as an academic in UK universities today means that expectations and opportunities to engage with external audiences are higher, and more widespread, than they have ever previously been. Multiple external funding schemes relating to knowledge exchange activities, public engagement and research impact have emerged, and most of the large grant schemes require applicants to provide detailed information about the likely non-academic beneficiaries, the likely impacts and/or public engagement plans. Most UK universities have introduced internal mechanisms to support research impact, including internal funding opportunities (the extent to which these initiatives can narrow the scope of engagement as part of strategic efforts to meet new performance measures is an issue we consider in this book). Many UK universities have also invested in new roles and centres that focus specifically on knowledge exchange and impact, with a view to both achieving grant income and performing well in the Research Excellence Framework (REF), which informs core research funding allocations to UK universities and which includes a focus on research impact assessment. Indeed, there now exists something of an 'impact industry' in the UK. The implications of this agenda affect not only research income but also prestige (Williams and Grant, 2018). It is increasingly hard to imagine university managers conceiving of permanent academic posts that do not include some expectations of outward-facing work, in the

1

pursuit of both grant income and highly sought-after REF impact case studies.

For academics with a commitment to effecting 'real-world' change, and working collaboratively with members of the public, policymakers, activists, businesses or practitioners, some of these changes feel very welcome. Indeed, the increased emphasis on research impact has been cautiously welcomed by some (e.g. London School of Economics Public Policy Group, 2011; Pain et al, 2011; Pettigrew, 2011), or at least accepted as inevitable (Bornmann, 2012). Others are supportive of the fundamental premise that academics ought to be encouraged to engage with external audiences and to account for the societal value of their work, especially that which is funded via the public purse or charitable sources (see, for example, Pettigrew, 2011). Some have noted the new skills and entrepreneurship that a focus on impact is engendering (Salter et al, 2010), while others still have suggested that the new resources and institutional support for research impact might increase opportunities to engage a wider range of audiences in research (e.g. Pain et al, 2011; MacDonald, 2017) and perhaps generally improve the status of, and support for, public engagement work (e.g. Watermeyer, 2012).

However, changes of this nature and scale inevitably bring challenges as well as opportunities. While some academics feel more supported to undertake the externally facing work they always wanted to do, or have newly discovered a propensity for, others feel the kind of work that motivated them to enter academia is now being sidelined in favour of that with more immediate, obvious or 'sellable' impacts. The kinds of work that academics have suggested is under threat in UK universities include curiosity-driven, 'blue skies' research, theoretically oriented intellectual work (which may not always require external funding but which certainly requires institutional support and desk time), critical analyses of external activities (e.g. of policy decisions and trajectories) and more broadly a dissenting type of public intellectualism (for examples of critical voices, see Chapter 5 and also Back, 2015; Chubb, 2017; Hammersley, 2014; Holmwood, 2011a; Oancea, 2013; Slater, 2012; Watermeyer, 2019).

This is no small threat. For some commentators, the UK's impact agenda represents a fundamental challenge to the role that universities have traditionally played, and in their view should play, in society; a challenge to the 'academic freedom and institutional autonomy [that give universities] the freedom to critique the moronic machinations of democracy' (anonymous, 2008, cited in Hofmeyr, 2008). From this perspective, the impact agenda is no less than a threat to academics' ability to contribute to social justice and critical citizenship (see Harris, 2005; Giroux and Myrsiades, 2001) and an opponent of curiosity-driven, 'intrinsic' research (McCowan, 2018).

Few have embraced UK articulations of how to incentivise and measure research impact wholeheartedly, but among those who appear broadly supportive there is a belief that an emphasis on impact can enable fruitful engagement with a range of potential beneficiaries, via the co-production of knowledge with government departments (Sasse and Hadden, 2018) and others, such as local communities (e.g. Pain et al, 2011), businesses or the wider public (Watermeyer, 2012). However, Watermeyer's interview-based study of research centre directors working in a social science setting found that most participants 'understood the impact of their work in relation to interactions with government and their ability to influence policy and policymakers' (Watermeyer, 2014: 364). Reflecting this, multiple commentators based in the social sciences (including some of us) have argued that an increasing emphasis on a need to be 'policy relevant' constrains the ability of social scientists to undertake critical, theoretical and longer-term research (e.g. Collini, 2009; Slater, 2012; Smith et al, 2011). In this chapter, we suggest that the origins and motivations for efforts to promote research impact in the UK help explain this perception. Later chapters return to this issue, exploring how perceptions regarding common target audiences for impact appear to vary with academic discipline and research topic.

For now, we take the following premises as our starting point: there is a widely held view that a series of reforms in the higher education funding landscape in the UK over the past fifteen years collectively constitute a new 'research impact agenda'; this agenda is innovative and is changing academic working lives and practices in UK universities; this, in turn, is informing the kinds of work that is supported and the kinds of academics who are appointed and promoted; and the UK's experimental approaches to research impact are being closely observed by a number of high-income countries with an interest in ensuring academic work is used beyond academia. In this book, we draw on our collective experiences as academics working in UK universities living through, and researching, these changes. We bring together our various empirical data and analyses to assess the controversies, consequences and challenges of the current UK approach to incentivising, assessing and rewarding research impact. We were inspired to write this book together for the following reasons:

1. We are part of the system that we are critically reflecting upon: as academics who peer-review grant applications and research outputs, and (in some cases) contribute to institutional preparations for the upcoming REF. As Chubb (2017) notes, academics are complicit in, and are shaping, the UK's research impact agenda. Crucially, as Darby makes clear, citing the recent UK REF review – known as the Stern report (Stern, 2016) – 'the evolving impact agenda remains alterable' (Darby, 2017: 231). It is therefore incumbent upon us, as academics participating in these systems that govern academic research and funding, to critically reflect on present and future developments.

2. The impact agenda has prompted a great deal of academic debate but, so far, much of this, including that written by us, has taken the form of individual opinion pieces or empirical research focusing on singular disciplines or particular aspects of research impact. We hope that the more collective, cross-disciplinary and empirically informed basis of this book will enable us to move beyond silos and the deeply contested nature of some of these debates.

3. It is clear, as we discuss in more detail in Chapter 2, that interest in research impact is increasing internationally, and that other countries are looking to the UK experience for lessons that might inform their own approaches to research impact. It is also clear, even to strong proponents of the UK's impact agenda, that the current approach has drawbacks and can (and should) be refined and revised. We therefore use this book as an opportunity to outline what we see as the key lessons to emerge from UK experiences and to put forward some suggestions for alternative approaches.

Plenty has already been written, and is currently being written, about research impact and we try to engage with as much of this emerging literature as we can. However, to help readers navigate this burgeoning literature, we also want to make clear how this book differs from other publications on this topic. We are concerned with the UK's impact agenda as a multifaceted 'whole', which we take to include (i) changes to funding schemes and funding application processes, (ii) changes to academic working practices and career prospects, (iii) changes to the organisation of, and roles within, UK universities, as well as (iv) changes to the process for assessing the research performance of UK universities via REF impact case studies (and, in turn, core research funding). Hence, the focus of this book is broader than an assessment of impact case studies submitted for REF2014. Rather, we see REF impact as one small (albeit significant) part of a much wider agenda, and assessment of the narrower REF approach has already been undertaken by others (e.g. Dunlop, 2018; Greenhalgh et al, 2015; Haux, 2019; Meagher and Martin, 2017; Smith and Stewart, 2017; and Robbins et al, 2017). However, we do engage with various publications reviewing the REF2014 impact case studies (which, indeed, includes work by some of us). Since our interest is in the real-world consequences of the UK's approach to research impact, we do not attempt to comprehensively or thoroughly review the various approaches and frameworks that have been developed as means of assessing research impact. For readers whose interests lie here, this book provides a brief overview of popular approaches and signposts key contributions to the literature. Finally, we must note that, while our data sources incorporate a wide range of perspectives, across multiple academic disciplines, we ourselves are all social scientists which means, inevitably, that the book has a social science 'flavour' to it. In some sections, for example, we focus especially on efforts to promote and reward policy impact, which is one of the most obvious types of impact within the social sciences but not (as we discuss elsewhere in the book – see, especially, Chapter 4) such a core concern to some other disciplines.

We hope that the book will be of interest to academics navigating this new environment, and to those making critical decisions about its future shape. In addition, since the UK is widely considered to be a leader in technologies of research governance and a model for imitation (or, according to a Canadian interviewee who features in Chapter 6, a model for resistance/avoidance), we hope that the book will be of interest to academics and higher education policy communities internationally, at least among those considering the governance and incentivisation of research impact.

Overview of the rest of the book

In Chapter 2, 'The rise of research impact', we chart the origins and emergence of the research impact agenda, noting some of its historical antecedents to explore the motivations and rationales underpinning the various dimensions of the research impact agenda, and the associated expectations that different actors appear to have.

In Chapter 3, 'Debating the UK impact agenda' we build on the brief overview of debates presented here, providing a more in-depth assessment of critiques of the research impact agenda. This includes concerns expressed in the Stern Review and debates regarding the possibility of applying 'metrics' to impact. We then consider how the impact agenda has been defended and amended in the context of these critiques.

In Chapter 4, 'Do experiences and perceptions of research impact vary by discipline?', we widen the focus of the book to explore whether there appear to be any disciplinary patterns among perspectives on, and experiences of, research impact in UK academia. This chapter includes an analysis of whether published perspectives on the impact agenda appear to vary by discipline (as predicted by Nowotny et al, 2001), informed by new focus group and interview data conducted for this book.

In Chapter 5, 'Impact on whom? Contrasting research impact with public engagement', we consider how the concept of research impact has been developed and articulated with respect to two, potentially very different audiences: policymakers and the broader public. This chapter includes an analysis of recent REF and research funder guidance, statements and opportunities relating to these two groups. This chapter also draws on interview data with a range of research funders.

In Chapter 6, 'Public intellectualism and the impact agenda: international perspectives', we use six in-depth interviews with high-profile academics in a range of countries that have an interest in the notion of research impact: Australia, Canada, the UK and the USA. Three of our interviewees are what we term 'public intellectuals', while the other three, each of whom works at the intersection of research and policy, we term 'academic interlocutors'. These perspectives allow us to consider how academics working within and beyond the UK, with some contrasting views about external engagement, view notions of 'public intellectualism', 'relevance' and 'impact'. As we discuss, much depends on the issue and the kind of 'public' academics feel they are working with and speaking to, something that is key to understanding whether public intellectualism may cohere with, as well as diverge from, prevailing impact agendas, and support as well as critique policy agendas.

In Chapter 7, 'Academic life in the impact vanguard: the view from knowledge exchange organisations', we focus on academics working in university-based groups that have been charged with, and funded to achieve, knowledge translation and research impact. These are, we suggest, academics working at the vanguard of the impact agenda, who we might consider as experimental subjects from whom we can learn. This chapter includes a summary of the types of knowledge brokerage roles and organisations that have been created in the UK and the perceived and stated rationales for these new roles and organisations, and an analysis of interview data providing insights into the perspectives of academics working within two such groups. These experiences raise a series of concerns about the way the UK's approach to knowledge exchange and research impact agenda is functioning, especially in terms of the impact on career development.

In Chapter 8, 'Looking back: evolving public health perspectives on research impact', we take a more historical approach, using public health as a case study to explore how views of efforts to stimulate and reward research impact have changed over time. To achieve this, the chapter compares the views of academics interviewed in 2003–7, the run-up to the Research Assessment Exercise (RAE) in 2008, just before the emergence of research impact, with the views of academics working in the same field in 2011–15, who experienced REF2014 and the first attempt to assess impact case studies. This comparison shows that, in this relatively applied research field, an initial scepticism about the likely impact of efforts to promote and reward research impact has given way to a mixture of delight (among academics who feel far more enabled to undertake external-facing work than they once did) and concerns about the broader consequences of this agenda.

In Chapter 9, 'Telling tales of impact: as seen through the eyes of user assessors', we turn our attention to those charged with the task of *judging* the 'reach' and 'significance' of impact claimed by academic researchers in narrative case studies in REF2014. Knowledge pertaining to how the societal and economic impact of scientific research is evaluated is sparse. This is especially true in the context of the UK's national system of research assessment, the REF, in light of the confidentiality and rules of non-disclosure enforced by Research England and UK Research and Innovation (UKRI, a quasi-autonomous non-governmental organisation created in 2018, replacing the Research Councils UK, RCUK, and some functions of HEFCE, the Higher Education Funding Council for England). This chapter therefore draws on a particularly important and under-researched set of perspectives on research impact. It includes an analysis of post-hoc interviews with sub-panel members and a retrospective construction of the experience of evaluating impact in the REF. The focus of these conversations was on the experience – which for many panel members was the first and was in fact a first in the REF – of evaluating impact, and the challenges involved in the application of evaluation criteria and the treatment of evidence in generating credible and robust adjudications. It also explores how impact evaluation in the REF, as one aspect of a wider audit and performance-based culture for higher education, intensifies a (survivalist) compulsion among academics for 'scholarly distinction' and engenders forms of opportunistic behaviours that are paradoxically antagonistic to what many hold to be ideal scientific conduct – particularly in service of the public good.

Bringing the book to a close, Chapter 10, 'Conclusion: what would an evidence-informed impact agenda involve?', seeks to apply the critical perspectives of the previous chapters to provide some pragmatic and practical suggestions for redeveloping the UK research impact agenda. To do this, the chapter summarises the key concerns about, and support for, research impact identified in the book and situates these findings in the context of existing literature/debates. It then draws on suggestions from each of the book's five authors to outline alternative potential approaches to incentivising, monitoring and rewarding research impact, informed by the ideas evident in their respective research and subject areas. The final section of Chapter 10 provides a comparative, reflexive discussion of these different suggestions and makes concrete suggestions where there appear to be areas of consensus.

Data sources employed in the book and authorship of chapters

Throughout the book, we draw on published literature and 'grey' literature documents such as policy statements, guidance documents and blogs (all of which is clearly cited to enable follow-up by interested readers). In Chapters 4–9, we also draw on various interview data sources, as we outline here (reminding readers via footnotes at the start of each chapter).

Chapters 4 and 8 both draw on focus groups and interviews conducted at a Russell Group university by Justyna Bandola-Gill and Kat Smith. This part of the research was funded by a University of Edinburgh School of Social and Political Science Strategic Research Support Fund award specifically for the purposes of this book. In total, this research included two focus groups (involving twelve participants), both of which were jointly facilitated by Justyna and Kat, and twelve individual, semi-structured interviews (ten of which were undertaken by Justyna, two by Kat), covering a range of disciplines, as summarised in Table 1.1.

The focus groups and individual interviews were all digitally recorded and transcribed, before being thematically coded and analysed in NVivo 11 by Justyna and Kat, using a coding framework developed with this book in mind. The framework focused on perceptions of impact, the origins of, and rationale for, the impact agenda in the UK, views about the conceptualisation and theoretical foundations of research impact, accounts of perceived practical implications of the impact

Table 1.1: Summary of the disciplinary context of the twenty-four participants who contributed to the qualitative data employed in Chapters 4 and 5

Research context	Total number of participants	Disciplinary working context/ training, as self-identified by participants
Focus Group 1 (held in November 2016)	7	Informatics (1) Knowledge exchange professional (1) Languages (1) Nursing (1) Public health medicine (1) Political science (1) Psychology (1) Sociology (1)
Focus Group 2 (held in November 2016)	5	Animal science (1) Biomedical science (1) Dentistry (1) Neurology (1) Psychiatry (1)
Individual interviews (held between November 2016 and May 2017)	12	Chemistry (1) History (1) Informatics (1) Law (1) Maths (1) Physics (3) Knowledge exchange professional (1) Education (1)
Total	24	18 disciplines plus knowledge exchange professionals

agenda, including efforts to monitor, incentivise and reward impact (e.g. on day-to-day working practices, funding and other opportunities, institutional support structures, appointments and promotions) and suggestions for changing the current approach.

Chapter 6 draws on interviews from senior academics in Australia, Canada, the UK and the USA, who we categorise as either critical 'public intellectuals' or 'academic interlocutors'. The three interviews with 'academic interlocutors' were undertaken by Kat in 2013–18, funded through a combination of an Economic and Social Research Council (ESRC) Future Research Leaders project and the University of Edinburgh School of Social and Political Science Strategic Research Support Fund mentioned earlier. The three interviews with 'public intellectuals' were undertaken by Nasar in 2015 and were funded by the British Sociological Association.

Chapter 7 draws on doctoral research conducted by Justyna and funded via the Principal's Career Development Scholarship at the University of Edinburgh. The data include fifty-one interviews with academics involved with two publicly funded knowledge exchange organisations as well as policymakers targeted by the organisations. The two organisations were chosen based on their diverse disciplinary focus – genomics and public health – and the timescales, reflecting different points of the development of the impact agenda (funded in 2004 and 2008). The interviewees within the organisations were selected based on their level of association with the organisations (e.g. management, employees and affiliated members), seniority (ranging from postdoctoral research fellows to professors) and their institutional affiliation (e.g. Russell Group vs post-1992 universities). The results discussed in this chapter are part of a larger, grounded-theory-based study.

Chapter 8, which tracks changing academic perspectives over time, draws on interview data gathered by Kat in a series of interviews with academics working in the interdisciplinary areas of public health and health inequalities. This includes a set of thirty interviews with academics undertaken between 2003 and 2006, twenty undertaken between 2011 and 2013 and seven in 2014. Two individuals were interviewed in the first and second set of interviews, totalling fifty-seven interviews with fifty-five academics. Although they all worked on public health and health inequalities, the disciplinary training and institutional settings of these fifty-five academics varied enormously. The most common five disciplinary backgrounds of participants were geography, epidemiology, public health medicine, political science and sociology, though many described themselves as having moved between disciplines during their career or as interdisciplinary researchers. All of the interviewees were themselves research active but they worked across a variety of UK university settings, including longstanding Russell Group[1] universities, the so-called 'plate glass' universities established in the 1960s and post-1992 universities.

Chapter 9 draws on data collected by Richard on the basis of funding provided by the UK Society for Research into Higher Education for a retrospective interview study of the experiences and attitudes of academics and user assessors populating REF2014 disciplinary subpanels, in respect of judging the quality of REF2014 impact case studies. Over forty interviews were conducted with panellists drawn from across social sciences and arts and humanities subdisciplinary panels. However, in Chapter 9 we focus on two of these interviews in particular, as illustrations of wider trends within the data.

Although the final book represents a collective endeavour, there are variations by chapter in our respective input, which we outline here for transparency. Kat was the lead author of Chapters 1, 3 and 8. Justyna was the lead author on Chapters 4 and 7 (the latter of which draws on Justyna's PhD research and received minimal input from the rest of us). Chapter 2 was jointly authored by Kat and Justyna, with Justyna producing the first draft. Ellen was the lead author of Chapter 5 and Nasar the lead author of Chapter 6, with Kat adding interview data and some further analysis to both chapters. Richard was the lead author of Chapter 9. We collectively authored Chapter 10.

Note

[1] The Russell Group is a self-selecting cohort of research-intensive universities in the UK, most frequently recognised as the UK's research elite.

2

The rise of research impact

In this chapter we consider early and evolving rationalisations, the conceptual underpinnings and historical antecedents of an impact agenda in the UK. We note also the salience and exportability of the UK's impact agenda as a policy with growing appeal and traction across the international higher education community.

The emergence of research impact as an idea

The emphasis on research impact has been increasing steadily in the UK since the late 1990s (Cabinet Office, 1999), intensifying in a context of growing frustration that, despite apparently mutual political and academic interest in strengthening the links between research and policy, the actual use of evidence in policy remained limited (e.g. Katikireddi et al, 2011; Husband, 2016; Naughton, 2005). Academic critiques of policy often position responsibility for this dissonance on the policy side, noting the availability of relevant research that appears to have been ignored. Yet, the persistent sense of a large gap between research and policy has also served to intensify longstanding policy concerns about the lack of 'return on investment' from publicly funded research in UK universities.

As Chapter 1 outlines, one means of addressing this concern is that research impact now forms a significant section of grant application processes for all the major UK funding councils. This means that academics are required to set out how the work they will undertake will benefit non-academic audiences and what they will do to help achieve this in advance of undertaking the research, in the knowledge that this part of the application informs reviewer assessment. Meanwhile, in the run-up to 2014, it was decided that the system for nationally appraising university research, REF, would award 20 per cent of overall scores to institutions on the basis of impact case studies. This is rising to 25 per cent in the upcoming REF (REF2021, 2017). Hence, obtaining core research funding (largely distributed on the basis of REF scores) and project-specific research funding from UK research councils are now *both* strongly dependent on academics' abilities to respond adequately to questions about the broader (non-academic) value of their work. These changes represent the contemporary backdrop for this book.

However, as this chapter explores, a range of historical developments informed and shaped this context.

Defining research impact

Defining the UK's research impact agenda can be difficult, but the following features are common in documentary guidance from REF2014, the research councils (AHRC, 2014; ERSC, 2014a, 2014b, 2019; MRC, 2013, 2014; REF, 2011b, 2012; Research Councils UK, 2011, 2014; UKRI, undated) and guidance for REF2021 (e.g. REF2021, 2017):

1. A consensus that researchers should be able to articulate the impact of their research beyond academia, with a particular focus on achieving societal and economic impacts.
2. An assumption (sometimes implicit, sometimes explicit) that this impact will/should be positive (the possibility that research impact could be negative, or even open to interpretation, is almost never articulated).
3. A belief that it is possible for reviewers to comparatively assess academics' accounts of research impact and that it is appropriate to metricise the results.
4. An agreement that the distribution of research funding should, while remaining primarily focused on supporting 'excellent' research, be at least partially reflective of researchers' ability to achieve demonstrable 'impact'.

At the time of going to press, the UKRI (a quasi-autonomous non-governmental organisation created in 2018, replacing the Research Councils UK, RCUK, and some functions of HEFCE, the Higher Education Funding Council for England) definition of impact was:

> the demonstrable contribution that excellent research makes to society and the economy. This occurs in many ways – through creating and sharing new knowledge and innovation; inventing ground-breaking new products, companies and jobs; developing new and improving existing public services and policy; enhancing quality of life and health; and many more. (UKRI website, 2019)

However, multiple empirical studies of how impact is being interpreted by academics and assessors find there are substantial variations, including between disciplines (e.g. King's College London and Digital Science, 2015; Oancea, 2013; Terama et al, 2016), a claim we explore in Chapter 4.

Situating research impact internationally

Although much of this book focuses on the situation in the UK, a forerunner in implementing an assessment framework for impact, it is clear that there is international interest in the idea of incentivising and rewarding research impact (see also Chapter 6). Indeed, the decision to incorporate impact case studies into the UK university research assessment exercise, REF2014, was closely informed by an approach for assessing 'impact' that was developed and trialled (though not, ultimately, implemented) in Australia (Penfield et al, 2014). Williams and Grant (2018) trace the first use of the word 'impact' to denote 'the broader benefits or contribution of research' to a 2005 Australian report summarising these initial ideas (Commonwealth of Australia, 2005) and argue that the research impact agenda has subsequently developed synergistically and iteratively between Australia and the UK. For example, although the approach to assessing 'impact' in Australia's 'Research Quality Framework' had been abruptly dropped within Australia, following a change of government in 2007, an HEFCE-commissioned review of international practices, undertaken by RAND Europe, identified it as one of the most promising options for developing impact assessment within REF (Grant et al, 2010).

The UK's subsequent approaches to implementing measures to assess research impact have, in turn, informed developments within Australia, although there are also emerging differences. For example, the most recent approach to assessing impact being rolled out in Australia distinguishes between 'engagement' and 'impact' and sets out different processes for assessing each (Williams and Grant, 2018), whereas the UK's impact agenda often appears to conflate these concepts (as we discuss further in Chapter 5). The current Australian approach also has a clearer focus than the UK's REF exercise on the mechanisms institutions (universities) use to promote and support impact. Separately, the main government-funded research funder in Australia, the Australian Research Council (ARC), has recently incorporated research impact plans into its grant assessment processes, having sought to learn from UK experiences (Chubb, 2017). It is perhaps worth noting that this shift is being implemented at a time of growing controversy regarding government decisions to block grants awarded by the ARC (Karp, 2018) and to introduce a 'national interest' test for grant funding (Hutchens, 2018).

Interest in research utilisation is also high in Canada (e.g. Lomas, 2000), where major health research funders have placed an increasingly strong emphasis on research utilisation and impact (Tetroe et al, 2008). For example, the Canadian Institute of Health Research (2005) and the Panel on Return on Investment in Health Research (2009) have both set out preferred frameworks for achieving, and indicators for demonstrating, research impact. More broadly, leading Canadian universities are employing 'knowledge brokers' to promote better links between research and the wider world (Phipps, 2011). These shifts lead Eakin (2016) to argue that the funding focus on utility-based research is squeezing the space for more critical, qualitative scholarship.

Meanwhile, in the USA, the National Science Foundation has included societal benefits as part of its grant assessment process since 1997 (De Silva and Vance, 2017) and the past decade has seen a broader trend towards assessing 'societal impacts' in peer-review processes for grant applications (Holbrook and Frodeman, 2011). More recently, key federal agencies and funders in the USA have developed a means of gauging impact known as STAR METRICS (Science and Technology for America's Reinvestment: Measuring the EffecT of Research on Innovation, Competitiveness and Science).[1]

In Europe, Denmark's Frie Forskningsfond (the Danish Council for Independent Research), the Irish Research Council, Science Foundation Ireland and a coalition of research funders in the Netherlands have all begun exploring ways of promoting and assessing research impact (ERiC, 2010; Brereton et al, 2017; Pedersen, 2017). In the Netherlands, this work builds on a longer-standing investment in 'boundary organisations', which sit between research and policy and are intended to facilitate research translation and use (e.g. Bekker et al, 2010; Van Egmond et al, 2011). Regionally, the Seventh Framework Programme of the European Union (FP7) included 'science and society' as a funding theme and supported a 2009–11 research project, involving organisations from France, Spain, the Netherlands and the UK, to examine social impact assessment methods for research and funding instruments. This collaborative project, referred to as SIAMPI, recommended an approach to assessing impact that promotes 'productive interactions' rather than demonstrable impact (i.e. which, in recognition of the serendipity often involved in achieving impact, places more emphasis on evidence of engagement and knowledge exchange work than on the ensuing results) (Spaapen et al, 2011). The follow-up tranche of European research funding, Horizon 2020, placed an emphasis on research that can achieve societal and economic impacts and included some contractual obligations for grant holders, supported by guidance on how to achieve impact (European IPR Helpdesk, 2018). A discussion paper on the likely direction of future EU research funding suggests that research impact considerations should play a greater role (European Commission, 2017).

In this context, the UK's efforts to formally incentivise, monitor and reward research impact, and the consequences of these efforts for academics and the work they produce, is of international relevance and interest. With this in mind, throughout the book, but particularly towards the end, we reflect on the potential lessons emerging from the UK's experiences of incentivising, assessing and rewarding research impact.

Tracing the emergence of research impact as an idea in the UK

As noted already, the emergence of specific incentives to achieve research impact in the UK reflects a much longer-standing concern with the societal return on investment from the public funding of science (Bornmann, 2012; Clarke, 2010; Wilkie, 1991), as well as an awareness of some of the international developments outlined earlier. This recurring policy anxiety has stimulated a variety of institutional arrangements and incentives intended to increase the social and economic value of science in the UK. This includes the creation of the Department of Scientific and Industrial Research in December 1916 (Clarke, 2010), through to the establishment of the research councils (which took place across the twentieth century, starting with the Medical Research Council in 1920 – see Figure 2.1) and, more recently, the UK's research assessment exercises of universities (Wilkie, 1991).

The 1980s represented a key period in which the UK government was fundamentally questioning the value of academic research and significant budgetary cuts were proposed (Bulmer, 1987). It was in this context that the Research Assessment Exercise was initially developed, with the first results published in 1986 (five further rounds took place in 1989, 1992, 1996, 2001 and 2008, before it was replaced by the REF in 2014). In one account of its provenance, MacDonald (2017) repeats a previously cited anecdote from Christopher Ball (then warden of Keble College, Oxford) about a dinner he attended with Peter Swinnerton-Dyer (then chair of the University Grants Committee) and David Phillips (then chair of the Advisory Board for the Research Councils) to explain the origins of the Research Assessment Exercise:

Figure 2.1: Timeline of key developments in the emergence of research impact in the UK

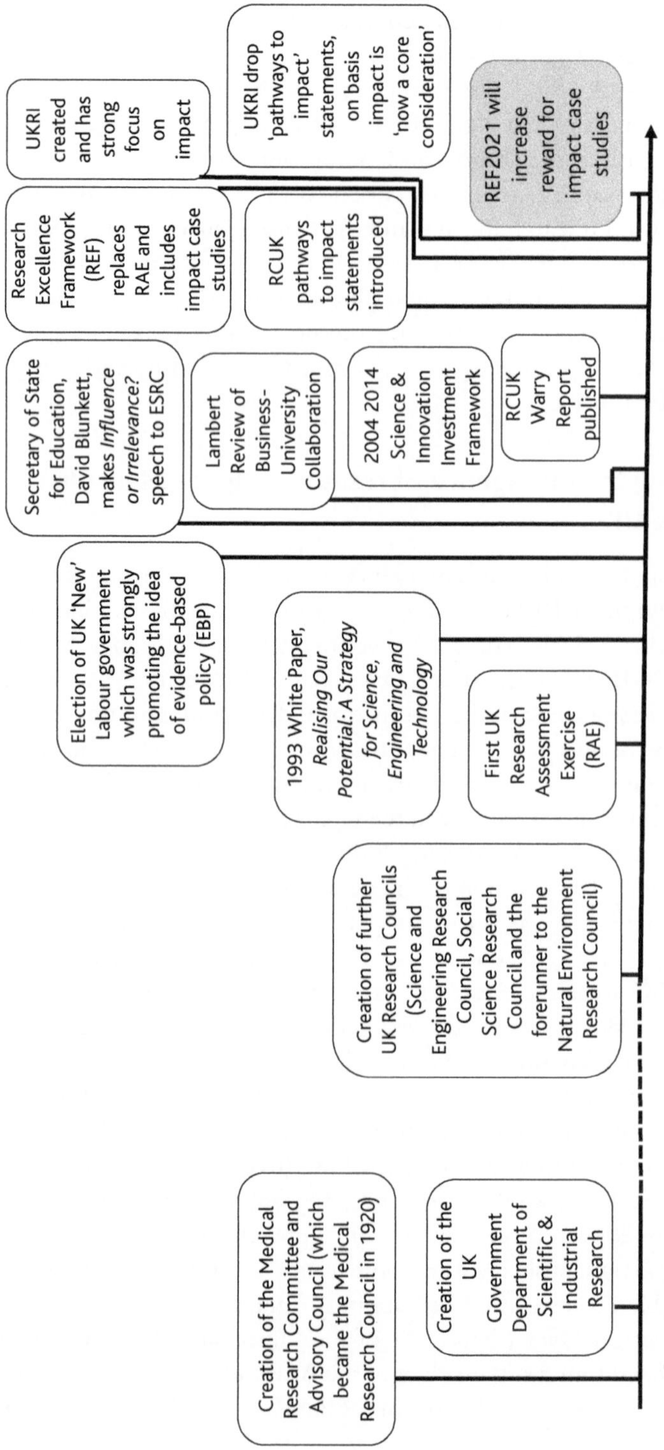

> [W]e used to have dinner together and plan our strategy. One evening Peter said: 'I can no longer defend the funding of universities [...] without real accountability to government' [...] So we discussed it and I suppose at that dinner we invented the research selectivity exercise. (Attributed to Christopher Ball in Kogan and Hanney, 2000: 97–8; cited again in MacDonald, 2017)

Against this backdrop of increasingly explicit research assessment, and greater monitoring of university activity, a 1993 White Paper, published by the Conservative government, *Realising Our Potential: A Strategy for Science, Engineering and Technology* (Cabinet Office, 1993), marked the start of a series of documents concerned with maximising the social and economic benefits of science. Hence, we can see the 1980s as a period in which the foundations of the UK's current approaches to assessing research impact were laid.

In May 1997, a 'New' Labour government was elected on a manifesto that included a clear commitment to taking a more 'evidence-based' approach to policymaking, signalling a deepening policy interest in ensuring the direct policy utility of publicly funded research. Once in power, several further statements expanded on this commitment (e.g. Cabinet Office 1999, 2000), the contents of which suggested that New Labour's notion of evidence-based policy was informed by a simple (some might say naïve), linear conceptualisation of the relationship between research and policy (discussed in more detail below). Within policy settings, specialist advisors, including leading academics, were appointed and research use was further promoted through newly created units, such as the Centre for Management of Policy Studies and the Social Exclusion Unit (see, for example, Lister, 2005). Various documents and initiatives in this era made it clear that the government of the day expected academics working in the UK to become more responsive to policy demands for evidence, with a particularly clear focus on the prospects for economic and social science to help address policy problems that were perceived to have economic and social roots and/or solutions (Smith, 2013).

In a much-cited speech to the ESRC in February 2000, New Labour's David Blunkett (then education and employment secretary) suggested that there was an opportunity to 'transform both the standing of social science research and its relationship to policy development and implementation' (Blunkett, 2000). While Blunkett accepted that 'fundamental blue-skies research that thinks the unthinkable' needed to retain a place in academia, he criticised researchers for addressing 'issues other than those directly relevant to the political and policy debate' and for appearing to 'set out to collect evidence that will prove a policy wrong rather than genuinely seeking to evaluate or interpret its impact' (Blunkett, 2000). Instead, he argued that researchers needed to improve 'the focus, relevance and timeliness of research' in order to make it 'more accessible and intelligible to users', while also accepting a need to change policymakers' attitude to research. Blunkett used this speech to promote a strongly positivist vision of research and research use, in which studies measuring 'the size of the effect of A on B' would be welcomed as 'genuine social science', in contrast to 'worthless correlations based on small samples from which it is impossible to draw generalisable conclusions' (Blunkett, 2000). In sum, the New Labour government's discourse of evidence-based policy involved a rational, instrumental model of research use that demanded a policy-focused, positivist social science (Hodgkinson, 2000).

The approach to incentivising academics to meet these demands for economic and social research reflected New Labour's broader approach to governance at that time, which centred on the establishment of targets and performance indicators. The *2004–2014 Science and Innovation Investment Framework* (HM Treasury, 2004), published by the Treasury in response to a *2003 Lambert Review of Business-University Collaboration* (Lambert, 2003), introduced knowledge transfer targets, called on publicly funded research to do more to meet 'the needs of the economy and public services' and specifically recommended that research council programmes 'be more strongly influenced by and delivered in partnership with end users of research' (HM Treasury, 2004: 6). This recommendation prompted the UK Research Councils to publish Delivery Plans (e.g. ESRC, 2005; MRC, 2005) and to introduce a more systematic approach to knowledge transfer, on which the ESRC took a lead (e.g. ESRC, 2005; ESRC, 2006). In 2005, the ESRC organised its first symposium on impact (Pettigrew, 2011), with various impact-related initiatives being evident in the run-up to this. Although the specific emphasis on the concept of research impact was new, these ESRC activities also appeared to respond to longer-standing concerns within the research council, expressed in a report by an ESRC Commission over a decade earlier (ESRC, 1994).

The subsequent Warry Report (officially titled *Increasing the Economic Impact of Research Councils*), published in 2006, argued that the UK's 'excellent science' was being accompanied by 'poor implementation' and suggested that research councils should be more diligent in their approach to measuring and communicating their impacts. Watermeyer (2016: 203) sums up the stratagem of the Warry Report as follows:

1. 'Influenc[ing] the behaviour of universities, research and Funding Councils in ways that will increase the economic impact of Research Council funding.'
2. 'Promot[ing] more extensive interchange of people and ideas between the research base, industry and public services. Research Councils should influence universities and Funding Councils to reward business interactions when allocating resources.'
3. 'Engag[ing] Government, business and the public services in a wide-ranging dialogue to develop overarching, economically relevant "research missions".'
4. 'Allocat[ing] a substantial part of their funding to programmes relevant to their user communities' (although no mention is made of user communities other than economic stakeholders).

The Warry Report's recommendations combined to trigger a series of changes to assessing funding applications. This informed, first, a brief UK Research Councils experiment with 'impact plans' in 2007–8 and then, following criticism that the requirement to anticipate societal impacts was too prescriptive (see Chubb, 2017), the development of pathways to impact statements and related guidance, from 2009 onwards (Payne-Gifford, 2014). The 'pathways to impact' and 'impact statements' required applicants to UK Research Council funding to outline target beneficiary groups, likely impacts and the plans for achieving these impacts (Phillips, 2010) At the time of going to press, UKRI had just announced plans to discontinue these specific sections since 'impact is now a core consideration throughout the grant application process' (UKRI, 2020).

The efforts by funders to encourage researchers to build research impact into proposals for specific projects have been complemented by efforts to trace and reward research impact through the main university assessment exercise in the UK, REF, as outlined earlier. The decision of the higher education funding councils to introduce the 'impact' case studies in REF2014 appears to have been informed by a proposal in the 2004–14 Science and Innovation Investment Framework to develop a new approach to evaluation (within what was then the RAE) that would provide 'greater reward, and thus stronger incentives, for academics to work on [...] research relevant to users' (HM Treasury,

2004: 11). This, in turn, appears to have been informed by an approach developed and piloted in Australia, as outlined earlier (see Williams and Grant, 2018 for a more comprehensive overview).

The declarations to implement impact as an assessment criterion to the UK REF were first announced in 2009, by the HEFCE:

> The REF should continue to incentivise research excellence, but also reflect the quality of researchers' contribution to public policy making and to public engagement, and not create disincentives to researchers moving between academia and the private sector.[2] (Quoted in HEFCE, 2009)

Following an initial consultation about the possibility of assessing research impact in 2007,[3] HEFCE conducted a second consultation on the impact element of REF in November 2009. This was followed by an impact pilot in 2010, which essentially established the efficacy of the REF's approach to impact assessment. HEFCE (2009) then worked with the UK Research Councils to develop the framework further, particularly in terms of research excellence and impact.

It is a result of these changes that the UK now has the 'dual' approach to incentivising and assessing research impact outlined in Chapter 1. This environment shapes the institutional context for all UK university-based academics (via REF) and the funding landscape for all academics applying for funding from UK Research Councils or the UKRI.

In its final form, REF2014 defined impact as: 'an effect on, change or benefit to the economy, society, culture, public policy or services, health, the environment or quality of life, beyond academia' (REF, 2011b: 31), a definition which remains in place for REF2021 (REF, 2019/01). For both REF2014 and REF2021, Unit of Assessment panels are asked to assess impact case studies on the basis of their "reach and significance" (REF, 2011b: 8; REF, 2019: 90). The REF2021 guidance states that, 'impact includes, but is not limited to, an effect on, change or benefit to':

- the activity, attitude, awareness, behaviour, capacity, opportunity, performance, policy, practice, process or understanding
- of an audience, beneficiary, community, constituency, organisation or individuals
- in any geographic location whether locally, regionally, nationally or internationally. (REF, 2019: 83)

Guidance for REF2021 makes clear, as guidance in REF2014 did, that 'academic impacts' are excluded but, in contrast to REF2014, notes that impacts on students and teaching are considered to be within scope. This is one way in which the definition of research impact appears to be broadening in response to recommendations within a government-commissioned review of the REF (Stern, 2016). The Stern Review, as the report is commonly referred to, highlighted the importance of connections across research and teaching for most UK universities (in which the idea of research-informed teaching is generally held in high regard), arguing: 'How a subject is taught, and what is taught in a discipline could be an important indicator of research impact' (Stern, 2016: 17). Guidance for REF2021 has also been developed around the role of public engagement in research impact (REF, undated), again reflecting a Stern Review recommendation (Stern, 2016).

In sum, the UK's evolving research impact agenda represents an innovative programme of changes to research governance structures and funding streams, with a view to encouraging particular kinds of research and particular kinds of uses and 'impacts'. As Chapter 1 notes, while some academics working in the UK have welcomed this shift, others are concerned about the consequences (see Chapter 3). Our interview data suggest that pockets of resistance are evident, with some academics refusing to engage in institutional efforts to develop REF impact case studies, and others seeking to reshape the meaning of research impact or to draw attention to the deficits of the current approach.

Indeed, in response to the introduction of impact plans by UK Research Councils, a group of nineteen senior academics wrote a letter to *Times Higher Education* arguing strongly against this development and calling for academics to revolt by refusing to peer review these parts of these grant applications (Braben et al, 2009). The letter, which informed a supportive leader article by the then *Times Higher Education* editor on the topic, Mroz (2009), largely focused on arguing that this requirement would curtail UK support for curiosity-driven ('blue skies') research. However, it also argued that these developments were overly bureaucratic and noted that, since the rationale to undertake basic research is usually to address questions for which the answers are not clear, it would be difficult for researchers to know what the results, and therefore the impacts, might be in advance, casting pathways to impact as akin to fortune-telling: '[I]n research worthy of the name, we are not aware of anyone who would be competent at foretelling specific future benefits and therefore in complying with the request in any meaningful manner' (Braben et al, 2009).

On a much larger scale, when it was first announced that REF2014 would include a measure of research impact, a UCU-led[4] petition against the development was signed by 17,570 academics (a number equivalent to a third of the total number of academics returned to the earlier incarnation of the exercise – the 2008 Research Assessment Exercise). Much like the *Times Higher Education* letter (Braben et al, 2009), a key argument in the UCU petition was that it is often difficult to predict which research will create the greatest practical impact, and that curiosity-driven research needed to be protected against efforts to prioritise research that is more obviously impactful in advance.

There have also been some strident responses from individual academics, the following two of which have been particularly widely cited (there are multiple others, especially within the pages of *Times Higher Education*, from 2009 onwards). For example:

> It is astonishing that the ostensibly intelligent and knowledgeable people who are responsible for higher education policy should evince the combination of philistinism and ignorance responsible for the ridiculous and deplorable ideology of impact now being foisted upon us. (Ladyman, 2009: 4).

> Unless these guidelines are modified, scholars in British Universities will devote less time and energy to [deepening understanding] and more to becoming 'door to door' salesmen for vulgarised versions of their increasingly market oriented 'products'. (Collini, 2009: 18–19)

Despite these protestations and criticisms, research impact assessment largely proceeded as planned in REF2014 (with the exception of the reduction from the 25 per cent weighting for impact case studies that HEFCE originally proposed to 20 per cent for 2014).[5] As we note above, it has also become a clearer and more consistent part of UK Research Council funding applications, and achieving impacts (particularly economic impacts) has been a central feature of the UKRI (which sits above the UK Research Councils and which also issues its own calls) since its creation in 2018, with many UKRI-led calls encouraging, and sometimes requiring, collaboration between academics and non-academics. A central component of this has been the Industrial Strategy Challenge Fund,[6] which encourages researchers to work with businesses and to address challenges that have been identified by industry partners, thus increasingly linking impact with the UK's innovation and economic agendas.

Reflecting these changes, the idea that research impact is a core part of academic activity in UK universities feels increasingly institutionalised.

And, while concerns about the consequences of this for academics continue to play out within the pages of academic journals and *Times Higher Education*, Murphy and Sage's (2014) analysis of UK media coverage of the REF found that broader media interest in the issue was limited (with the exception, to a degree, of the left-of-centre *Guardian* newspaper). At this stage, it is unclear how feasible it is for individual academics to resist an agenda so closely intertwined with institutional and research funding, in which broader public interest seems (perhaps understandably) rather limited. Meanwhile, as outlined earlier, other countries are looking to the UK's experiences for research impact assessment insights and inspiration, with Australian, Canadian and European Union funders all signalling their growing interest in this area.

Notes

1. For more details, see: https://www.starmetrics.nih.gov/Star/About.
2. Source: http://www.hefce.ac.uk/news/newsarchive/2009/Grant,letter/ (accessed: 17 March 2016).
3. Source: http://www.ref.ac.uk/about/background/ (accessed: 17 March 2016).
4. UCU, the University and College Union, is a British higher and further education trade union and the largest of its kind in the world.
5. As we note earlier, the weighting for REF impact case studies has risen back up to 25% for REF2021.
6. See https://www.ukri.org/innovation/industrial-strategy-challenge-fund/ for more details.

3

Debating the UK impact agenda

Introduction: key concerns with, and critiques of, the UK's impact agenda

As Chapter 2 began to outline, the announcement of REF's inclusion of impact assessment ignited intense debate among academics. Statements outlining how research impact would be retrospectively assessed via REF appear to have generated particularly widespread concerns. In contrast, responses to the adoption of pathways to impact statements by UK Research Councils and the UKRI have, since Braben et al's (2009) *Times Higher* letter, been comparatively muted. Sociologist John Holmwood has questioned this, since it is in shaping new research that such changes have the potential to have their greatest repercussions for academic activity (though of course, advance knowledge about what REF is trying to measure and reward may also shape research activity):

> Whereas the REF impact agenda is the one that has generated most comment within the academic community, it is the [UK Research Councils'] 'pathways to impact' that should generate most immediate concern. The former is an ex post judgement, whereas the latter seeks to transform the research culture. (Holmwood, 2011b: 14)

Although the majority of voices commenting on the UK's approach to research impact are critical of specific aspects, this does not mean that they disagree with the basic, underlying assumption: that science should be, in some way, beneficial to society. Indeed, the idea that academics should be subject to something like a 'social contract' (Martin, 2011), in which they receive public funds and, in return, provide society with useful innovations, seems to be broadly supported, with some academics themselves articulating a moral or ethical obligation to work towards achieving (socially beneficial) change. For example, Eynon (2012: 2) reflects that researchers have 'always wanted to make a difference', while Smith's research on public health researchers cites multiple examples of academics expressing a desire to achieve impact (see Smith, 2013; see also Chapter 6).

The issues with the UK's research impact agenda that we have identified in existing literature rarely challenge the fundamental premise that academic research and other intellectual work should be socially beneficial. Rather, concerns tend to focus on the potential consequences of current efforts to incentivise, measure and reward research impact in the UK. As we delineate below, despite the key role of the ESRC, the UK Research Council most closely associated with social science, in developing and promoting the UK's impact agenda, the tools and frameworks for assessing research impact appear remarkably uninformed by the wealth of empirical and theoretical work on research and policy processes within the social sciences. Here, we sketch out what we see as ten key areas of concern in existing literature.

Concern 1: the theoretical challenge to research impact

Despite an extensive literature on research–policy relations in sociology, science and technology studies, social policy, political science and public management (among others), only a very narrow range of these contributions appear to have informed the guidance on incentivising, achieving and assessing research impact. Hence, a key critique of the UK's impact agenda is that guidelines and models appear to be based on simplistic, largely discredited ideas about how research can be 'utilised' (Smith and Stewart, 2017; Boswell and Smith, 2017).

Boswell and Smith (2017) argue that the absence of engagement with more sophisticated theories about research use partly reflects the fragmentation of relevant literature and an associated failure to systematically synthesise and compare key contributions across disciplinary fields (a limitation that this book seeks to address). There is an issue of commensurability here since different empirical accounts of research use are often premised on quite different concepts and theories, making comparison, appraisal and synthesis challenging. This is exacerbated by the fact that there is (as yet) no recognised field of research–policy relations, so academic debates on similar questions occur within multiple discrete settings, each approaching the topic with the tools in the literature they have been exposed to (see Oliver and Boaz, 2019). Thus, social scientific accounts of research–policy relations do not speak with one voice, reducing their influence over the public bodies developing impact guidelines.

In their article, Boswell and Smith (2017) seek to advance the debate on impact by setting out four different approaches to theorising research–policy relations, each of which synthesises a larger area of social science research. Each set of theories is categorised according to its core assumptions about the interrelations between the two spheres. The first approach focuses on a 'supply' model of research–policy relations, examining how knowledge and ideas shape policy. The second challenges the idea that research is independent of politics and policy, instead focusing on how political power shapes knowledge. The third approach takes this line further, suggesting that research knowledge and governance are co-produced through an ongoing process of mutual constitution. And the fourth approach offers a radically contrasting account, suggesting that there is no overarching causality between science and politics, but that politics only selectively appropriates and gives meaning to scientific findings.

They go on to argue that current approaches to research impact have been informed by simplistic supply-side models within their first category of 'knowledge shapes policy', despite the fact that such accounts have been widely discredited by theorists of research–policy relations, as well as by many empirical studies of research use. Both the second and fourth accounts suggest that the very idea of trying to incentivise the use of research in policy is flawed. Indeed, on these accounts we should be cautious about adopting systems that reward researchers for influencing policy. From this perspective, such impacts are viewed as spurious, in that their apparent influence is likely to be down to pre-given interests or independent political dynamics; or the result of researchers aligning research questions and approaches to pre-fit political agendas (as we discuss more below). Hence, Boswell and Smith (2017) conclude that, by rewarding researchers for achieving impact via REF, the UK is adopting an arbitrary incentive system that is at best decoupled from research quality, and at worst, threatens the integrity and independence of social science.

For those more sympathetic to the idea of research impact, the first and third theoretical approaches at least offer some potential. Neither method suggests that the current UK approach is likely to achieve its intended goals, however, and both caution against rewarding individual researchers for 'achieving' research impact based on narrow indicators (e.g. citations in policy documents). The enlightenment model (which forms part of the first theoretical approach outlined) suggests that research impact involves subtle, incremental and diffuse ideational adjustments over a long period of time, which are generated by a wide range of research insights rather than specific individual findings. This suggests that a system for rewarding impact should not focus on individual research projects or groups and their linear effects on particular policies. Rather, impact frameworks should reward collaborative endeavours that build incrementally on a wider body of work; that develop longer-term relationships with a range of non-academic audiences (not only policymakers and other 'elites'); and that may bring about subtle conceptual shifts, rather than clearly identifiable policy changes. This in turn implies the need for more complex research designs and methodologies for charting such influence over a far longer time frame, avoiding incentives to over-claim credit for particular groups or projects. The notion of co-production similarly suggests the need for more in-depth, ethnographic or process-tracing methods for reconstructing the complex relationships between research and policy. A focus on co-production additionally calls attention to the idea that social science can itself affect the social and political world, imagining and enacting new social problems; an idea that stretches rather beyond current approaches to research impact.

Taking as their focus the growing 'how to' guides for academics interested in achieving policy impact, Oliver and Cairney (2019) likewise highlight that much of this available guidance lacks an empirical or theoretical basis, appearing to be uninformed by available bodies of work on policymaking and evidence use. They argue that this leads to 'significant misunderstandings, and advice which can have potentially costly repercussions for research, researchers and policy' (Oliver and Cairney, 2019: 8). They also note that such advice tends to focus on what individuals can do, despite evidence (in the existing empirical and theoretical literature) that engagement between research and policy tends to be driven by more systemic factors.

In sum, the UK's current approach to research impact does not appear to be grounded in available (empirically informed) theoretical conceptualisations of the various ways in which research, and broader academic work, influence activities and ideas beyond academia. The differences suggest that the UK's approach may: (i) encourage academics to engage in activities that are unlikely to achieve research impact; (ii) mistakenly reward academics and institutions for achieving 'impact' that is actually a result of other, serendipitous or interest-based factors; (iii) fail to capture particular forms of 'impact' (e.g. more conceptual influences); (iv) facilitate external interests and politics in shaping academic work (politicising research); and (v) ignore the potential for research to imagine and enact new social problems (rather than responding to existing problems). Several of these concerns are, indeed, evident in existing literature, as the remainder of this chapter makes clear.

Concern 2: the problems with demonstrating and attributing 'impact'

As Penfield and colleagues (2014) note, concerns over the attribution of impacts have been raised repeatedly (e.g. The Allen Consulting Group, 2005; Grant et al, 2010). The kinds of questions that have been raised include: (i) can academics adequately demonstrate, and assessors judge, research impacts and academics' role in achieving these? (ii) will accounts of impact sufficiently distinguish between significant and incremental impacts, or between significant and minor roles in achieving impact? (iii) who will be rewarded for the impact of synthesised research outputs? (iv) how, if at all, will the serendipitous nature of impact be reflected in assessing case studies (see Concern 1 for the theoretical underpinnings of this concern and Concern 3 for further discussion)? And (v) does the ease of demonstrating impact vary with the time/significance of impact?

In response to the last question (v), Hughes and Martin (2012) use Figure 3.1 to argue that the ease with which impact can be attributed decreases with time, whereas the impact, or the *effects* of the impact, is likely to increase over time. Figure 3.1 highlights both the basic problem of persuasively demonstrating that impact has been achieved and the fact that there may be a significant time lag between research outputs and ensuing impacts (see Concern 8).

Penfield and colleagues (2014: 26) argue that the problem of attribution 'presents particular difficulties in research disciplines conducting basic research, such as pure mathematics, where the impact of research is unlikely to be foreseen'. They conclude that assessments of impacts in these disciplines need to do more (compared to applied disciplines) to reflect the cumulative nature of the intellectual advances underpinning research impact.

Similarly, Smith and Stewart (2017) use Figure 3.2 to explain why the ease of demonstrating policy impacts may decrease with the significance of the impacts achieved. This reflects the propensity of social science to inform what Weiss (1980) called 'conceptual' change or 'knowledge creep' (see discussion of the 'enlightenment' function of research in Concern 1 and also Davies et al, 2005). As Pettigrew (2011: 350–1) explains, 'conceptual impacts can […] include reframing policy issues in order that new policy options and pathways to implementation open up or close down in a policy domain. This closing down of policy options through intellectual challenge can be a very important scholarly contribution, especially when robustly evidence based.'

Figure 3.1: Time, attribution, impact

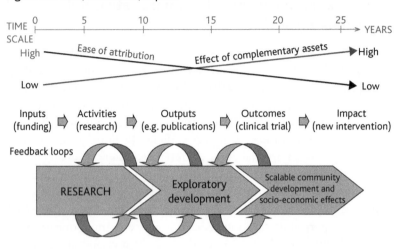

Source: Reproduced from Hughes and Martin (2012).

Figure 3.2: 'Impact ladder': significance versus demonstrability

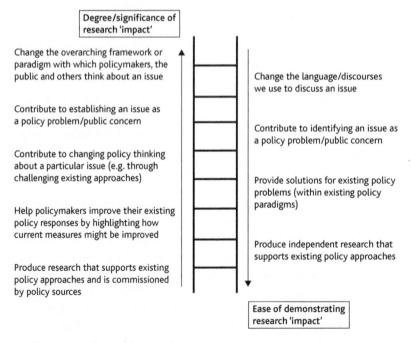

Source: Reproduced from Smith and Stewart (2017).

However, this kind of ideational shift can be far harder to demonstrate than contributions prompting more immediate, incremental changes since changes in fundamental ways of thinking about an issue are not necessarily documented to the same degree as shifts in specific approaches to tackling an issue.

Overall, these various assessments underline concerns put forward by Fielding at an early stage of the research impact agenda's emergence in the UK:

> My sense is that it valorises what is short-term, readily visible and easily measurable. My sense is also that it has difficulty comprehending and valuing what is complex and problematic, what is uneven and unpredictable, what requires patience and tenacity. My sense is that it finds difficulty in distinguishing between levels of change, between what is fairly superficial and what is, to coin another already over-used, increasingly presumptuous phrase 'transformational', between what, in the management literature, is second-order rather than first-order change. (Fielding, 2003: 289)

The fundamental problem is that the UK's approach to assessing research impact (both in research council funding applications and, retrospectively, via the REF) appears to assume a simple, linear relationship between research evidence (see Concern 1) and positive social or policy change (see Concern 6); a relationship that can be easily demonstrated and, therefore, appropriately rewarded (see Concern 3). The reality, as multiple commentators have articulated (e.g. McCowan, 2018; Mhurchú et al, 2017; Oancea, 2013; Smith et al, 2011), and as a wealth of empirical studies demonstrate (see Weiss, 1977 or Smith, 2013 for overviews), is usually far more complex. This poses a major challenge to the idea that research impact can reasonably be captured via short impact case studies in REF. It is notable that Chubb's (2017) participants (academics in Australia and the UK based in a range of disciplines) seemed more comfortable with the term 'knowledge exchange' than 'impact'; a preference that seemed linked to concerns with how to define and assess impact. Chubb (2017) also reports that participants felt that the impact agenda favoured short-termism and implied an overly linear process of innovation and impact.

Concern 3: the difficulty of meaningfully measuring research impact

The perceived problems with the measurement of impact are multiple, reflecting the very obvious problem that stems from trying to measure something that is elusive, complex and context-dependent (see Concerns 1 and 2). Even researchers who are supportive of some of the impact agenda's aims have queried whether the current approach to assessing impact in the UK, via case studies in the REF (an approach informed by the Australian Research Quality Framework – as outlined in Chapter 2), captures impact in a sufficiently meaningful way. For example, an empirical study exploring the impact of developments in research policy on higher education, which drew on email interviews with seventy-one academics specialising in higher education, found that, while 'there was a good deal of support for the idea that research should have impact, serious concerns were raised about how "impact" is conceptualised and measured' (Leathwood and Read, 2012: 4).

To take a more specific example, MacDonald (2017) believes that a REF2014 impact case study that he was involved in, which feedback indicated had been awarded 4★ by assessors, actually achieved very little impact. The underpinning research empirically challenged myths within policy and media debates that some areas of the UK are populated by communities in which there is a 'culture of worklessness', with families experiencing multiple generations who have never worked (e.g. MacDonald et al, 2013; Shildrick et al, 2012). As MacDonald (2017) explains, this research was widely cited, being much discussed in the mass media and policy contexts, including the UK Parliament. Yet, despite this, and the substantial efforts that the researchers involved clearly made to promote their findings, MacDonald (2017) argues that the myths continued to achieve public, media and policy traction, both locally and nationally. This leads MacDonald to conclude that the methods of assessing the research impact in the REF 'can be pollyannaish and simplistic' (MacDonald, 2017: 706), rather than meaningful, at least when it comes to critical social science.

The issue of measurement is important not only because it might be insufficient and/or invalid but also because, as sociological studies of science and metrics have repeatedly demonstrated, measuring something in itself often changes what is being studied/measured (Berman and Hirschman, 2018). Indeed, Martin (2011) argues that introducing the evaluation indicator is more effective in changing the behaviour of the actors to fit the new criteria than it is in helping to achieve the actual goal. In sum, trying to perform well against evaluation criteria concerning research impact guides researchers to ask certain questions or to undertake certain types of scholarship:

> [REF's] framing is currently more likely to encourage geographers to ask 'how can we strategise for maximum impact on users with our research?' rather than 'how can we open up academic knowledge and collaborate with other (non-academic) researchers with shared political goals?' (Pain, 2014: 20)

As soon as any form of measurement is introduced, there are risks that game playing will ensue (particularly in the context of the relatively high value of REF impact case studies for institutions – see Watermeyer, 2016). It is perhaps unsurprising, therefore, that Chubb's (2017) interview-based study with academics in Australia and the UK found that game playing for impact is already occurring. Linked to this, there are risks 'that the forms of measurement that are possible (or are seen to be preferable) end up determining what we understand [...] impact [to be], conditioning our work in practice' (McCowan, 2018: 290).

In this view, debates about how research impact should be measured have distracted attention from the more fundamental question of whether we can meaningfully measure research impact and, if not, whether it makes sense to try: 'Even if it were to be shown that impact can be achieved by universities, and that it were desirable for them to achieve it, there are still significant doubts about our ability to identify, assess and evaluate this impact' (McCowan, 2018: 290).

As outlined in Chapter 2, the approach that the REF employs takes the form of a series of case studies which require a narrative account of impact that links to underpinning research. This kind of case study approach leaves open the decision of whether or not to employ quantifiable indicators of impact. This was deemed preferable to both simpler and cheaper bibliometric approaches, which cannot easily be used to distinguish academic from non-academic impacts (Penfield et al, 2014) and the various more specific frameworks for assessing research impact that are available, including:

- The Payback Framework, developed by Buxton and Hanney (1996), which has been used to assess the impact of health-focused research and which consists of a logic model, seven stages of research and five categories of 'payback' (see Greenhalgh et al, 2016, for a succinct overview).

- The Dutch-led SIAMPI approach of focusing on 'productive interactions' (see Chapter 1) as opposed to assessing subsequent impacts.

There are multiple further approaches to assessing impact in existence and there have been efforts to challenge and/or refine the approach REF takes by drawing on some of these approaches (see, for example, Greenhalgh et al's 2016 review of six established frameworks for assessing the impacts of health research).[1] Penfield and colleagues (2014) outline four basic approaches to capturing research impact for assessment, each of which has strengths and limitations. Table 3.1 broadly summarises Penfield and colleagues' assessment, although their original paper distinguishes between 'metrics' and 'citations', whereas we consider these collectively (since citations are commonly considered in a metricised form). We also supplement this overview with findings from more recent literature:

Penfield and colleagues concluded that the mixed-method case study approach was probably the best available approach to assessing impact at that time since it allows 'a comprehensive summary of the impact within context' (Penfield et al, 2014: 30). This suggests that the approach to assessing research impact within REF2014 and REF2021 is better than many alternatives that have been considered (although we should note that there have been a range of relevant developments since then, particularly in terms of altmetrics). The case study approach is certainly more sophisticated than bibliometric measures and enables a variety of forms of evidence to be employed in the articulation of impact (so REF impact case studies are less restrictive than some frameworks). Nonetheless, Smith and Stewart's (2017) research suggests policy-focused academics often struggle with the tension between their own experience of the interplay between research and policy as complex and almost impossible to influence, and the simplistic and reassuring ways they feel compelled to tell what Dunleavy (2011) has called 'fairy tales' of academic achievements. The hesitation that academics report feeling, combined with the emphasis that a narrative case study approach places on good 'storytelling', help explain why Watermeyer (2019) found that an 'army of impact administrators' were often also involved, resulting in a situation in which some of the academics featuring in REF2014 impact case studies were not even aware of their inclusion. This suggests that some impact case studies are being 'ghost-written' by professionals hired by institutions to promote the achievements of their academic staff. It also points to the emergence of an 'impact industry', with an operational blueprint analogous to what

Table 3.1: Penfield et al's (2014) account of the strengths and limitations of four approaches to capturing research impact for assessment

Approach	Strengths	Limitations
Employing metrics (including, potentially, citations and altmetrics)	• Cost-effective • Enables a comparison of impact against baseline data • Rapid developments in altmetrics (which capture social media citations, etc.) are increasing the availability of impact-relevant metrics • Enables monetisation	• Only captures quantifiable evidence of impacts and may fail to capture qualitative evidence • Metrics have generally been better at capturing academic impact, rather than non-academic impacts and, while some claim altmetrics are changing this, others claim the current value of heterogeneous altmetrics (Haustein, 2016) is limited (Barnes, 2015) • Likely to focus attention towards generating positive metrics rather than delivering real value • If monetised, there are risks this approach will inform attempts to compare the costs/benefits of completely different kinds of research and impact (e.g. artistic events versus health gains)
Employing narratives (e.g. in impact case studies)	• Enables quantitative and qualitative data to be employed • Allows evidence to be contextualised and a story told • Enables assessment in the absence of quantitative data • Allows collation of unique datasets • Preserves distinctive account or disciplinary perspective	• Automated collation of evidence is difficult so this approach is likely to be more resource and time intensive • Incorporating different perspectives and types of data can make it difficult to assess impact comparatively • Potentially rewards those who can write well, and/or afford to pay for external input
Surveys and testimonies	• Can help establish a path from research to impact • Responses could help inform the development of systems to better capture research impact	• Resource intensive • Responses are likely to be hampered if surveys/testimonies are captured retrospectively

Lee (2015) calls the 'public engagement industry', and a prioritisation, at least in the run-up to institutional REF submissions, not merely on the scaffolding of impact generation but its 'storyboarding'.

Donovan's (2019) commentary piece, which she developed on the back of discussions about research impact with colleagues, concurs with the idea that impact case studies are better than current alternatives, but comes with a warning that 'impact fatigue' among academics may lead to what she calls 'metricide'. By this she means an increasing willingness to allow impact to be assessed in more imperfect, metric-based ways, to avoid having to undertake the work involved in developing REF case studies. The financial cost of the mixed-methods case study approach to assessing impact creates a further potential pressure to simplify the approach. Indeed, one of Smith and Stewart's interviewees wryly stated that one consequence of the UK impact agenda has been to make 'people lie more convincingly on grant applications' (Smith and Stewart, 2017: 118). However, for now at least, key reports have recommended the continued used of narrative-based impact case studies that allow for impact to be evidenced in a range of ways (Wilsdon et al, 2015; Stern, 2016).

Overall, while the case study approach to assessing research impact seems better than many of the alternatives, it still has limitations. It is no small feat to persuasively and clearly narrate a tale of impact that can be directly linked to underpinning research evidence and specific impact-related activities within the short space provided in REF impact case study forms. Hence, as Penfield and colleagues (2014) note, it seems likely that case studies may perform better than others simply because they are written more persuasively. So, it is worth noting that key reports from REF2014 chairs raised concerns about variations in the way impact case studies had been written (REF2014 Main Panel A, 2015; REF2014 Main Panel B, 2015; and REF2014 Main Panel C, 2015).

Concern 4: the potential to encourage and reward 'symbolic' research use or 'performative impact'

Studies of the relationship between research and policy have long demonstrated the potentially high value to decision makers of evidence that supports decisions, or trajectories, that have already been agreed on (e.g. Weiss, 1977, 1979). This is 'spray on' evidence use according to Halpern (2003). The wider literature concerning the relationship between research and policy often reflects these accounts. In her overview of various 'models' of the relationship between research and policy, Weiss, for example, describes what she calls the 'political model', where research is deployed to support pre-given policy preferences; as well as a 'tactical model', where research is used as a method of delaying the decision-making process, providing policymakers with some 'breathing space' (Weiss, 1979). In the first case, the research process itself is not necessarily informed by politics, but the decision to employ research (or not) is entirely political. In other words, politics informs the ways in which actors respond to research evidence (e.g. Bambra, 2013). Boswell (2009) highlights the significance of 'symbolic' (or 'political') use of evidence for immigration policies in the UK and Germany. In the second, the commissioning of research might itself be understood as a political act (or, at least, an act that creates political benefits – see Bailey and Scott-Jones, 1984). In either case, efforts to reward researchers for 'achieving' research impact would seem misplaced and might be understood as a means of facilitating the influence of politics/elite interests over academic research. Moreover, as Watermeyer (2016: 209) points out, it can be 'difficult to determine where research has influenced symbolically or instrumentally, when decision-making processes are the denizen of multiple actors, social and environmental factors and are largely opaque'.

Accounts of symbolic evidence use build on a broader political science and sociological literature that demonstrates the ways in which state-building and modern techniques of governance shape the production of knowledge (e.g. Heclo, 1974). In simple terms, this may involve political (or other powerful) interests looking to academics and their research to bolster their predetermined positions and preferences (while discarding or ignoring research that challenges these positions). More sophisticated accounts of the influence of political and elite interests over research production and utilisation highlight the potential for this influence to occur via the production of self-regulating subjects (as Foucauldian analyses illustrate) or the dominance of particular ideologies (as Gramscian analyses tend to posit). From this perspective, research utilisation in policymaking is understood as profoundly constrained; although those involved in the construction of policy are not necessarily consciously aware of the forces shaping their decisions. In this view, any attempt to engage with research must be understood as part of a wider political project.

Theories highlighting the ability of organisational and decision-making structures to influence the construction and translation of knowledge help explain how this kind of ideological influence can occur (which may not be obvious to those working within elite systems). For example, the various forms of institutionalism (see Immergut 1998 for an overview) suggest that policy processes (including efforts to engage with research) are significantly shaped by the historically constructed institutions, procedures and ideas within which they are embedded (Schmidt, 2008). Those who have contributed to the development of this genre of work have emphasised that such theories do not suggest that particular policy outcomes are *inevitable*. However, such theories do suggest that it becomes increasingly difficult to change the overall direction of a policy trajectory as previous decisions become ever more deeply embedded in institutional structures and ways of thinking (e.g. Kay, 2005). Employing these kinds of theories, Smith (2013) has demonstrated how the institutionalisation of particular ideas about health and economic policy function as filters for research-based ideas about health inequalities, encouraging those ideas that support existing institutionalised ideas (or 'policy paradigms') to move into policy, while blocking or significantly transforming more challenging ideas.

In effect, policymakers may be citing research to lend authority to decisions that have already been made. Without the kind of insider insights that anthropological studies bring, it may be impossible for outsiders assessing impact case studies to determine whether contributions claiming policy change are describing instrumental policy influence or this kind of symbolic, post-hoc support. Since symbolic influence has generally been found to be common within policy (e.g. Boswell, 2009), the high-stakes financial rewards of REF impact case studies may be enough to persuade academics to reframe research use they suspect to be symbolic as impressively instrumental. At the very least, such analyses suggest that only research that can be used to support politically dominant ideas and interests will be employed in policymaking, while research that challenges dominant ideas will be discounted (see Wright et al, 2007). A stronger interpretation would hold that the research process *is itself* shaped by the 'powerful interests' directing policy agendas (e.g. Navarro 2004), as we discuss next, in Challenge 5.

For those who are supportive, meanwhile, of the fundamental idea that academics and universities in the UK ought to be doing more to engage, and work with, external audiences, studies report a concern that the current impact agenda is simply facilitating dissemination and publicly oriented 'PR work'. Watermeyer (2014), for example, reports that some of his social science interviewees who worked in more applied settings were critical of colleagues who they felt approached impact 'as something engineered merely to satisfy the demands of regulators/funders', which they 'mobilised in largely unimaginative or unengaging ways' (Watermeyer, 2014: 367). In this context, Watermeyer (2014) notes that the UK's impact agenda can be seen to share many of the same criticisms levelled at the public engagement agenda, 'where academics perform and claim social responsibility, altruism and philanthropy while being motivated by matters of self-aggrandisement and self-perpetuation' (Watermeyer, 2014: 367).

Concern 5: impact as a challenge to the autonomy of academia

Many of the concerns expressed about research impact are not primarily about specific policy developments but about a more fundamental desire to protect the autonomy of academic work. The evolution of the impact agenda demonstrates how changes in resourcing streams and assessment processes enable policy to shape academic practice (Cozzens and Woodhouse, 1995). This has triggered a concern that the impact agenda is limiting academics' ability to ask questions other than those that directly address accepted (implicitly short-term) policy issues (e.g. Watermeyer, 2014). Such contributions are often framed with reference to the importance of protecting 'curiosity-driven research' (Phillips, 2010), 'blue skies'/'intrinsic' research (McCowan, 2018; Wilkinson, 2019) or 'critical' research and analyses (Leathwood and Read, 2012). The fear here, clearly evident in the initial negative responses to the UK Research Councils' decision to require pathways to impact statements and to the higher education funding councils' decision to include research impact assessment in REF2014 (as discussed in Chapter 2), is that the impact agenda will change not only how academics engage with non-academics but the type of scholarship being produced in UK universities (McCowan, 2018).

As noted in Chapter 2, the *Times Higher Education* letter signed by nineteen eminent academics that called on academics to 'revolt' by refusing to peer-review 'pathways to impacts' when assessing grant applications (Braben et al, 2009), implied that this dimension of the impact agenda would lead either to funding research that was not worth pursuing (since the answers are already known; and the impacts, therefore, feasibly predictable) or that applicants would have to engage in fictional accounts of what the impacts of their research might be (assuming potential options for impact are informed by the results of questions not yet answered). An interview-based study with academics working in the UK and Australia indeed found that, 'where the impact was not obvious several academics intimated that they might feel forced to embellish the claims of potential funding in order to secure professional advantage, describing it as "smoke and mirrors"' (Chubb, 2017: 175). Similarly, Williams argues that 'there are strong incentives to produce positive messages' within REF impact case studies that belie the messy nature of engagement and create pressure 'to stretch claims of how much grass-roots users have benefited or how much policy has been influenced' (Williams, 2012: 493).

It has also been argued that not all types of research have an equal chance of being impactful and, as research impact increases in academic 'value', academic work that does not have obvious potential for impact may become both less attractive and less supported. In a recent survey of active research staff working at the University of West of England (UWE), Wilkinson (2019) reports that over half of the respondents felt that evidencing impact undermines 'blue skies' or basic research. As Watermeyer's social science interviewees warned, 'too integrated a relationship between academe and government could undermine the critical and objective propensity of researchers and result in manipulated and/or preordained outcomes intended to satisfy the expectations of contractors' (Watermeyer, 2014: 365). Yet, Williams believes that, 'citation of research by high-profile public figures or within policy documents, international exposure and invitations to join "exclusive policy networks" appear to be the new hard currency of "high-impact" research' (Williams, 2012: 493). In this context, Williams warns that an impact agenda which 'encourages us to perform our relevance by demonstrating our interaction with and influence upon [...] policy makers, and other powerful agencies' fails to acknowledge the ways in which these relationships 'can directly constrain our ability [...] to openly criticise public policy' (Williams, 2012: 494).

Perceptions of the impact agenda as a threat to academic autonomy build on the broader political science and sociological literature outlining the influence of politics and interests on knowledge production and utilisation. This way of thinking about the relationship between academia and policy suggests that research is constantly being influenced by policy and politics, and that efforts to bring researchers and policymakers closer together are likely to exacerbate this in ways that are undesirable. At best, from this perspective, the research impact agenda seems likely to reward some academics (and not others) for achieving impacts that have far more to do with political interests and agendas than the research or impact activities of those academics (see Concern 2). At worst, the impact agenda will lead to the increasing politicisation of research (and an associated reduction in academic freedom). Indeed, some of the most critical responses to the impact agenda are informed by these kinds of concerns. Cohen (2000) and Hammersley (2005), for example, put forward early warnings that placing restrictions on publicly funded research to be 'useful' would limit the potential for academics to promote ideas that are out of line with current (policy) thinking. Likewise, Davey Smith et al (2001), argued that efforts to achieve evidence-based policy may, in fact, do more to stimulate research that is shaped by policy needs than to encourage better use of research in policy making.

From this perspective, the UK's impact agenda can be understood as a conscious effort by policymakers and research funders to shift academic attention away from what Gibbons and colleagues (1994) call 'Mode 1' (traditional, intellectual) work, refocusing efforts on 'Mode 2' (applied, problem-solving) work. Such a shift is viewed by many as an extension of broader neoliberal reforms in UK universities (Collini, 2012; Evans, 2004; Holmwood, 2011b; Shore, 2008); changes which have reduced the financial security of many research staff (Collinson, 2004) and increased the pressure to secure research funding (Nixon et al, 2001), compelling academics to be more responsive to the demands of potential funders.

Empirical evidence of the ways in which political and economic interests can shape research is perhaps even more overt in research that analyses the influence of actors with specified interests on research that they have directly commissioned or funded. Reviews have, for example, repeatedly demonstrated that research funded by commercial sources, such as the pharmaceutical (e.g. Lundh et al, 2012) and tobacco industries (e.g. Bero, 2005), is more likely to present findings that are useful to those interests (see also Bailey et al, 1984). In other contexts, it has been suggested that researchers may struggle to maintain their independence where research is commissioned directly, or indirectly, by government sources (e.g. Barnes, 1996; Smith, 2010). As an example, a survey of 205 academics who had recently undertaken government-commissioned research in the UK found evidence of government sponsors making significant efforts to achieve politically congenial results from research, across multiple stages of the research process (LSE GV314 Group, 2014). While the survey findings suggest that, for the most part, the academic respondents claimed to be able to resist this pressure, the authors urge caution here, noting that it is in academics' own interests to be able to maintain a sense of academic autonomy.

This kind of political influence may be felt both overtly and subtly, with researchers responding to signals from research funders as to what is likely to be funded (and what is not), what they are hoping (or expecting) to be found and what they are not (Knorr-Cetina, 1981; Smith, 2010). Viewed critically, the UK's current research impact agenda can be understood as intentionally increasing the responsiveness of academics (especially those applying for research funding) to these kinds of external interests.

Some commentators, such as the sociologist Michael Burawoy (2005), have expressed confidence that, despite such challenges, the 'originating moral impetus' of academic work 'is rarely vanquished' as a result of career and institutional pressures. Murray and Harkin's (2017) reflections on their approach to influencing police stop-and-search policies in Scotland certainly demonstrates that, where policy and practice audiences become hostile to research, alternative, external routes to achieving policy influence remain possible. Indeed, Kath Murray was awarded an ESRC and SAGE publishing award for 'Outstanding Early Career Impact' for this work (ESRC, 2016), which initially met with significant policy concern (Murray and Harkin, 2017).

Moreover, recent interview-based studies with UK academics provide evidence that 'impact' is not (yet) a driving force for academics but, rather, an additional dimension that they are weaving into their work (e.g. Marcella et al, 2018). Yet, as we have seen, others remain concerned (e.g. Collini, 2012), outlining evidence that suggests academics in the UK are becoming increasingly restricted in the kinds of intellectual work they can pursue. Chubb's (2017) research with academics working in the UK and Australia paints a rather confusing picture on this point. When asked about the potential for the impact agenda to restrict academic freedom directly, Chubb found around half of her fifty-one participants said they did not feel compromised by the impact agenda (and UK respondents often seemed more concerned by the restrictions stemming from 'themed' calls for research funding). However, looking at her data more broadly, Chubb concludes:

> [T]wo thirds of interviewees described how an impact agenda was 'strangulating' research and used words such as 'confine', 'constrict', 'force' and 'inhibit' when describing the effects of the agenda on their freedom. This was largely attributed to a perception that government was in control of the research agenda. (Chubb, 2017: 166)

Such a trajectory has long been foretold. Max Weber, for example, positively described a 'uniquely free-thinking' intelligentsia (1995 [1906]), while noting that the institutionalisation evident in Western societies seemed likely to limit the abilities of individuals to think outside the boundaries of contemporary rationality. While, in the 1993 Reith Lectures, Edward Said suggested that academia was experiencing an increasing tendency towards 'professionalisation':

> By [which] I mean thinking of your work as an intellectual as something you do for a living, between the hours of nine

and five within one eye on the clock, and another cocked at what is considered to be proper, professional behaviour – not rocking the boat, not straying outside the accepted paradigms or limits, making yourself marketable and above all presentable, hence uncontroversial and political and 'objective'. (Said, 1994: 55)

As we discuss in Chapter 6, Said went on to outline the pressures within academia which he felt were contributing to this trend, including a warning that to be considered an 'expert' increasingly required being 'certified by the proper authorities'. As a result, Said (1994: 59) suggested there would be an 'inevitable drift towards power and authority' within academia, 'towards the requirements and prerogatives of power, and towards being directly employed by it'. Viewed from this perspective, efforts by authorities and funders to ensure that British universities are actively contributing to the economy and society (e.g. HEFCE, 2009) are deeply concerning.

It is this kind of perspective that informs Slater's (2012) argument that the impact agenda represents a serious threat to the autonomy of researchers, for "[p]recious to scholarship is the ability to ask our own questions" (Slater, 2012: 118). In direct contrast to guidance relating to research impact, Slater (2012) argues that the idea that there needs to be a two-way relationship between research and non-academic audiences represents an invitation to censorship, especially in cases where researchers are collaborating with policymakers (an idea for which there is some empirical evidence – see, for example, Smith, 2010). Similarly, it has been argued that limiting the scope of the research questions to existing policy/public concerns might be detrimental to work challenging the existing status quo (Eynon, 2012).

In sum, there is a fundamental concern that being required to demonstrate achieving, or having the potential to achieve, research impact inclines academics to try to maximise their contribution to political, social and/or business activities. As such, Williams (2012) notes that the push for 'more impact' might lead to ethically questionable power relations.

On the other hand, some academics have interpreted the challenge to academic autonomy posed by the research impact agenda as an opportunity to reflect on the power vested in academics, suggesting that frameworks and incentives for research impact can be used to justify building more collaborative relationships with less powerful actors. For example, Pain and colleagues (2011) have argued that the impact agenda might be an opportunity for academia to develop more participatory relationships with local communities, calling for more socially accountable universities that cooperate with different stakeholders in knowledge production (co-conceiving and co-producing research). While Chubb (2017) notes that some of her academic interviewees suggested they were comfortable with the idea that academics should not have complete freedom (in some cases, this was because they linked total freedom with dangerous practices, in others, it was informed by a sense of frustration that the concept was used as a catch-all case against change or was simply unhelpfully 'nostalgic').

In this context, it seems important that the REF2014 and REF2021 guidance for assessing impact case studies states that evidence of influence on 'the work of NGOs' (non-governmental organisations), as well as policy and commercial organisations, will be taken into consideration, as will research that challenges conventional wisdom' (REF, 2012). In theory, this provides more room for rewarding research impact that challenges existing policy directions. However, NGOs, which are themselves often dependent on policy and commercial funding, may not always represent an alternative channel for critical research. If no clear audience exists for challenging and critical research, it seems feasible that the impact agenda could function to actively discourage this kind of academic work. As currently articulated, the UK's 'impact' agenda appears to be framed by funders as apolitical; a framing which appears to ignore empirical accounts of the relationship between academics and research users (policymakers, businesses, etc.) that consistently emphasise the important role of ethics, interests, politics and values (Sanderson, 2009; Hallsworth and Rutter, 2011; Smith and Joyce, 2012).

Concern 6: the assumption that research impact is necessarily 'positive'

Those academics who have put forward arguments supporting the idea of research impact have often contributed another key assumption underpinning the impact agenda – the idea that it is high-quality research that will (or should) have impact (e.g. ESRC, 2015; HEFCE, 2009, REF, 2011b) and that the impacts achieved will necessarily be positive. As a recent reflection on the UK's research impact agenda notes:

> The notion of impact has an exclusively positive sense.
> It is understood as the process by which the beneficial
> knowledge generated by the university brings desirable

change in society (negative impacts – the so-called 'grimpacts' – although certainly possible are not generally contemplated). (McCowan, 2018: 283)

Using the example of the drug thalidomide, Penfield and colleagues (2014) highlight how perceptions of impact can vary over time. Thalidomide was widely prescribed to women experiencing morning sickness (among other things) in the 1950s but withdrawn in the 1960s due to a link to birth defects. More recently, it has been found to have beneficial effects in treating some cancers. Hence, 'the impact of thalidomide [research] would have been viewed very differently in the 1950s compared with the 1960s or today' (Penfield et al, 2014: 22).

Similarly, focusing on the potential for research to impact variously on different groups, McCowan (2018) uses an example of a (fictional) research project on natural sweeteners in which leads to the following impacts:

- Significant economic benefits for the company the researchers are working with.
- Some financial gain for Paraguayan farmers.
- A new variety of low-calorie fizzy drink for consumers.
- Loss of lands and environmental destruction for indigenous groups in Paraguay.

Reflecting on this, McCowan concludes the example demonstrates:

[T]hat it is unhelpful to see 'impact' in a unitary way. In fact, it is a multifarious process that operates through diverse channels and involves multiple actors and that cannot be determined to be inherently positive or negative. 'Having impact' is, therefore, a woefully inadequate criterion for universities or for research, in terms both of understanding descriptively what is happening and of evaluating it normatively. (McCowan, 2018: 286).

Yet, the definitions of research impact put forward by UK research funders appear to assume that, so long as research impacts are informed by 'excellent' research, they will necessarily be positive.

Relatedly, although the ESRC has claimed that 'you can't have impact without excellence' (ESRC, 2014c), Smith and Stewart's (2017) study found that many academics felt that this was not only possible but, in many ways, actively incentivised by the current impact architecture. For example, current incentives seem to encourage researchers to seek impact for single studies, almost regardless of how these findings relate to larger bodies of available research. Several of Smith and Stewart's (2017) interviewees contrasted this with the notion of academic excellence implied by medical 'hierarchies of evidence', which prioritise syntheses and meta-analyses of research evidence (see Black, 2001; Murad et al, 2016).

Consequently, some (including the recent Stern Review) have called for impact incentives to do more to promote the dissemination of syntheses of evidence from multiple studies (systematic reviews, meta-analysis, etc.) (Smith and Stewart, 2017; Stern, 2016). Yet, both the decision of UK research councils to require academics to articulate the potential relevance, impact and pathways to impact of their work, and the articulation of impact within the REF2014 and REF2021 assessment criteria, appears to encourage the promotion of original studies to non-academic audiences. Crucially, it remains unclear, when researchers do undertake systematic reviews (or otherwise synthesise bodies of research) that go on to have some impact, whether it should then be the academic reviewers/synthesisers or the authors of the original studies informing the review conclusions that are awarded credit in 'impact' terms.

Here it is worth noting that the individuals we interviewed who work at UK research funders promoting impact were keen to highlight that applicants for funding can say that they do not think their research findings will (or should) result in research impact. Yet, the UKRI website initially said (and many of our interviewees agreed) that a pathways to impact statement was 'essential' (UKRI, undated). The emphasis being placed on research impact in the UK has been sufficient to open up a space for new commercial companies who provide training and advice on achieving and narrating research impact. As might be expected, these companies then work to further underline the need for academics to engage with research impact. To take one example, the Fast Track Impact company website says, 'you cannot get away without producing an impact summary and pathway to impact if you want funding from the Research Councils' (Reed, 2017). Since social studies of the research process consistently demonstrate that, when applying for funding, researchers will often do everything possible to maximise their chances of success (Knorr-Cetina, 1981; Latour and Woolgar, 1986; Smith, 2010), the ability of academics working in the UK to ignore notions of research impact seems increasingly slim. If a funding call indicates that it will reward commitments to knowledge translation and 'impact', there is inevitably a temptation to articulate these kinds of commitments in a grant application, regardless of how appropriate a researcher may actually perceive this to be. Somewhat unexpectedly, in January 2020, UKRI announced they were discontinuing 'pathways to impact' and 'impact summary' sections of grant applications, with immediate effect. However, their advice that impact remains a 'core' requirement that will be considered 'throughout' grant applications (UKRI, 2020), suggests the requirement for applicants to focus on impact remains.

To some extent, the peer-review process for research grant applications ought to guard against researchers achieving credit for the potential impact of poor-quality research, while the REF2014 and REF2021 guidance on assessing impact applied a threshold of 2★ quality for impact case studies. This means that, to qualify as a potential impact case study, research outputs must demonstrate a thorough and professional application of appropriate research design, investigation and analysis, plus the potential for providing valuable, incremental advances in knowledge in the field. However, Smith and Stewart's (2017) interviewees felt that 2★ outputs cited within policy documents (i.e. where a clear 'impact' can be demonstrated) were likely to score more highly in the REF2014 'impact' assessment than 4★ (i.e. supposedly higher quality) outputs which had influenced policy debates in ways that were less obviously auditable. Whether this is fair or desirable is debatable.

An additional concern relates to scenarios in which research evidence is misinterpreted or misapplied by non-academics. Smith and Stewart (2017) found this was relatively common for public health researchers, several of whom described being bewildered at journalistic, political and policy interpretations of their work and one of whom described feeling that an advocacy group had deliberately reframed the implications of their research (despite their protestations). This poses a significant dilemma: should such researchers promote the 'impact' of their work (e.g. via REF case studies), thereby reaping rewards, even if they feel the work has been misinterpreted (and are researchers themselves the best people to judge how accurately their work has been interpreted)? If the consensus is that they should not, then questions arise as to how to define 'misinterpretation' or 'misapplication'. So far there is little evidence to suggest that the reward systems for impact that are currently being implemented in the UK have adequately considered either how to capture the relative quality of research in assessments of their impact or how to deal with varying (and potentially misleading) interpretations.

A final example of 'bad impact'[2] or 'grimpact' (Derrick and Benneworth, 2019) might be high-quality research with ethically dubious applications/impacts. For example, the fact that REF guidance states that evidence of the impact of research on 'commercial organisations' can be submitted means, in theory at least, that researchers may be rewarded for evidence that their work is being used by businesses profiting from the sale and use of socially harmful products, such as alcohol, tobacco and arms manufacturers. Hence, in theory at least, the current REF impact guidance seems to allow for positive rewards to be attributed to research assisting tobacco companies in understanding what attracts young people to begin smoking their products. While some may agree this is entirely appropriate, it is clear that many do not (e.g. Collin, 2012; Freudenberg et al, 2009; Hastings, 2007). The point, as McCowan (2018) outlines, is that the UK's current articulation of research impact mistakenly assumes not only that research impacts will be positive (so long as the underpinning research meets a threshold of 'excellence') but also that we have societal agreement about what counts as positive. Derrick and Benneworth (2019) argue that the UK's approach to research impact means researchers are rewarded for research that enables impact to be quantified, rather than for achieving positive impacts, calling this a 'perfect storm' for so-called 'grimpacts'. Hence, we suggest more dialogue and critical reflection on the multifarious nature of research impacts, the propensity of impacts (and perceptions of impacts) to change over time and the role of values, ethics and beliefs in assessing impacts. So far, debates about the 'impact' agenda have largely been silent about these kinds of normative and ethical dilemmas.

Concern 7: overloading policy audiences and/or confusing 'more research use' with 'better research use'

Much of the current guidance on research impact seems predicated on the idea that improving the use of academic research in policy means increasing its flow into policy. Yet, empirically informed theories of the policymaking process, from Lindblom's (1959) concept of 'muddling through' to Kingdon's 'policy streams' model (1995 [1984]), paint a picture in which decision makers face a daily barrage of information, with advocates and lobbyists working to pull their focus in different directions. This is reflected in a much more recent, UK-focused report, which describes policymakers struggling to process unmanageable levels of information (Hallsworth and Rutter, 2011). In this context, policymakers may not welcome increasing numbers of academics sending more research outputs their way or seeking their involvement in research projects (through co-production, etc).

Yet, as the research impact agenda evolves and beds in, there is evidence of a growing push for academic researchers to develop ongoing relationships with potential research users, involving them from the start of projects and maintaining interactions throughout. From a research utilisation perspective, such a steer is empirically informed since this kind of collaborative working relationship does appear to increase the chances of research impact (Innvær et al, 2002; Greenhalgh et al, 2004; Walter et al, 2005; Mitton et al, 2007; Contandriopoulos et al, 2010). And for many researchers with an eye on achieving impact, policymakers are often the most likely, or obvious, users of their research (e.g. Lavis et al, 2004; Macintyre et al, 2001). The tension between acknowledging the limited capacity of policymakers to engage with research in a meaningful sense, and the growing impetus to achieve such engagement, has not yet been empirically explored.

Concern 8: unnecessary exclusion of impact examples via the application of an arbitrary time limit

As numerous commentators have highlighted (e.g. Gunn and Mintrom, 2017; McCowan, 2018), the impact of research can come many years (even decades) after the research was produced. In articulating this point, Smith and Stewart (2017) use the example of research on the links between smoking and lung cancer, while Penfield and colleagues (2014) use the discovery of DNA. In both cases, practical/policy developments only followed around thirty years after the original research. Reflecting these kinds of time lags, the UK's Russell Group universities recommended that no time limit should be applied to REF impact case studies. For reasons that were unclear, REF2014 applied a twenty-year cut-off point (i.e. impact case studies submitted in 2013 for assessment in REF2014 had to have been informed by research published since 1993) for all disciplines except architecture (which was granted an additional five years, again, with a rationale that was not especially clear). In REF2021, the twenty-year cut-off remains (so impact case studies submitted in 2020 for assessment in REF2021 must be informed by research published from 2000 onwards) and architecture no longer appears to have any special dispensation. Several commentators have suggested the unnecessary exclusion of research impacts with longer time lags is unhelpfully exclusive of research with very significant impacts that has, for a multitude of reasons, occurred over longer periods. It is worth noting that policy studies scholars often suggest that ten years is a minimum period over which substantial policy change can feasibly be studied (see Fischer and Miller, 2007). McCowan (2018) argues that a degree of insulation from immediate demands may be beneficial to longer-term agendas and specifically suggests that the imposition of a time limit is one of the factors likely to mean that the UK's impact agenda reduces support for 'blue skies', curiosity-driven research.

Concern 9: the resources required to achieve, demonstrate and assess research impact

Achieving research impact is resource intensive and can involve multiple activities beyond teaching and research. Reflecting on this concern, which was raised by his interviewees, Watermeyer (2014) notes that demonstrating or effecting research impact appears to be a 'full-time occupation'. This aspect of the impact agenda needs to be understood in the context of evidence suggesting that UK-based academics are generally struggling with burgeoning workloads (e.g. Leathwood and Read, 2012). Since the need to be able to achieve and demonstrate research impact in the UK is understood to be additional to teaching and research, and since many of the approaches for achieving research impact that are advanced as most likely to achieve results (building relationships of trust, close collaboration, etc.) are resource intensive, it is unclear how academics are meant to achieve impact alongside other demands (see, for example, Salter et al, 2010).

Resources are also a key factor in options of assessing and rewarding research impact. Indeed, from the outset, a key concern with the decision to retrospectively assess the impact of research outputs in the REF has been the resources required for this activity to be meaningful. Again, this concern needs to be understood in the context of broader concerns about the cost of research assessment-type exercises in the UK (see, for example, Sayer, 2015). Resource implications were a central consideration of RAND's review of internationally available impact assessment frameworks (Grant et al, 2010). The economic costs of the decision to incorporate impact case studies into REF2014 and REF2021 are difficult to estimate with any precision but Watermeyer reports that a freedom of information request submitted by *Times Higher Education* to UK universities 'revealed an estimated total spend on preparations for impact assessment at around £2.2 million' (Watermeyer, 2016: 205). A RAND-led assessment of the impact assessment in REF2014 estimates that the cost of assessing impact in REF is around £57 million (Manville et al, 2015). Penfield and colleagues (2014) argue that the initial costs for universities may be relatively higher due to the need to 'collate evidence retrospectively' (in the absence of baseline data, agreed indicators, etc.) but, unless the approach to assessing REF impact case studies changes substantially (which is certainly not the case for REF2021), the costs involved in assessing impact do not seem likely to reduce. One early assessment of emerging efforts to assess research impact in the UK argued that the financial costs would almost inevitably rise, following incremental refinements, with the consequence that costs would quickly outweigh benefits (Martin, 2011).

As we reflect on the costs of the UK's approach to research impact assessment in the REF, it is worth noting that approximately 88 per cent of all impact case studies in the REF were awarded either a 3★ or 4★ grade. In other words, the huge majority of claims of impact in the REF were awarded quality related (QR) funding, while only 12 per cent of research impact case studies submitted to the REF were deemed to have failed to reach the upper echelons of excellence. While this can to some extent be explained by the decision of some units of assessment to artificially deflate the number of academics returned to the unit of assessment in order to reduce the required number of impact case studies, it nonetheless paints a radically more positive account of academics' abilities to influence the external world with their research than can be found in either qualitative studies of this topic (e.g. Smith, 2013) or theoretical accounts (e.g. Boswell and Smith, 2017). Watermeyer and Olssen (2016) have written about how some universities employed an aggressively selective approach in putting forward their best candidates to the detriment of others. What we can ascertain from the partial submission of researchers to evaluation is that the process appears to be a zero-sum game: all those evaluated are already 'excellent' researchers. Their REF2014 assessment suggested that the impact of these researchers was also 'excellent', which may raise questions about the approximate £250 million spent on the whole REF process. Although this has been partially responded to in REF2021 via the principle of universal submission and a requirement that all staff 'with significant responsibility for research' are included within institutional submissions, the simultaneous move to widen the number of outputs associated with academics (from a minimum of one to a maximum of five per full-time-equivalent members of staff being returned) provides scope for the respective under and over representation of researchers within a unit of assessment to continue to be determined by REF managers.

Concern 10: reifying 'impact heroes' and traditional elites

Our final concern is the potential for an emphasis on research impact to reify traditional elites. This concern was identified in Smith and

Stewart's (2017) interview-based study, in which some academics (particularly those who were at an earlier career stage) suggested that impact reward systems may unintentionally reify traditional academic elites. This concern seemed to stem partly from a belief that it is easier to achieve research impact if you are already a senior academic with a strong reputation in, or connection to, policy circles or if you have personal connections with senior impact beneficiaries (if you have friends or relations who are ministers, senior civil servants, chief executives, etc.) (see for example Ball and Exley, 2010). Indeed, an ESRC report on work to evaluate the impact of research on policy and practice found that:

> [T]he most important factor contributing to the generation of impact was the pre-existence of networks and relationships with research users. Sustained contacts with users, based on personal relationships and built up over the long term were the most important channels for policy and practice applications. (ESRC, 2009: 15)

This is perhaps one reason why, after reviewing the REF2014 impact case studies for politics and international relations, Dunlop found two-thirds of submissions used a single academic as a 'key author of impact throughout the text' (Dunlop, 2018: 273). Similarly, after reviewing the REF2014 impact case studies for sociology, Les Back concluded that:

> In large part the 'impact agenda' has licensed an arrogant, self-crediting, boastful and narrow disciplinary version of sociology in public. This is impact through 'big research stars' that are scripted – probably by the editors of the impact case studies rather than themselves – as impact 'super heroes' advising cabinet ministers and giving evidence to parliamentary select committees. (Back, 2015)

Drawing on his interviews with research centre directors, Watermeyer reflects that:

> Quite possibly, the most successful conversations with government are managed by academics with the confidence, alacrity and artifice to traverse the comfort-zone of their native scholarly communities; and with fluency with the working culture and professional anatomy of government fostered through secondment or internship. This cohort

may tend almost exclusively however to comprise senior academic staff, prompting questions of how more junior or early-career academics go about impact. (Watermeyer, 2014: 369–70)

Here, we must acknowledge that some REF2014 case studies did attempt to situate the excellence of the impact they proclaimed by couching research achievements within larger bodies of work. Indeed, some narrative accounts showcase authors' attempts at realistically, perhaps even modestly, extrapolating impact claims from their research as one contribution among many. Moreover, we should acknowledge that, in the context of REF2021, the development of impact case studies (as well as that of outputs) seeks to move away from singular claims of excellence attributed to the lone academic as purveyor of impact. Such reorientations reflect an effort by the REF's architects to mediate concerns that it induces forms of individualistic and non-collegial behaviour among researchers desperate to avoid the precarity commensurate with a reputation of being anything other than 'excellent'. This aside, many case studies in REF2014 appeared to operate as a platform for academics' public celebrity (see Back, 2015), even if this was not the academics' intent or motivation. Early findings of current research into how researchers named within the REF2014 impact case studies perceive the effects of their inclusion suggest a sentiment among some of feeling exploited by their institutions (Watermeyer, 2019). Others claim to have even been ignorant of their inclusion (Watermeyer, 2019). The danger here is that impact in the REF appears to impose upon and engender among academics an articulation, or rather caricature, of themselves as existing in heroic and paternalistic isolation.

Williams is one academic who, having managed to successfully obtain a large ESRC-DFID (Department for International Development) grant on the basis of commitments to achieving policy impact via his networks, has expressed concerns about the implications of this for newer researchers:

Two Indian Government Ministers and a senior member of DFID-India with whom I had had prior contact about the planned research were named research users within my grant application: this helped to strengthen a narrative about the project's potential for impact, but should it count significantly? If funding success depends in part on having the social networks to produce a credible impact statement, this is likely to work against new researchers, and/or those who are relatively isolated in institutional terms. (Williams, 2012: 491)

Crucially, in this context, a recent interview-based study with early and mid-career (full-time, permanent) academics found that participants felt they lacked institutional support for developing their understanding of, and approaches to, research impact (Marcella et al, 2018). Similarly, a recent survey of research-active academics working at UWE found the majority of respondents (fifty-one out of sixty-eight respondents) reported having 'received no training, coaching or mentoring' on how to prepare grant funding pathways to impact statements or REF impact case studies, despite the fact that UWE (like many other UK universities) has multiple interventions in place to support academics in developing their approaches to research impact (Wilkinson, 2019). Others have highlighted that the work required to achieve impact is not yet adequately reflected in workload allocation models (e.g. Yarrow and Davies, 2018). All of this suggests that earlier-career academics, or those on part-time or fixed term contracts, may experience a disadvantage (although it's worth noting that Chubb's 2017 study identified mixed views on this topic, with some senior academics suggesting that earlier-career colleagues would be more immersed in activities and practices relating to research impact and, therefore, likely to become better at it than more senior colleagues).

Further issues arise when we consider the inflexible timing of key opportunities for 'impact' – evening events can, for example, be unfeasible for academics with caring responsibilities. Since evidence suggests that women still take on a disproportionate amount of caring work, this may also be a gender issue. This is perhaps why, in their assessment of the impact case studies submitted to the business and management studies unit of assessment in REF2014, Yarrow and Davies (2018) found women to be significantly underrepresented. This is despite the fact that Chubb's interview-based study with academics working in a range of disciplinary settings in Australia and the UK identified a fairly widely held assumption (though notably expressed more often by men) that women were better at outward-facing communication and engagement work. This linked to a sense that 'impact'-related work involved 'soft skills' and that this kind of work was still not valued in the same way as more traditional academic work. Reading Chubb's (2017) analysis evokes the sense of a circular set of assumptions and practices in which women are perceived (by some) to be better at a form of academic work that is relatively undervalued and therefore encouraged to do more of this work (despite caring/

family constraints), which further underlines gender hierarchies relating to this sphere of work within the academy. These kinds of concerns have informed a recent (widely supported) call for research impact assessment systems and processes to routinely incorporate an assessment of gender equity and to investigate gender bias (Ovseiko et al, 2016).

Shifting, now, to think about research impact from the perspective of people working beyond academia, it is worth noting that many of the incentive structures for research impact, particularly those that involve some provision of funding, require 'buy-in' from non-academics at an early stage in the research, ideally during proposal development. This can be resource intensive, requiring a great deal of time from individuals within non-academic institutions, who, at the proposal stage, are being asked to commit time and resources with no clear prospect of benefit. Even if a proposal is funded, there may be no immediate benefit for non-academics since funding is often predicated on non-academic partners providing resources (and if this is not feasible via match funding, then time and resource commitments are required). In a context of limited public and NGO funding, this is no small ask and seems likely to result in a bias towards larger, more resourceful non-academic partners. It is also, as Williams (2013) points out, likely to be particularly problematic in the Global South, where NGOs are often working with more limited resources than their Northern counterparts.

Further, as several of the concerns discussed above make clear, the current UK impact agenda is interpreted by some as being rather more oriented towards achieving policy and commercial impact than to achieving public engagement and dialogue or, indeed, broader social benefits (this perception, it should be noted, is challenged by Terama et al's (2016) analysis of REF2014 impact case studies). This leads Watermeyer to conclude that, 'It is not so clear [...] that impact in the context of the REF, encourages or incentivises academics' public citizenry or necessarily correlates with intentions of academics performing public accountability and transparency' (Watermeyer, 2016: 205). Likewise, Williams' (2012) reflections on his impact-oriented promises in applying for funding from ESRC-DFID, which drew on his links with senior officials in India (see p 55), are that this relied on the notion that seniority and status equate to 'reach' in some sense: 'Enlisting "high-profile" users also reinforces a particular politics of scale, whereby a project's "reach" is confirmed by the status, and assumed efficacy, of the people with whom it engages' (Williams, 2012: 491). Reflecting on these kinds of concerns, Back (2015) expresses a sense of embarrassment that he ever felt impact could be employed to support the kind of 'public sociology' that Burawoy

(2005) advocates. His assessment of REF2014 sociology impact case studies leads him to conclude that the impact agenda, 'puts us on the side of the political elite, Ministers of State, Job Centre Managers, Immigration Officers and the apparatchiks of prevailing government policy. Bluntly, it puts us on the side of the powerful.'

Finally, researchers based at UK institutions who collaborate with colleagues, and undertake research, in low- and middle-income (LMIC) settings have expressed concerns about potential international inequities in the context of research impact. Reflecting on his ESRC-DFID project in India, Williams (2012), for example, recounts how a member of the research team was approached by a politician seeking election for information which they deemed likely to be used in his election campaign. On this occasion, the team member declined to provide the requested information, with the team judging that their research 'would almost certainly have been used instrumentally' to support a particular political agenda and that this, in turn, 'would have […] labelled Indian members of our team as open critics of the (outgoing) government, a risk that would be entirely borne by Southern institutions and academics, for the sake of benefits accruing to their Northern counterparts. Williams' (2012) concern, here, is that the impact agenda provides researchers with a strong 'push' to take up opportunities such as this, despite the potential risks involved and the possibility that both the burden of demonstrating (Williams, 2013) and the risks may be unevenly born by local team members or even research participants, rather than the UK researchers reaping the benefits. The more important gap, Williams argues, is not between researchers and the architects of policy change (officials, politicians, NGO policy leads, etc.) but 'between the "middle-class" lifestyles researchers share with policy makers, and the altogether different life worlds of those on whose behalf poverty-alleviation policies are being made.' In response, Williams (2012) suggests that academics do more to bridge *this* gap: 'taking time to listen to the voices and perspectives of marginalised groups, and using this to question assumptions built in to policy and governance practices' (Williams, 2012: 494); a suggestion we return to in Chapter 5.

In sum, there are five distinct ways in which the UK's impact agenda is potentially reifying traditional elites: (i) by requiring accounts of research impact that are clearly linked to single projects or research groups (thereby narrowing the accounts of who is involved) (see Dunlop, 2018); (ii) by rewarding advantages bestowed on academics due to their personal and professional connections (which seems likely to advantage senior, white, male, public-school/Oxbridge-educated academics over others); (iii) through the expectation that non-academic organisations engaging in key schemes will be able to mobilise resources to support research engagement; (iv) via the relative ease with which it seems commercial impacts and incremental impacts on policy can be demonstrated over more challenging, critical or publicly oriented impact; and (v) by not actively considering the burden and risks that may fall on colleagues working to achieve impact for UK-funded research in LMIC settings, where that research is deemed to criticise or challenge those in, or seeking, power (e.g. governments, politicians, armed factions, etc.). This suggests that the current incarnation of the UK's impact agenda is at odds with efforts to make the kinds of democratic, egalitarian contributions that many academics express a commitment to (e.g. Smith, 2013). As McCowan puts it:

> [G]iven the critical challenges facing the global community and the severe inequalities, there is an onus on universities to contribute wholeheartedly to enhancing well-being, reducing poverty and promoting social justice. [...] [R]esponsibility and openness are not equivalent to the orientation of the work of the university towards immediate and direct impact, narrowly conceived, and the latter may indeed work against the former in unexpected ways. (McCowan, 2018: 293)

If we accept these concerns as valid (and it is worth noting that MacDonald's 2017 example of 4★ being awarded to a REF2014 case study that directly challenged some 'elite' myths – discussed in more detail in the context of Concern 5 in this chapter (pp 41–46) – suggests that concerns regarding the difficulty of demonstrating 'REFable' impact on the back of critical research may be overstated, at least for now), then academics working in the UK who seek to challenge existing power inequities are on tricky terrain. As MacDonald argues, citing Pain and colleagues' (2012) earlier defence of the research impact agenda, 'ignoring the progressive possibilities of the REF impact agenda, in favour of a commitment to clearer intellectual autonomy, [itself] smacks of an "Ivory Tower" elitism' (MacDonald, 2017: 701). Moreover, it is essential to note that, while some academics have expressed strident opposition to the UK's impact agenda, empirical research also identifies significant academic support for the fundamental aims of this agenda and for at least some of the specific mechanisms and implications (see, e.g., Chubb, 2017).

Conclusion

A wealth of studies on research utilisation developed from the 1960s onwards offered an opportunity for the UK's research impact agenda, developed around the turn of the twenty-first century, to be theoretically and empirically informed. Had this body of work been used as a foundation for the UK's impact agenda by its various architects, and had the intention been to genuinely improve the societal contribution of academic activity, it is possible to envisage the development of an agenda with broader support and fewer drawbacks.

Yet, while the UK's impact agenda has almost certainly made it easier for academics to undertake outward-facing work (since resources and institutional support are now easier to secure), opening up conversations between academics and non-academics on a scale not previously feasible, the approach is manifestly not evidence based. A more theoretically robust, evidence-informed approach to incentivising and rewarding research impact would not, for example, have ignored all the sophisticated and complex theories and models of the relationship between academic knowledge (e.g. Blume, 1977; Caplan, 1979; Rein, 1980; Weiss, 1977, 1979) in favour of simple, instrumental notions of research use, articulated in simple impact 'plots' within the concise REF impact case studies.

Any genuine acknowledgement of the literatures on knowledge diffusion, policy studies and social change would have implied that rewards and incentives should focus on achieving research engagement but not necessarily impact (since the latter is widely agreed to be informed by a multitude of factors beyond academic control). Likewise, a research-informed impact agenda genuinely committed to achieving better outcomes on the back of research evidence would have avoided incentives that encourage individual researchers and projects to try to achieve demonstrable research impact, in favour of rewarding efforts to synthesise large bodies of research evidence for non-academic audiences. A more socially conscious and democratically oriented approach to research impact would have had a greater focus on public engagement (as we discuss further in Chapter 5) and done more to guard against the potential to reify traditional elites by excluding non-academic actors with limited resources. Far greater consideration to the potential for 'bad' impact would also have been evident and more would have been done to enable the capacity of academics to continue undertaking work without immediate social, economic or policy impacts (protecting spaces for critical and 'blue skies' endeavours). We outline what we feel a more desirable approach to research impact might look like in more detail in Chapter 10.

In sum, the UK's research impact agenda generates tensions which go to the heart of questions about what academic research, and universities, are for. At present, academics responding to these new incentive structures:

> stand accused by detractors of the impact agenda, of reducing their scholarly vision and ambitions, their capacity to be impartial and critical, preferring instead the less complicated or be that contentious route of research suppliers – facilitating the kinds of policy-led evidence or 'spray-on' (Halpern 2003; Henderson 2012) evidence preferred by many of those in political office. (Watermeyer, 2016: 208)

In contrast, more supportive commentators suggest that the impact agenda is, despite its limitations, providing a much-needed corrective to the inward-focusing pressure to engage in academic publishing (Pettigrew, 2011). It should also be acknowledged that the limited number of case studies required in REF does not actually incentivise the kind of wholesale shift that some might like to see. Empirical research with academics often captures this range of views, providing evidence that there is substantial academic support for aspects of the UK's research impact agenda, as well as concerns about specific aspects, including, notably, the difficulty of predicting, demonstrating and assessing research impact (e.g. Chubb, 2017).

Notes

[1] We do not describe this review, or the included approaches, in detail here due to the clear focus on health research (and our intention to focus on impact across disciplines).

[2] The idea of 'bad impact' is attributed to Ben Baumberg Geiger (Smith and Stewart, 2017).

4

Do experiences and perceptions of research impact vary by discipline?

The understanding of any academic phenomenon would be incomplete without an exploration of its disciplinary character. Yet much of the existing published literature assessing the UK's approach to research impact focuses on single disciplines or areas of research (e.g. Dunlop, 2018; Greenhalgh and Fahy, 2015; Haux, 2018; Pettigrew, 2011; Watermeyer, 2014; Smith and Stewart, 2017), institutional research groups (Biri et al, 2014) or particular professions (e.g. Kelly et al, 2016; Marcella et al, 2018). In particular, there is a high number of studies relating to the research impact agenda that focus on health (Haux, 2018). Such a strong disciplinary bent in the existing analyses fails to capture, or allow comparative consideration of, the diverse ways in which impact and impact initiatives are experiences across different disciplines. This chapter starts to address this gap by focusing specifically on the role that disciplinary training, preferences and context appear to play in perceptions and experiences of the UK's impact agenda.

The limited existing literature that has explored experiences and perceptions of the UK's impact agenda across disciplines has reached mixed conclusions. A recent survey, which focused on research–active staff at a single UK institution (UWE), found only nuanced differences between academics based in different disciplines, concluding that 'much can be shared and learned by and amongst researchers in different settings regarding impact best practice and its evidencing' (Wilkinson, 2019: 83). In contrast, an interview–based study with academics in the UK and Australia found that disciplinary orientation can 'dictate the type of activity associated with [impact]' (Chubb, 2017: 22). For example, Chubb found that participants working in arts and the humanities emphasised the 'public good', a sense of the general value of research work, public engagement activities and cultural enrichment, while participants working in life and earth sciences emphasised policy impacts, practical improvements and working with industry, participants based in physical science, maths and engineering emphasised society, applied/useful research and an economic contributions, and, finally, participants in the social sciences stressed policy impacts, the direct use of research, societal change and broader engagement.

Another interview-based study with academics working in seven different disciplines in the UK found that 'norms and traditions shared within disciplines, fields and modes of enquiry frame what can count as worthwhile "impacts" and as desirable or acceptable impact-oriented activities for individuals and groups' (Oancea, 2013: 248). Similarly, Chowdhury and colleagues' (2016) study of 363 impact case studies submitted to REF2014 (spanning five research areas) found differences between disciplines in terms of approaches to assessing and scoring impact case studies, as summarised in Table 4.1.

In the end, Chubb concludes that:

> [A]ssuming one should group the arts, humanities and social sciences together, whilst grouping the physical, life and earth sciences together with respect to impact (commonly the case in research support structures in institutions and for training purposes) is not necessarily appropriate. (Chubb, 2017: 270)

Instead, Chubb argues, it is potentially useful to think about impact as a two-by-two matrix, onto which she maps disciplines, according to her interview findings (Figure 4.1). Although Chubb (2017) notes that only some aspects of her research findings could be easily mapped onto the matrix, suggesting that simple binary divisions cannot easily be applied.

Disciplines manifest themselves in almost every aspect of academia, both structurally (in terms of departments or research councils) and epistemologically (in terms of knowledge production and cognitive styles) (Becher, 1989). One way of categorising academic disciplines is with reference to their position on 'real-life problems', a division which is often simplified as a basic/applied research dichotomy. Basic research is usually depicted as that which aims to improve understanding of phenomena and is guided by a quest for a new discovery or idea. By contrast, applied research is aimed at solving concrete problems and therefore is guided more by the needs articulated by concrete users (for example governments or firms) (Roll-Hansen, 2017).

These characteristics should – at least potentially – determine the fit of different disciplines to the research impact agenda. For example, Gibbons et al (1994), in their influential work on the new modes of knowledge production, have argued that different disciplines will move to Mode-2 production of knowledge more easily than others.

Table 4.1: A summary of Chowdhury and colleagues' (2016) account of the contrasting forms of impact preferred in different disciplines, based on REF2014 impact case studies

Discipline/area	Types of impacts that assessors appear to prefer/reward	Target groups rewarded by assessors	How impact was evidenced in high-scoring case studies
Clinical medicine	Indicators/evidence of improvements in quality of life and/or life expectancy; reductions in morbidity and/risks of future illnesses; improved knowledge transfer, efficiency, productivity or safety of services; evidence of contributions to UK industry/economy	- Patients - The public - The UK economy - UK industries	Successful impact case studies emphasised a link to research income and publications in high-impact journals
Physics and general engineering (note these were analysed as two distinct areas but the relevant findings for this table were presented jointly)	Indicators/evidence of public engagement activities and impacts on society (including health); impacts on the economy; impacts on culture or creativity; impacts on security; impacts on products or services; impacts on practitioners or professional services; impacts on the environment	- Society - The economy - Services and companies - The environment	Successful impact case studies emphasised levels of collaboration and research income and/or outlined spin-offs created/secured, and linked impacts to publications in high-impact journals
Communication, cultural and media studies and library and information management	Indicators/evidence of impact across civil society; impacts on cultural life; impacts on economic prosperity; impacts on education; impacts on policy making; impacts on public discourse and public services	- Civil society - Society / the public - Educators - Policymaking - Key communication platforms (mass media, etc.)	Successful impact case studies emphasised research income generated and grants secured
Anthropology and development studies	Indicators/evidence of influence on sustainable development; regulatory reform; poverty alleviation; child protection; public policies; public opinions	- Regulators - Policymakers - Civil society - The public	Successful impact case studies emphasised research income secured

Figure 4.1: Chubb's 'two-by-two' cultures of research impact

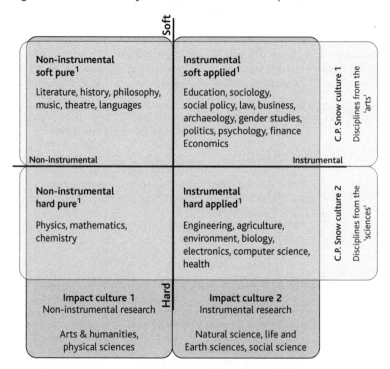

Source: Reproduced from Chubb (2017: 239); informed by Becher and Trowler (2001) knowledge domains.

The authors argue that the Mode-2 (transdisciplinary, contextualised) model of knowledge production would be more suitable for disciplines that are already closer to 'the context of application' – such as engineering or computer science. Other disciplines – within, for example, the humanities – are more deeply embedded in Mode-1 production (disciplinary, detached). This assumption suggests that "research impact" may be relatively easy to attain for some disciplines and more difficult for others. Perhaps reflecting this way of thinking about research impact, HEFCE's initial panel guidance for REF2014 made clear that they expected diverse kinds of impacts achieved, and the underpinning evidence of these impacts to vary by discipline (REF, 2012).

At the same time, the impact agenda operates under the assumption that all disciplines could and should have an impact on non-academic audiences. This assumption manifests itself in the expectation placed on all disciplines to include impact submissions in the REF exercise and in the impact requirements of grant applications (RCUK, 2017; REF, 2011b). Furthermore, the definition of 'impact', and models of reporting, are unified across disciplines. This assumption prompts the question: is impact a universal disciplinary experience or do different disciplines perceive and experience the impact agenda variably? In this chapter, we explore this question by comparing the perceptions and experiences of academics working in different disciplines – both basic and applied. In order to assess the various disciplinary responses to the impact agenda, our research focused on asking participants how and to what degree the introduction of the impact agenda was influencing academic practices in their area.

This chapter is based on qualitative material gathered at a Russell Group university. This included data from two focus groups, one with academics working in social science and public health (plus one person working in a professional services knowledge exchange role within the social sciences), the other with academics working in medical and veterinary research, plus individual interviews (N=12) with people working in: art and design (2), chemistry (1), history (1), informatics (1), law (1), maths (1) physics (3) and education (1), as well as another person working in a professional services knowledge exchange role (this time across disciplines). Potential participants were selected primarily on the basis of their disciplinary background, but in our efforts to ensure that particular disciplines were represented in the interviews (which took place after the focus groups) we were regularly directed towards people who had an impact-related role (e.g. some had institutional roles relating to REF impact case studies and others were featuring in draft impact case studies). This relatively small qualitative data set is supplemented with reference to guidance relating to achieving and assessing research impact that was available at the time of analysis (2016–18) as well as the broader literature outlined previously.

Research impact across disciplines

Since the relationship between research and its application is complex and often difficult to capture and define (Nutley et al, 2007; Weiss, 1979), it is perhaps unsurprising that participants in different fields put forward distinct ways in which research impact was being defined and operationalised. The differences were most tangible when it came to discussions about target audiences, as we discuss later. However, there was also a surprising degree of consistency across the data. For example, participants across all of the disciplines contrasted research impact as an institutionalised practice linked to research income (via REF and funders) and research impact as an activity which, in different forms, has always been a part of much academic practice.

This point of departure informed our decision to focus this section on four areas: the perception of genuine versus 'REF' impacts; the importance of creating persuasive narratives of impact for funders and REF assessors; the perception of complexity in the research application process; and finally, the differentiation between various forms of outcome of the impact activities, in terms of cognitive or practical applications. Across all four of these issues, there appeared to be quite a lot of commonality across disciplines.

'Genuine impact' versus 'REF impact'

Over half of the participants differentiated between what they considered to be a 'genuine' impact and the impact produced or reported as part of the REF impact assessment exercise or articulated prospectively in grant funding applications. 'Genuine impact' was often framed as emerging almost spontaneously, without steering, control or monitoring. This type of impact was perceived by some interviewees as being of better quality and greater substance than research impact that was developed with impact frameworks and incentives in mind:

> 'My gut feeling is that [one of the case studies] was the best, because it was so genuine and so not manipulated. Because the person did whatever they did and the consumers [...] use it. That can be documented very easily. And that happened long before impact was invented; whereas the others were clearly created with that in mind.' (Academic, classics)

Correspondingly, some of the academics differentiated between impact understood as a bureaucratic exercise, for example as part of REF, and the broader impact of research on society. Even though formal documents explaining the impact agenda focus on achieving social and economic benefits, some of the academics perceived the process, in practice, to amount to little more than a 'box-ticking' exercise:

> 'You've got this general word of "impact", which is ... how well you serve society. But then there's something very specific about how well you tick the right boxes for the REF impact case studies. And it seems like other people are making decisions about that somewhere else in the university. I don't know, there's something slightly kind of odd about that, that this word carries two different

meanings for those – a more general and very specific sense.'
(Academic, social sciences)

At the same time, some of the interviewees pointed to the fact that this second, specific (funder-oriented) meaning was often linked to (even equated with) any potentially outwards-facing activities. As one of the social scientists participating in the focus group pointed out, impact "started more nebulous and then it became something associated very much with the REF" (academic, social science). Interviewees suggested this perceived shift may demotivate academics to do engagement work (or even research work linked to research impact), though few concrete examples were provided to support this.

Creating narratives of impact

This notion of genuine impact might stem from the perception of the vast majority of interviewees that an important aspect of impact work was the creation of rhetoric or narratives about impact. For example:

> 'It is difficult to do that [write an impact statement] and I think we never put as much effort into doing that as maybe we should do. Fortunately, the university has some expertise in wordsmithing to make these things appear better than they perhaps are and, as the years go by, we're getting better at working out how to write these things and I think we actually know what the difference between an impact statement and a pathways to impact statement is now. But in some cases you can actually talk about how your work is directly working, how you are actually integrated with a company and there's genuine knowledge exchange and those kind of things, but most of the time it's really pretty woolly and fluffy and you're making it up as you go along.'
> (Academic, particle physics)

The above extract seems to suggest that, in some cases, where the impact is a core part of the project, writing the impact statements is (as we might expect) rather easier. In other cases, impact statements require more manipulation or 'wordsmithing', as the above interviewee put it.

The perception of a need to create persuasive impact narratives, even for research in which impacts are not obvious, seemed (across disciplines) to relate to: (i) beliefs that REF impact assessment only captures a small proportion of potential impacts; and (ii) an expectation of more impact case studies being required than projects which convincingly fit REF definitions of impact (particularly in less applied fields). Some of the academics also indicated that 'role distance' (to use Goffman's 1961 term) may be at work, whereby academics take on the role of 'impactful researchers' but at the same time signal their distance from it, by indicating this is a duty that has to be fulfilled:

> 'We don't work towards those [impact] criteria; we just do research. So I think it's my responsibility to shift the research to meet that criteria. We carry on and every so often somebody takes a snapshot and it is what it is. If it suits the criteria, that's great. If it doesn't, I could be held accountable, but I'm not going to trouble myself with that too much.' (Academic, design)

Some of the interviewees saw the impact statement and impact case studies as rhetorical devices aimed at getting funding rather than specific plans which have to be followed by action. For example, during focus group discussion about funders' expectations that future impact activities would be predicted and planned, one of the social scientists pointed out:

> 'I think you can ignore it to an extent, or you can circumvent all these things that go to very specific impact statements. I don't know if people are ever held up for not adhering to a "pathways to impact" statement. I haven't heard about that.' (Academic, social scientist)

In sum, as shown in the two sections above, academics across the disciplines seem to differentiate between what they consider to be 'naturally' occurring engagement with and impact on external audiences, and strategically constructed accounts of impact that respond to the perceived needs and preferences of institutions and funders. While some interviewees did not seem to mind this compromise, it was clearly uncomfortable for some. This was sometimes due to various specific concerns (including many of those discussed in Chapter 3) but it was also, for the following interviewee, simply a matter of feeling constrained by the emergence of tools and processes for governing and monitoring impact:

> 'I suspect that the main reason most academics object is that they, academics, feel incredibly constrained by rules. I mean

we are under enormous, much, much greater rules about assessment and how we deal with students than we used to be. There's almost no discretion left in that respect. […] So the one area where they feel that they have some freedom is engaging with an audience outside the university where there are no rules really, and then suddenly, along comes this impact agenda.' (Academic, education)

As highlighted in the quotation above, the development of the impact agenda is a part of a larger shift towards monitoring and metrics in British academia (Shore and Wright, 2015). Ten to fifteen years ago, this academic felt that external engagement activities were one of the few remaining areas of academic life that was not formalised or closely monitored. For this individual, a requirement to create and report narratives of impact is meeting resistance among academics because it is further reducing academic discretion.

The complexity and collective nature of research impacts

Another characteristic of research impact that appeared to be relatively consistent across the disciplines was the perceived inadequacy of the REF approach to assessing impact. The issue that seemed to be most problematic for participants was not the definition of impact itself, but the requirement that researchers show a clear, documentable pathway between the research and social and economic benefits, since this was perceived to exclude some areas in which impact was occurring in more complex and diffuse ways:

'Those things [formal mechanisms to assess impact, such as REF] are extremely artificial because, at least in informatics, what you see is that all the work is very synthetic, that you'll be depending on work of other people, both in a kind of vertical direction, in a sense standing on the shoulders of others, and also horizontally, in order to get this thing to the point where it has an impact. Then you probably have to produce something that somebody can deploy in a company or do something like that. […] So you end up with these, where there are some things, there's some algorithms that you can definitely see, "here's when this theory is proved, and here's when the product happens". So Google is a good example, so page rank already invented by actually science citation index probably twenty years before Serge Brent and co got their hands on it.' (Academic, informatics)

In these cases, research impact was positioned as a collective and often cross-disciplinary endeavour (rather than something emanating from single individuals, projects, institutions or disciplines) requiring a broad spectrum of experts in different areas to reach a viable, useful application. In these cases, the process of achieving research impact was perceived to be a multi-stage process of synthesis and translation. This was frequently directly contrasted with REF impact case studies, which were understood as seeking accounts of simplified, linear and individualised impact achievements. Participants coming from physics, mathematics and informatics all pointed to the complexity of technological and social change and said they felt that the REF impact case studies could not adequately capture this. For example:

'Certainly, particle physics and astronomy find it very hard to be linked to individual, deliverable chunks of material that companies might make, whereas complex condensed matter group, that particular aspect of the condensed matter group find it much easier.' (Academic, particle physics)

These accounts are similar to those put forward by social scientists (both our interviewees and authors of existing literature) regarding the complexity and diffuse nature of social science impacts. This suggests a widespread, cross-disciplinary sense of frustration with the UK's current approach to assessing research impact stemming from its inability to sufficiently capture complexity and its tendency to obscure the long-term, collective nature of major impacts.

Conversations about the complexity of impact led several interviewees to also highlight a perceived role of serendipity in achieving impacts; often impacts that related to unexpected findings or events, which could not have been planned in advance. Accounts of unexpected and unplannable impacts (an issue repeatedly raised by social scientists concerned with policy impacts – see Chapter 3) was especially prominent in our data among interviewees based in physics, with all three emphasising the importance of unpredictable research outcomes, despite coming from distinct areas of physics (particle, soft matter and computational). For example:

'A Nobel physics prize winner [...] who accidentally discovered magnetoresistance. And you don't know what this is but actually your laptop benefits from it. So do you remember in this moment in time you could suddenly buy really big hard disc drives for your laptop? This chap discovered this. And he discovered it entirely accidentally in his research and it was research that has been funded by a company in Germany and he told them, "I've seen this really weird effect, are you interested in patenting it?" They said, "no, no interest at all". And ten years down the line, it was picked up and turned into this product. So it was entirely an accidental series of events and I don't think government understands the impact of accident. You know, it's more complicated than they think, definitely.' (Academic, computational physics)

Although there appeared to be a relatively widespread consensus that research impact is more complex and serendipitous than funders and REF architects appear to assume, these issues seemed to feel particularly challenging for academics in disciplines or subdisciplines concerned with producing what we might understand as 'transitional' knowledge; that is, knowledge that falls somewhere between applied impact and basic research. For example, in mathematics:

'The kind of statistical methods and optimisation algorithms that people use, they might not be doing applications themselves but they're usually algorithms and problems which are out there in the world. I'd say particularly a lot of the very strong, very serious methodological statisticians have done that by developing, innovating methodology that is directly needed for applications.' (Academic, mathematics)

Since this type of work was process oriented, rather than impact–related, academics working in these transitional spaces tended to see themselves and their work as not being well aligned with the UK's impact agenda. Other examples that interviewees put forward that they felt did not fare well involved various strands of research from multiple disciplines impacting on another discipline (and, therefore, the work that it was possible to do in that other discipline).

Conceptual versus instrumental impacts

A fourth area in which we can identify similarities across disciplines relates to the importance interviewees from a multitude of disciplines attached to conceptual uses of research. Conceptual uses of research (e.g. research informing new ideas, knowledge or understanding) were often contrasted with instrumental uses (such as practical outputs and specific changes to working practices or policies) (see Nutley et al, 2007 for a more detailed comparison of conceptual and instrumental impacts). Perhaps unsurprisingly, there was a widespread consensus that the current approach to assessing research impact in the UK is more suited to instrumental impacts. However, in contrast to Nowotny et al's (2001) suggestion that views on a shift from Mode 1 (more conceptual) to Mode 2 (more instrumental) knowledge production would be received differently across disciplines, our findings suggest that there are few areas of academia that do not attach substantial importance to conceptual impacts, and that a focus on conceptual impacts cuts across very different disciplines. For example, participants working in maths, particle physics, social sciences and classics all described the main impacts of their disciplines/areas as conceptual in nature. Of course, the notion of 'conceptual impact' is not directly transferable between disciplines. For example, for classics, impact was described as follows:

> 'I mean we talk a lot about ancient democracy, talking about this from the basis of our research. Not me personally but others, with members of the general public would hopefully make them reflect about their own democracy they live in, and what they think is good about it or bad.' (Academic, classics)

Whereas, for particle physics, the account given was as follows:

> '[T]hat's the biggest impact that our kind of research has. It's much longer term, it's much more, you're improving the deeper understanding of how the everyday aspects of the universe, how they work and so you can exploit those more efficiently to generate better technology.' (Academic, particle physics)

Unsurprisingly, the academics for whom conceptual impacts are perceived to be a priority tended to find the impact agenda more challenging. As one of the social scientists pointed out, the model on which the impact agenda is based depends on an assumption of social change that seems to ignore, or sideline, longer-term, conceptual learning:

'I do technology studies and I think that the way technology profoundly changes society over a long historical timescale [is important], and it's much more unpredictable than a lot of things we think about [in terms of] how do we impact on society? I think it's totally missed out of a lot of these discussions. So I think they've got the wrong model about how society changes and how the economy changes. And I think somehow we need to, that's why we need to challenge it.' (Academic, social science)

Other accounts emphasising conceptual impacts (and the need for an approach which better captures these) referred to critical academic work (i.e. contributions challenging the status quo in some way). This included an academic in law talking about the challenges of documenting long-term challenges to, and changes in, legal processes, policing and the justice system. In that case, the participant noted that even though they had recently taken a more collaborative approach to these endeavours, working with external actors, they were still struggling to capture accounts of impact in ways that they felt would work for REF.

While the importance attached to conceptual impacts seemed to cut across disciplines, our data suggest that academics in different disciplines had rather more variable views when it came to considering whether conceptual impacts will (or can) translate into more tangible impacts over time. For example, the extract from the academic in classics earlier in this section might suggest that igniting reflection is as far as the impact of historical research can go. Yet other extracts (e.g. from academics in informatics and particle physics) suggest that, while conceptual impacts might turn into social and economic benefits, these would not necessarily be traceable or measurable. Hence, there were variations in the focus of concern; some academics were concerned with a sense that conceptual impacts were not deemed as important as instrumental impacts in the UK's approach to research impact; others were concerned that the simplified, short-term approach to measuring and assessing research impact made it difficult to document the role of conceptual contributions.

Drawing on interviews with academics working on health inequalities, two of us – Smith and Stewart (2017) – explained the problem of instrumental and conceptual impacts in the context of social policy impacts by proposing the concept of a 'ladder of impact' (reproduced in Chapter 3). This ladder suggests that, as the complexity and societal importance of research impacts increases, it often becomes more difficult to measure and document the impacts. Correspondingly, smaller-scale, easier-to-achieve impacts tend to be easier to document and report. Data discussed in this chapter suggest that this perceived imbalance can be found across a wide range of disciplines.

Impact targets audiences

In contrast to the previous section, when it came to interviewees' accounts of primary target audiences for research impact, there were evident disciplinary differences. Both REF and research funder guidance documents[1] set out a broad range of potential targets for research impact. Nevertheless, and although a few of the participants said they felt impact targets should not be discipline-specific, most of our participants suggested that their disciplines tended to have 'core' audiences and types of impact. The data presented in this chapter suggest that perceptions and constructions of desirable impact audiences within disciplines are informed by a complex process of combining experiences of bottom-up collaboration (often traditional audiences for particular disciplines) with top-down considerations for maximising assessment scores (in both funding applications and REF).

Industry and technology

Across our data, target groups for impact activities were closely related to the meaning assigned to the term research impact, as well as to sets of 'impactful' practices. This multiplicity was summarised by one interviewee as follows:

> 'If you look at the different [research] councils, their approaches are quite different. […] ESRC tends to look for impact around policy issues. EPSRC [Engineering and Physical Sciences Research Council] tends to think about engineered products in some way or another. Whereas I think MRC [Medical Research Council] tends to be more structured around health interventions in some way. So it's more kind of on the ground.' (Academic, informatics)

Industry was considered to be a particularly valuable audience for research impact by many interviewees, with several participants suggested it was one of the preferred target audiences for UK funders. Collaboration with industrial partners was also seen as easy to measure in terms of monetary benefits and therefore preferred by the government:

> 'I think they're [targets of the impact agenda] discipline-specific. I think from the government point of view, I think they get more impressed if it is about contributing to the economy. So more jobs and more yeah, increase in the economy.' (Knowledge exchange lead)

This focus was particularly evident in science disciplines. All of our participants working in science – chemistry and different areas of physics – viewed two groups of targets as important: industry and publics. However, the REF impact model, requiring documentation and measurement of impact, was seen to prioritise industry over publics:

> 'Main targets? Well what I know from my colleagues I mean many of them are engaged with industry and so that's where the main impact I think here in this place is taking place. But at the same time many of us are engaged with outreach activities. But because of the difficulties I mentioned in kind of documenting that kind of impact, it almost runs in parallel in a way. We do a lot of activities here. We contribute to scientific festivals. We work with high schools. We create materials for web, etc. etc. But that is seen as an outreach or knowledge exchange activities which are not necessarily translated or linked to the impact in our minds.' (Academic, chemistry)

Interviewees from science consistently suggested that industry was both a priority target of the impact agenda, and the easiest audience in which their disciplines could achieve documentable impacts. All of our science-based interviewees also referred to longstanding traditions of science–industry collaboration. For example, the interviewee working in chemistry said they felt that academics were 'encouraged historically' to collaborate with industry, and that science disciplines have developed closer links with industry as a result. An interviewee working in physics made a similar point:

> 'We know how to engage with companies so we meet them at conferences. And we start talking to them and then we set up projects and we collaborate and so that's quite easy

for us to develop. Maybe other potential stakeholders don't come across our path, don't come to physics conferences and things like that so it's harder, but maybe there is no impact opportunity.' (Academic, computational physics)

Industry was also seen as the key target group for informatics, both in terms of collaborations with big technology companies and in terms of academic entrepreneurship and academic start-up companies. The issue of entrepreneurship seemed to be particularly important for this discipline, and the participants working in informatics were the only ones who named academic entrepreneurship as an important driver of the impact agenda.

Policy

Policy was also identified as an important target for the impact agenda, particularly in the social sciences, with participants suggesting that some disciplines were struggling with this focus: "There's a big debate now in particular in sociology about the extent to which it's just having a kind of policy impact and the way that particular departments kind of lost quite big from the last REF" (Academic, art and social science). Other examples seemed less discipline-specific, with an individual from politics and another from social policy both reflecting that the critical nature of their work, combined with current political trajectories (in the regions and countries on which their work focused), made it very unlikely that they could achieve policy influence, at least in the short term. This was deemed particularly problematic in a context in which collaborative approaches were being promoted as the most promising route to achieving policy impact; indeed, most of the social scientists participating in focus groups and interviews said that working with and for policymakers was the most common approach to achieving policy impact. This kind of collaboration was noted to be very challenging for a range of reasons, as explored in detail in the section on collaborative research (pp 86–88) and in Chapters 6 and 7.

Publics

Members of the public were identified by interviewees as the main impact target for a smaller number of the disciplines, particularly those that might be categorised as 'pure science' or humanities. However, while the scientists tended to differentiate between impact and knowledge exchange (as was evident in the extract from the interviewee working in chemistry cited earlier in this chapter), humanities scholars tended to describe a closer overlap: "I think [in my department] the common understanding is it's about talking to the general public about your work and somehow influencing their behaviour – knowledge exchange with results, put it that way" (Academic, classics).

Yet, even though impact guidance suggests that publics are a legitimate impact audience (see Chapter 5), documenting impacts arising from working with members of the public was perceived as difficult to measure and document, and thus problematic for REF (though less so for some research funders):

> 'There's public outreach. We can maybe do that which is, that's slightly different because obviously there's no dollar signs at the end of it but again instead of dollar signs there you need to have number of people who've engaged with the materials.' (Academic, particle physics)

The above quote illustrates an important limitation of the REF model. The core assumption behind the REF definition is the focus on outcome rather than on process, with the determining element of impact being the magnitude of change in the economy, policy, awareness, etc. (see Chapter 2). This type of change is difficult to capture for public engagement and this, in turn, informs the way impact is documented and reported in different areas. Within this variation, there was some consensus that merely reporting the numbers of people with whom the academics engage is not sufficient. This approach was criticised by some:

> 'We can go through lots of disciplines, history or something, where the impact, at the very best, the impact is in the form of maybe forms of public education, maybe through the BBC or museum exhibition or something like that, but that tends to not be highly regarded by the REF either, because they're looking for things that have an immediate and measurable impact. You can't much measure the impact of an exhibition. And the REF, I mean, a criticism I would certainly have of the REF definitions is that they didn't allow activity to count, sorry, they didn't allow merely an account of activity to be enough to create an impact case study. You had to measure the impact of that activity.' (Academic, education)

Participants' sense of how problematic this difficulty to measure this type of impact was varied, with some of the pure scientists suggesting that public engagement was valuable in increasing public recognition of the disciplinary area:

> 'I don't think they [particle physics] are necessarily worried because I think, as long as the public recognises that particle physics is important and doesn't necessarily link to applications, I think the public is interested enough in particle physics that the impact agenda is not too much of a problem for them, but I think they do feel pressure to engage with the public to make sure that is always something of interest.' (Academic, material physics)

In that sense, even though the public was seen as a challenging target for achieving demonstrable research impact for the REF, strong public support was nonetheless seen as important for sustaining popular support for more 'basic' disciplines.

Practice

Finally, interviewees in applied disciplines with strong links to practice (education, law and medicine) all highlighted practice audiences, often within the public sector, as the main targets of their impact activity:

> 'I think [...] especially social sciences, [it] is generally easier to have impact if there's a well-organised professional group that you can go and talk to. So if you're doing research on education, there are school teachers; if you're doing medical research there's doctors and nurses, social workers. I've mentioned engineers, there's engineers.' (Academic, education)

Generally, as might be expected, interviewees working with both policy and practice audiences suggested that impact was easier to achieve where longstanding disciplinary–professional practice links exist.

Targets, impacts and REF panel preferences

As discussed in this section, participants' accounts suggest that research impact targets are selected partly on the basis of the perceived prospect for achieving impact (for example because of existing links with particular groups) and on the basis of perceptions as to how feasible it is likely to be to demonstrate any ensuing impact. Here, participants' comments suggested that their perceptions of REF panel membership and assessment processes informed their sense of where to target their impact efforts.

For example, the interviewee based in informatics explained that their department intends to shift the approach to research impact in preparation for REF2021 (compared to REF2014), focusing more on policy impacts than on industry. This shift was informed by a perception that the department had underperformed on research impact in REF2014 and that other informatics departments at UK universities had fared better due to their inclusion of policy impacts. Likewise, a participant working in a professional services knowledge exchange role noted that case studies from a business school that had involved collaboration with industry had not scored as well as expected in REF2014 and suggested this might have been due to issues with perceived reach and significance. These accounts seemed to contrast with several others, in which participants said they felt impacts on industry would be well received in light of the current government focus on economic impacts. In these instances, the bottom–up motivation to collaborate with certain groups, for example due to historical patterns of engagement and perceived ease of achieving impact, was contradicted by the perceived preferences of REF assessment panels.

Indeed, the review panels were perceived by the majority of interviewees as central in constructing and shaping the target impacts. These accounts emphasised the subjectivity of the term research impact. For example, an interviewee working in the arts said they thought panels produced refined (working) definitions of impact for the panel assessment, which informed their belief that different REF panels were applying distinct versions of impact, even though this was not necessarily articulated formally. This view was also put forward by the following interviewee:

> 'I've heard from the sciences that it was very difficult to get high scores for any cases linked to public engagement or policy impact. And there's been some discussions, there were, they could learn something from us [social science and humanities] in terms of evidencing that. And it might be, but to be honest, I have seen some of those cases that didn't do well, and I think if they were put forward in any of our panels, they would have done [well]. So I think that was those panels just being more impressed with [certain kinds of] commercial impact. But I think that is, I don't

think there was anything in the guidance suggesting that you should do that. So I think that's probably a bit of a bias in the panels.' (University professional services, knowledge exchange)

The above quotation underlines the subjective nature of the UK's approach to assessing research impact; the same REF impact case study might well be assessed differently, depending on the panels (and panel members) assessing it. As highlighted in the introduction to this chapter, there are multiple academic cultures, each of which is strongly shaped by the disciplines and institutions involved. The findings presented in this section suggest that discipline-based models of engagement and knowledge exchange existed prior to the emergence of the UK's research impact agenda and that these have informed disciplinary approaches to research impact. At the same time, perceptions around the kinds of impacts and impact audiences that funders and REF panels prefer is leading to changes in how knowledge exchange and research impact are approached in some areas. While there are multiple possible models of engagement, and while much of the guidance appears relatively open to different forms of impact and different beneficiaries, the process of assessing research impact (or plans for research impact) and the institutionalisation of these processes appears to be informing decisions to shift activities and investments away from some kinds of activities and audiences, towards others. Yet, the direction of shift does not appear to be uniform across disciplines (e.g. the interviewee from informatics discussed a shift away from commercial impacts to business impacts, while interviewees described shifts within science disciplines away from public engagement and policy, towards commercial impacts).

'Easy' and 'difficult' impacts

The various disciplinary differences and similarities discussed thus far point to an emerging understanding of certain types of impacts being easier or more difficult to achieve. The factors that participants identified as allowing research impact to be achieved and demonstrated relatively easily are listed below:

- Having a clear target or a 'natural' audience.
- Having an target audience falling into one of the following categories (as opposed to members of the public): industry, practice, policy.
- Experience or opportunities to engage with relevant non-academic audiences.

- Being involved in research that enables instrumental impacts.
- Being able to easily link research to a product/impact.
- Having means to measure/quantify the impact(s).
- Producing research that addresses specific questions or problems that relevant impact audiences had already identified.

To avoid creating a sense of binaries (which would not really reflect our data) we have not listed the factors that participants suggested made achieving and demonstrating impact in the UK system difficult. However, these factors were often the contrary of the list above. With these kinds of factors in mind, all of our participants seemed to agree that some disciplines are more aligned with the UK's approach to research impact than others. However, it was also clear that most disciplines have subdisciplinary areas of work with obvious impact strengths. The REF approach to research impact, which requires a much smaller number of impact case studies to be returned than their research-active academics, was therefore broadly appreciated, allowing some areas within disciplines to continue without worrying too much about research impact.

The most obvious exception here was mathematics, which was commonly named as an area of academic work for which the impact agenda was posing particularly acute challenges. For example, the participant employed by a mathematics department noted that they felt their own appointment was informed by their strong, individual impact track record. This interviewee also reported that some UK mathematics departments had opted not to return all of the academics they could have returned to REF2014 because they lacked a sufficient number of impact case studies. However, mathematics appeared to be an unusual case and the vast majority of participants agreed that there is usually enough variety among the academics within different units of assessment to produce an adequate number of case studies.

Linking research to impact

Issues with documenting a link between impact and underpinning research consistently emerged as one of the largest perceived challenges for creating REF impact case studies, regardless of how applied or close to practice different disciplines were. Nevertheless, disciplinary differences emerged regarding the precise nature of the problem of linking research to impacts. Interviewees from more basic disciplines described finding it difficult to document impacts that were not tangible or were too diffuse to present a clear link between the original research and the final outcomes (e.g. new products or technologies). In contrast, interviewees from more applied disciplines described being able to present measurable impacts relatively easily but challenged the notion that impact should be based on individual papers, produced within the same institution, by the same people. These academics described finding it difficult to fit accounts into REF impact case studies because they were drawing on a broader pool of knowledge, which went beyond their own research. For example:

> '[Our centre] works with about 700 companies. So a shiny example of impact on the economy and almost none of those interactions were reportable through REF[2014], because our work was based on scientific research which was done elsewhere in the world. We were just taking it and applying it. Some of it, very difficult stuff, so not the stuff that you could buy commercially, exactly the sort of stuff that [our centre] is good at. But because we don't publish and because in this university the work we do isn't that much, you know, blue skies academic research, it was more difficult than we thought to find situations where we had taken something that had been developed, initially published in the university, and then we'd taken that and deployed it to some company and then write it up. That proved much more difficult than we thought – which is silly.' (Academic, computational physics)

Interestingly, reflecting the above observation, the academic working in education argued that the fact REF impact case studies require a link between research and impact has positive disciplinary consequences, as it pushes the applied academics to produce more original research:

> 'For [academics working in education], although they have an impact, these academics, it's not an impact based on their research or indeed necessarily on any research at all. I think the impact of the impact agenda on that kind of discipline is really beneficial because it forces them to think in a more fundamental and I would argue truly academic way, [to] stand back from the practice and evaluate it. But [it] would certainly be quite a disruptive force in these areas of activity.' (Academic, education)

Figure 4.2: The 'upside-down' pyramid of impact

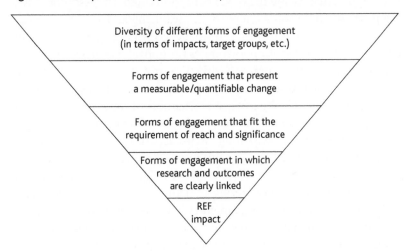

The issues discussed thus far might be illustrated by an upended pyramid of impact (Figure 4.2), which illustrates how the REF model considerably narrows down what 'counts' as research impact.

The Figure 4.2 pyramid highlights an apparent paradox in the UK's approach to research impact via REF assessment: the REF guidelines set out a broad and encompassing definition of impact in the REF guidelines (as a reminder, the definition of impact in REF2014 was: 'All kinds of social, economic and cultural benefits and impacts beyond academia, arising from excellent research' REF, 2011a: 4). Yet, there appears to be a perception across academic disciplines and REF units of assessment that the kinds of impact that score highly in REF is far more constrained. The gap appears to stem from the combination of this broad definition with a range of other expectations and demands, for example the requirement for research impact to be linked with specific research, undertaken by those submitting the case study within the institution submitting the case study, to present a measurable change and to be significant. What this chapter demonstrates is that, across disciplines, each of these criteria in effect narrow the work that can be included (or, at least, which is expected to fare well) in the REF impact assessment.

The consequences of the impact agenda for academic practices

This chapter has looked into how different disciplines understand and approach impact in the context of the UK's chosen method. So far we have argued that, while the broad definition might suggest otherwise, the processes and tools for reporting, measuring and assessing impact (especially within REF) appear to be constraining the forms of engagement regarded as opportunities for impact. Several participants highlighted that this approach risks limiting the scope of external engagement for UK academics. In the remainder of this chapter we examine in more detail participants' accounts of the consequences of this agenda for academic practices in the UK. Reflecting the fact that these findings did not have strong disciplinary differences, the focus on disciplines is somewhat lesser in this section (though continues to be a strand of our analysis). The findings suggest that the UK's approach to research impact is not only altering academics' approach to engagement but is also shaping the way academics perceive and practise science/academic scholarship (changes informed by a shifting sense of what counts as academic work and what the purpose of universities, and academics, is).

Increased engagement and collaborative work

As might be expected, and as the architects of impact appear to have intended, nearly half the participants described an increase in levels of engagement with non-academic audiences resulting from the impact agenda. This was the case across basic, theoretical and more practically oriented, applied disciplines.

Unsurprisingly (and as contributors to the existing literature, discussed in Chapter 3, suggest), academics who had already been involved in this type of work tended to feel that they were benefitting from the impact agenda and that their work was now gaining legitimacy in the eyes of their university employers and peers:[2]

> 'I'm very positive about the move towards impact. In the past I did teaching, I did research, but I also did a lot of advisory work, and I felt the university wasn't really valuing that. And in fact they were asking: "Why are you spending your time doing this advisory work? It's not bringing in students or research". Whereas now you can make a clear case that you're advising the change policy, and that's going to have a wider public impact. And actually the university values that. Maybe ten years ago here I couldn't have said that. I would have felt slightly under pressure to spend less of my time doing these things.' (Academic, medical science)

Some academics working in applied areas argued that, even though they had collaborated with non-academic audiences in the past, the impact agenda encouraged them to seek partners in a more systematic way:

> 'The impact agenda basically almost kind of brought this to the minds of people more than OK, well it happens that you come across something then yes, we will apply it in the world of industry. But now we are actively encouraged so that basically has an effect on our everyday life of academics.' (Academic, chemistry)

As we have already discussed, while official definitions of research impact do not appear to promote particular types of engagement over others, the more specific requirements embedded within guidance, and the perceived preferences of panel members, are informing specific modes of engagement within disciplines. Adding to this is a shift in the focus of funding calls towards requiring collaboration and co-production with external partners (particularly policy and industry partners):

> 'The feeling is more and more that, and there's a lot of public-private bodies in my area that you have to collaborate with. Like I'm doing some work now with one of [a public-private body], and they are essentially business driven. So there's a sense going forwards now that for us to be relevant to that agenda we have to be much more kind of what's the benefit for UK PLC of doing sustainable technology and so on. I think post-Brexit as well, that's becoming more and more clear that the future research calls in our area are going to be how are you assisting business development, local economic growth.' (Academic, social science)

This perception is confirmed by the higher education market analysis, showing that collaborative research is one of fast-growing sources of research income at UK universities (HEFCE, 2016a). This points to a broader change in academic practice in the UK, with co-produced research becoming a far more commonplace and significant part of academic life.

Reflecting some of the concerns around academic autonomy discussion in Chapter 3, not all academics saw the increasing acceptance of co-produced research, or even the pressure to undertake external engagement work, as a positive trend. For those who were less comfortable with the shift, two sets of (interlinked) problems were often put forward: a sense that this shift was limiting the scope of critical academic work, and a sense that it was compromising important principles of academic autonomy and independence. For some interviewees these concerns were great enough to warrant resistance. The following social scientist, for example, was keen to stress that they were working to maintain a clear sense of academic autonomy and that they were reframing impact accordingly:

> 'I want to preserve the independence, so what is considered good in terms of the way the rules are being interpreted and the direction of travel, for me that doesn't necessarily count as good impact. I've got an idea of what good impact might be, [a] more critical form of engagement.' (Academic, social science)

Overall, the pressure (or incentive) to engage with audiences beyond academia, including via collaborative endeavours, appeared to be experienced across disciplines. Whether this pressure was perceived to be positive or not, however, varied across our participants, and while this appeared to be linked partially to disciplinary norms, individual experiences, preferences, beliefs and values were also at play.

Co-production as a restriction on critical scholarship

The academics who wished to engage with policymakers more critically certainly viewed the model of co-production as problematic. Such academics reported the need to ignite a change in the existing systems and institutions, rather than to work directly and collaborate with the institutions. They were cautious about incentives to engage more closely with policymakers as they viewed this approach as likely to reproduce the status quo.

> 'There have been some other scholars who've taken a very, a strong view, saying well actually if criminology, most criminologists and indeed most -ologists – say that, ultimately, they're seeking to create fairer and more equal societies, then […] it [impact] should be about resistance, not collaboration with institutions. So it becomes a kind of, "we have to smash existing capitalist arrangements". That's

what it's about. And these kind of relationships with the status quo, as it were, are viewed quite, are viewed extremely negatively.' (Academic, law)

This points to the issue of incompatibility between the immediate relevance of research and its critical, transformative qualities (Smith, 2010). These two qualities represent different ideals of the roles that academics should be playing in society. The co-production model, strongly promoted in the current UK impact agenda, inherently expands the boundaries of expertise by inviting different groups to participate in the process of knowledge and policy production (Jasanoff, 2004; Wynne, 2006). But the underlying assumption is that the outcomes of co-produced research process should lead to a form of consensus with a clear policy recommendation (which might be practically challenging; see Irwin, 2006). However, the assumption of reaching consensus through co-production or deliberation poses a challenge to academics who see the role of academia as providing dissent and critique, rather than consensus. For example, one focus group participant said they felt that some of the simplistic, linear notions of research impact that were evident in early UK guidance served a purpose in maintaining a separation between academic and external audiences and noted that, as such, they preferred this approach to more recent efforts to respond to complexity via co-production:

'I think there's one thing about the impact agenda is that it has a knowledge transfer idea in it, which in some ways can preserve independence because it suggests that the knowledge creators are the academics almost, and you go out and impact on. So it's quite a linear model in some ways, which I quite like. Because the other option is this co-productionist, very transdisciplinary thing which starts to get even more difficult I think in terms of academic independence and what our role is. So I think there is a safeguarding in some ways professionally in the impact agenda.' (Academic, social science)

From this perspective, co-production poses a risk to the role of academia as a critical voice in policy and practice. Autonomy and separation, rather than co-production, are seen as a guarantor of academics' ability to provide critical ideas that might be useful to society. This issue will be further explored in the context of more specific concerns about academic independence and autonomy.

Research impact as a restriction on academic freedom and autonomy

Reflecting many of the published debates about research impact (see Chapter 3), several of the participants brought up the issue of academic independence in connection with the impact agenda. As highlighted in the preceding section, this issue was particularly salient in the accounts of co-produced or government-sponsored research, where participants suggested (in line with some of the existing literature we discuss in Chapter 3) that academic independence often had to be carefully and constantly negotiated.

As such, our academic participants did not perceive autonomy to be a binary concept, but rather put forward rather more nuanced views on the desirable distance between the government and academia. Most participants did not assume a need for absolute academic freedom and even criticised academics who might claim a need for complete isolation of science from society (though this inevitably reflects our approach to recruiting participants):

> 'I think you get a very good example with the olden-day academic freedom, which had the advantage of so to say academics not following just what's the flavour of the day, but a disadvantage that they can just spend the next fifty years doing something which they think is important but no one else does. And I think what we have now is exactly the opposite.' (Academic, social science)

Overall, while there were variations within our sample (e.g. more social scientists expressed these types of concerns), most participants expressed some concern about academic independence in the context of the impact agenda. For some participants, their concern to protect academic independence seemed to relate to concerns about the perceived quality of academic work. Linking research quality with autonomy reflects the deep-rooted assumptions of the so-called 'social contract for science' – a funding paradigm that dominated after the Second World War. The social contract for science contained an implicit assumption that the autonomy and self-regulation of science will lead both to assurance of the quality of science and to its social and economic benefits (for example, see Guston, 2000). The autonomy of science is one of its most important signifiers, and a basis of its claims to epistemic authority. This model was based on the assumption that science could regulate itself through a value system, described most famously by Robert Merton as universalism, disinterestedness, communitarianism and organised scepticism (Merton, 1942).

Yet, at the same time, the reality of knowledge production has regularly been shown to be contrary to the Mertonian rules. As highlighted by Jasanoff (1987: 196): 'Much of the authority of science in the twentieth century rests as well on its success in persuading decision makers and the public that the Mertonian norms present an accurate picture of the way science "really works"'. Viewed from this perspective, efforts to encourage and incentivise external engagement pose a challenge to a longstanding basis of scientific authority. The notion of co-production, in particular, appears to require scientists to drop Mertonian values around disinterestedness and organised scepticism.

The Mertonian values have long been challenged within social sciences and humanities and, reflecting this, our data suggest that there are significant disciplinary differences in the perception of academic autonomy. Interestingly, within our focus groups it was generally not scientists who appeared to be most concerned about academic independence; rather, this issue was more dominant in the accounts of social scientists and humanities scholars (social science, law and education). These academics focused particularly on the importance of independence from government intervention and accountability. In contrast, the only natural scientist discussing this looked at it from the perspective of freedom to do basic research.

> 'Well, certainly in universities and the research is there to generate the knowledge which drives the progress. And that definitely requires a balance between giving the academics the freedom to do whatever they want. But I can understand that there is a need also for closer collaboration and transfer of that knowledge to the industry for the building of society basically. Not only to industry but general to society, so. But it cannot happen without this big pool of freedom and basic research ideas because – so the question is to strike the balance.' (Academic, chemistry)

In considering why social science participants seemed relatively more concerned with academic independence and autonomy than other participants, we suggest one reason might be the contested and political nature of much social science work. For example, one of the social scientists reported that, because they are working in strongly politicised areas, they are expected to get involved in public policy debates, whether or not they want to:

> 'I work on food policy and in a way the nutrition research evidence is taken up into public policy. And the politics of it are murky. And I'm also an early-career researcher and it feels like quite an exposed place to go into what is a very well entrenched set of politics. So you can end up being slotted into positions that you don't necessarily agree when you talk in public. And I think about in my case the most obvious way to do impact is through, either through the media or giving expert advice. So it is that kind of high profile, and it makes me a bit anxious.' (Academic, social science)

At the same time, while discussing constraints on academic freedom and autonomy, it was clear that research impact was far from the only threat (e.g. participants talked extensively about the constraints stemming from funder decisions to prioritise particular themes and areas). Hence, we suggest that while expectations regarding academic engagement with non-academic audiences are considered by academics across disciplines to be a potential threat to academic autonomy, these concerns are raised in a context of an ever-changing funding landscape and they are far from the only threat.

Research impact and academic careers

Participants across disciplines noted that universities increasingly reward impact work, for example in promotion criteria (although members of our sample were working, at the time of their participation, in one particular university, several had recently moved from other institutions and others made explicit reference to situations in other universities). However, the issue of career benefits from impact work is complex, as universities still require traditional forms of academic performance measures, such as publications and grant income. Yet, doing impact work requires time that is not spent publishing. Therefore, as pointed out by some participants, academics who are involved in impact work might not be as well published as their peers. There were some indications in the data that this might not be as detrimental to one's academic career as it was in the past, but this was not a clear and consistent finding. This view is illustrated by the following quote:

'I suspect partially why I've got this job is to do to an extent with impact. But I know for a fact I wouldn't have this job if I'd never published anything. And obviously the way impact is framed, there's got to be papers or books. There's got to be research that has impact. So in some ways, you know, this is kind of what I was saying before, impact kind of goes with the grain of how academics and how institutions operate already.' (Academic, arts)

The intertwined nature of formal and informal university values and rules is further illustrated by the story of an academic from physics who received his professorship based on the income from collaborative projects with the industry:

'I got my professorship based on the grounds that I brought a vast amount of money into the university in project money [with industry], £54 million over the years when I added it all up. But when the [Vice Chancellor] gave me my professorship [based on engagement activities], you had to go to this ceremony and all this, he said I was a very unusual case – and I wasn't sure whether to take that as a compliment or not. But I thought it was an interesting comment from him. If the impact agenda is here to stay, the university needs to work that out. And I don't think it's just this university, I think it's all universities.' (Academic, computational physics)

This issue raises a question of what is perceived to be an acceptable way of doing academic work. Even though official university declarations confirm that knowledge exchange should be valued, our data suggest that many academics still do not consider impact work to be as 'academic' as publishing. This was particularly evident during the focus group discussions that included medical and veterinary scientists (focus group 2 in Table 1.1), with one of the participants strongly objecting to the idea of academic promotion based on public engagement:

'It's the public engagement. And now the university is awarding professorships for public engagement, which does cause a big impact. But I am personally totally against it, to call it as a scientific professorship, because then you're not a scientist anymore. I mean now the scientists are supposed to do two things. They are supposed to do research and do public engagement. And there is nothing wrong, public engagement is important, it has to be done. But I think that it's not necessarily a job of a scientist. It's still my opinion that they should be seen as a professor in public engagement.' (Academic, clinical medicine)

As exemplified in this quote, for some academics, the impact agenda means the criteria of academic distinction that they are used to are shifting in ways that they are not necessarily comfortable with. Reflecting this, several interviewees discussed a need to refine career progression criteria.

The impact agenda and research quality

One of the big concerns expressed by our interviewees was the problem of research produced for policy or for industrial partners and the difference between this type of research and academic research. This does not necessarily mean that the research is of lower quality, but that the quality criteria are different in these two types of social settings. For example, as explained by one of the social scientists:

'I noticed, as I was giving a talk to the Scottish government health department in April, I'd prepared a talk very much with scientific slides. And I realised in the last five minutes that's not what they're interested in at all. They want to have very practical things. They say OK you come from university, don't show us the evidence, show us exactly what [the recommendations are] and so on. So I think we, and the problem is, so we'll be judged more in academic terms or in real society terms, and the two sides can be very different.' (Academic, social science)

Additionally, some of the participants linked the lower quality of research with the increase in funding for small-scale, applied or collaborative projects that might not be as rigorous as research projects funded through bigger, more competitive grants. A final way in which the impact agenda was suggested to be potentially detrimental to perceived research quality was through its impact on academics' workloads, with a few interviewees pointing out that the time they dedicate to impact is not directly translatable into research or research grant applications.

Research impact shaping research projects

As signalled above, one way in which the impact agenda was viewed as shaping academic work was by increasing the availability of funding for specific types of research. For example, an academic in classics commented:

> 'I would think that many areas in which people work are perhaps not as obviously attuned to creating impact than others. And they may simply decide to put in a funding application for a topic that is sexier that might have a greater public appeal, as opposed to what they would have otherwise done for that reason.' (Academic, classics)

Some of the participants pointed to the issue of increasing pressure coming from the government to focus on certain priorities. These priorities were seen as science funding for scientific projects lacking direct application:

> 'Science funding has become very prescriptive over the last fifteen or so years and everything seemed it had to have some sort of industrial impact. I don't think that's really right. I've always felt that I think we need to get the balance right between the sort of research funding that leads to direct impacts for companies and blue skies curiosity-driven science and I think the balance is wrong at the moment. The problem is you stoke up those troubles a long time in the future. The lack of curiosity-driven science we're doing now will only be felt in ten or fifteen years' time.' (Academic, computational physics)

Another participant made a similar point with an example of how adding a clinical aspect to the grant proposal increased the potential to get funded:

> 'I apply for grants where a very strong, it wasn't my site, very strong laboratory sites case got rejected, rejected, rejected. I just came along and sprinkled some clinical transition on it. I didn't do anything substantial. It [was] funded. And a clear idea that if you suddenly, if you give them the means by which they can go back to the government and say, well whichever government [department] funds [*Engineering and Physical Sciences Research Council*] and say this is the one.' (Academic, medical sciences)

A few of the interviewees pointed to the fact that basic science funding is important, even for the applied disciplines (e.g. education, law, physics) because it provides the applied academics with a knowledge base and/or research inspiration.

The pressure to produce research impact also encourages academics to choose collaborative approaches to research projects, since these seem to be linked to impacts that could be easier to achieve:

> 'I think some of the more highly theoretical philosophical work within this school and within other schools simply might not fit that kind of model. I think almost the kind of, the direct line between research and impact, and the way pathways to impact I think is encouraging this more collaborative integrated approach to the research process fits certain kinds of research more than others.' (Academic, law)

Finally, as noted by the participant from education (discussed earlier), in some cases the impact agenda's focus to link impact to research is encouraging more fundamental research.

Conclusions

This chapter has looked into disciplinary differences in perceptions and assessment of the impact agenda, comparing the perceptions of people working in multiple disciplines. The findings presented in this chapter have highlighted a cultural diversity around the idea of research impact which broadly maps on to academic disciplines and subdisciplines. We have argued that different traditions of scholarship translate into different models of engagement with non-academic audiences. As a result, the implementation of the impact agenda consists of multiple different, distinct, but overlapping processes of implementation, across different disciplinary cultures. In this sense, our findings overlap with existing analyses, which have consistently found a level of disciplinary variation in how impact is interpreted and experienced (e.g. Chowdhury et al, 2016; Chubb, 2017: Oancea, 2013: 248).

However, we also identified what we felt were a surprising number of issues that were either across participants or varied in ways that did not appear to relate to discipline. One area of consensus we identified is that participants in this chapter suggested that simpler, often less impactful research impacts were easier to capture within the UK's impact governance system (see also Smith and Stewart, 2017). This is particularly important for considering the unintended consequences of the UK's impact agenda and the associated tools of research governance. As multiple studies document, although tools such as setting targets, monitoring, grading and rewarding a particular outcome may aim solely to measure and encourage particular activities, they also have the power to construct reality, especially where structures are created to incentivise certain practices (Bevan and Hood, 2006; Boswell et al, 2015; James, 2004). In effect, such tools can steer behaviour to fit what is perceived to perform best in the chosen forms of assessment. In the context of the impact agenda, the requirement to report on impact might support practices that would be more easily measured and documented but less socially important (Smith and Stewart, 2017). This problem of decreasing plurality of academic practices as a result of the REF and its predecessor the RAE has already been demonstrated in the context of academic publishing (De Rijcke et al, 2016; HEFCE, 2016b). As a result of these assessments, academics changed their publishing patterns in order to fit what was perceived as a desirable outcome – for example journal articles rather than books, reports or conference proceedings. The data presented in this chapter suggest that a similar process of decreasing plurality of practices is happening in terms of the impact element of REF, as some activities are perceived as more acceptable to the assessors and as yielding a bigger return on investment.

Gibbons and colleagues (1994; Nowotny et al, 2001) argued that applied disciplines are more likely to be open to moving to Mode-2 knowledge production, as they have already had closer relationships with research users (so that the knowledge is already being produced in the 'context of application'). The findings in Chapter 8 found that academics working in an applied area, public health, were indeed relatively supportive of the UK's research impact agenda. However, the findings presented in this chapter suggest that the relationship between the attitudes to impact and the disciplinary background is more complex than the Mode 1/Mode 2 literature discussed earlier suggest. The perception of a better fit to the impact agenda depends also on the type of audience that the discipline aims to impact upon, the structure of the problems it deals with, the ways in which academic work is divided up (which, in turn, affects the ease with which research can be linked to impact) and perceptions of funder and assessor preferences.

How the concept of "research impact" translates into working practices is shaped by two simultaneous processes. One is the bottom-up expansion of patterns of relationships and forms of collaboration that have been historically shaped within disciplines. The other consists of sets of formal or informal rules of assessment, which are perceived to assign unequal value to different types of engagement and impact. In the more extreme cases, as appeared to be the case of public engagement activities in some disciplines, these processes draw clear boundaries around what counts as an impact activity and exclude other forms of engagement (see also Chapter 5).

Generally, our findings suggest that the UK's impact agenda has not introduced completely new engagement practices; rather, they have been practices build on historically developed forms of engagement. Academics in some disciplines have historically worked with industry partners, while others have long-term experience of organising public events or providing advice to policy or practice audiences. Nevertheless, the impact agenda does appear to have institutionalised and appropriated these types of activities as increasingly legitimate practices for academics. At the same time, the impact agenda, as an evaluative tool, has influenced these bottom-up activities. Most importantly, by imposing definitions of impact, and rules for measuring and documenting it, it appears to be informing a decrease of plurality in forms of engagement in some academic areas, as illustrated in Figure 4.2. Accordingly, the UK's approach to research impact risks having unintentional and undesirable consequences, akin to the increasingly homogeneous publication patterns that were documented in response to the RAE/REF assessments of academic outputs.

Notes

[1] For example, 'Panel Criteria and Working Methods – the Final Guidance Document to REF 2014' http://www.ref.ac.uk/media/ref/content/pub/panelcriteriaandworkingmethods/01_12.pdf.

[2] Although we note a recent study by Watermeyer 2020, that reveals far greater ambivalence among impact case study researchers, in terms of how their status as REF-impactful has caused them to ameliorate their status at an institutional and managerial level, and among their peers.

5

Impact on whom? Contrasting research impact with public engagement

As Chapter 2 showed, the current policy interest in research impact can be traced back to efforts to ensure that academic research provides a return on investment to the public purse. This agenda has risen alongside, and often rather separately from, a wider tradition of public engagement with, and in, academic research. The extent to which public engagement is seen as part of, or separate from, research impact appears to vary by discipline, as Chapter 4 discussed. This chapter explores the overlaps and elisions between these two fields of practice in more detail, comparing their articulation in guidance from research funders and regulators in the UK[1] with how researchers from different disciplines describe the experiences, pressures and opportunities of each. We conclude with a brief reflection on continuing shifts in these unstable fields, as, in the UK, 2017's industrial strategy reorients research impact towards economic competitiveness.

Definitions: the relationship between impact and public engagement

It is not always clear or consistent what different actors seek to signify when they use the terms research impact or 'public engagement'. Harmonising definitions of research impact between funders and evaluators of research, particularly with regards to public engagement, is one of the stated goals of REF2021 (HEFCE et al, 2017). The terms include distinct 'targets' (the public and, e.g., policy, practitioners or industry), and two 'processes' (impact versus engagement). These are contested terms; the notion of 'the public' (singular, coherent) is, in contemporary social science, almost always pluralised to recognise the dynamic and relational nature of societal groupings (Felt and Cochler, 2010; Newman and Clarke, 2009). There are other resonances and disagreements here: engagement implying a two-way process, impact seeming more didactic. However, the combinations that have come to dominate contemporary universities are for policy to be 'impacted' and 'the' public to be engaged.

The relative paucity of definitions of the term research impact in official guidance has been commented on before (Terama et al, 2016). By contrast, the work of the National Coordinating Centre for Public Engagement, an organisation funded by a consortium of HEFCE, UK Research Councils and the Wellcome Trust, has gone some distance to clarifying and harmonising definitions of public engagement. They have published a series of outputs which define and elaborate a considered and thorough definition. For example

> Public engagement describes the myriad of ways in which the activity and benefits of higher education and research can be shared with the public. Engagement is by definition a two-way process, involving interaction and listening, with the goal of generating mutual benefit. (Wilson et al, 2014: 3)

This definition emphasises diversity in process and, in other publications, the NCPPE (National Coordinating Centre for Public Engagement) emphasises the long roots of contemporary public engagement in practices including community engagement and lifelong learning (Duncan and Manners, 2017). Importantly though, this definition insists upon the idea of public engagement being an interactive process. Indeed, interactivity is a feature of understandings of public engagement within guidance from all the UK research councils and the Wellcome Trust. (Regarding other major funders, the Leverhulme Trust website emphasises instead impact on other academic disciplines, and the British Academy, while having several funding streams which emphasise public engagement, does not, at the time of this analysis, discuss their understanding of it at any length.) A 2015 report commissioned by a consortium of research funders including both the Wellcome Trust and the British Academy (see Wellcome Trust, 2016) cited the definition of public engagement used in the 2010 RCUK (Research Councils UK – a body that formally represented the UK's research councils from 2002 until it was replaced by the creation of the UKRI in 2018) strategy on public engagement. This dialogic definition distinguishes public engagement from, for example, impactful, publicly oriented dissemination work (see for example Pickett and Wilkinson, 2015), and is a shift from the same consortium's predecessor report on science communication (Royal Society, 2006).

A focus on research both shaping and being shaped by publics creates some peculiar recursive moments when subsumed within wider discussions of research impact. For example, in ESRC guidance, public engagement becomes a route to impact (rather than an intrinsically impactful activity): engagement, it is argued, should 'shape your research agenda so that it is more meaningful and useful to these groups. As a result, it is likely to have more of an impact' (ESRC, undated). When it comes to the public, the permeability of the academy is presented as necessary to increase the academy's ability, in turn, to permeate other arenas. And yet within research council guidance, this permeability is far less often presented as a feature of the policy world. The MRC, for example, discusses policy impact exclusively as a one-way process, with no reflection on how its scientists might in turn be influenced by policy actors:

> The MRC regularly submits evidence to consultations by government departments and House of Commons and House of Lords Select Committees, drawing on the expertise of researchers and research boards as necessary … Our researchers are also often called upon as experts in particular areas of research to give advice or evidence. (MRC, 2016: 1)

An emphasis on impact on, rather than engagement with, policymakers resonates with other research suggesting academics should open up their own working practices to policymakers, rather than simply package their findings for one-way dissemination (Matthews et al, 2018).

Rationalising public engagement

Most of the UK research councils present public engagement as one potential tool towards research impact, and yet there are nuances in their approaches. For the MRC, engagement is simply 'required' to implement one's scientific findings:

> All scientific achievements, from those arising from discovery science to those with research origins in the health sciences, require engagement with the public or policymakers to be successfully put into practice. (MRC, 2016: 1)

For the ESRC, an intrinsic, normative value to the work, and recognition of the need to open up research to be influenced *by* publics, is much more frequently present:

> Reasons for engaging with the public extend beyond the benefits to the research and researchers themselves. Some argue that if research is publicly funded, society has a right to shape research agendas and be involved in decisions about how discoveries are used. (ESRC, undated)

This contrasts slightly with independent funders. The Wellcome Trust, for example, often keeps public engagement ('Encouraging conversations about science, health and the human condition') separate from influencing policy ('Making research and healthcare as effective as possible') on their website and funding guidance (see, for example, Wellcome Trust, undated a: 8). Indeed, much of the Wellcome Trust's guidance on public engagement assumes, rather than elucidating, a rationale for public engagement. Their webpages and reports focus much more on encouraging researchers to reflect on their own motivations for conducting public engagement activities than on elaborating the trust's own rationale: 'There's one important question to ask yourself before you begin: "Why do I want to engage the public?" Thinking about your answer will make your public engagement easier and more successful' (Wellcome Trust, undated b). The Wellcome Trust website also demonstrates a strong interest in evaluating and improving public engagement activities:

> Engagement is an integral part of health research. Many people who fund and conduct such research are increasingly accepting and promoting engagement. With engagement firmly established, it is time to think about the quality and impact of these activities. (Aggett et al, 2012)

Again, evaluation is generally presented as being specific to the (varied) aims for individual activities, rather than to a funder-wide vision of what public engagement is for (see Wellcome Trust, 2015).

Safer bets? A perceived preference for policy and commercial impacts

An early reflection on public engagement by one of us, in the context of the emerging research impact agenda, optimistically predicted a positive shift in the perceived status and utility of engagement efforts:

> Where public engagement 'pre-impact' was viewed by sections of the academic community as frivolous, faddish and tokenistic, it is now elevated as an integral component of impact-capture work and in plotting the pathways between research producer and research intermediary/end-user/collaborator. (Watermeyer, 2012: 115)

However, as the 'impact agenda' became incentivised in REF2014, fears began to be voiced that governmental priorities, rather than a sense of societal gain, would shape the reception to impact case studies. That is, as Belfiore puts it, the impact agenda would reward 'a particular, pragmatic and economically inflected articulation of … value to the public' (Belfiore, 2015: 97). Such fears were evident in our focus groups and interviews, with academics generally appearing to believe that particular kinds of impacts are more likely to be well received in REF impact case studies than impact achieved through public engagement (see Chapter 4). These included policy and commercial impacts, which were sometimes contrasted very directly with the more amorphous notion of engaging with, or impacting on, members of the public. In more traditionally scientific fields, participants generally indicated that they felt commercial and other economic impacts were the most coveted forms of impact and that this preference was becoming more obvious with recent policy changes. For example:

> 'I've heard, but that's not my field, but I've heard from the sciences that it was very difficult to get high scores for any cases linked to public engagement or policy impact. And there's been some discussions there where they could learn something from us in terms of evidencing that. [...] So I think that was the panels just being more impressed with commercial impact. But I think that is, I don't think there was anything in the guidance suggesting that you should do that. So I think that's probably a bit of a bias in the [science] panels.' (University professional services, knowledge exchange)
>
> 'In my area [...] there's a very strong, we have a department for industrial strategy at the UK level. So, used to be Department of Energy and Climate Change, which has now been absorbed into the Department of Industry, Business and something else, strange acronym.[2] And so the feeling is more and more that, and there's a lot of public-private bodies in my area that you have to collaborate with.

> Like I'm doing some work now with one of the Innovate UK catapults, and they are essentially business driven. So, there's a sense going forwards now that for us to be relevant to that agenda we have to be much more kind of, what's the benefit for UK PLC of doing sustainable technology and so on? I think post-Brexit as well that's becoming more and more clear that the future research calls in our area are going to be, "how are you assisting business development, local economic growth?"' (Academic, social science)

In sum, our research suggests there is a widely held belief (which, in our data, was most overt among participants working in the natural sciences) that economic impacts from research are viewed as the most valuable form of impact, at least from a funder perspective (and sometimes, some participants suggested, an impact assessor perspective), while evidence of public engagement was often depicted as both harder to capture and, ultimately, less likely to be valued by assessors. This perception has been challenged by Terama et al's (2016) assessment of REF2014 impact case studies submitted by one university – University College London (UCL) – which concludes:

> [T]he spread of case studies and the results of their assessment indicate the REF has been able to recognize and reward a diverse range of impact types, with a diverse basis for submission across faculties. Despite the lack of more specific guidance, no single type of impact was more rewarded than others – there is no evidence to suggest that the REF2014 exercise was designed to focus academic research towards commercial or economic goals, for example. (Terama et al, 2016: 4)

Indeed, Terama et al (2016) found that public engagement formed a central component of impact across UCL within REF2014. Yet, an interview-based study with academics working across a variety of disciplines in Australia and the UK, found interviewees held the same kinds of perceptions that we identified: 'There was also a sense that public engagement did not 'count' towards impact and that many would use it in their pathways to impact as an aside rather than a core activity' (Chubb, 2017: p145). Chubb, like us (see Chapter 4), notes some important disciplinary variation here, with academics working in the arts and humanities being more likely to view public engagement as a valid approach to impact. What appeared to unite participants across disciplines in both our own research and Chubb's (2017) study was a concern that it might be difficult to be able to persuasively document research impacts achieved through public engagement. This suggests that, no matter how REF impact case study panel assessors actually review public engagement work, academics and institutions may be restricting their submissions (and possibly their underlying activities) due to a perception that public engagement is likely to perform less well than other outward-facing activities.

Some of the panel overview reports from REF2014 also highlight this concern, with the report from Main Panel A (covering medical, health and food sciences) reporting:

> One aspect of impact assessment on which panellists felt there was need for further clarification within the guidance was on the nature of evidence required to show that public engagement-based research impact had gone beyond 'business as usual' in engaging audiences. (REF2014 Main Panel A, 2015: 11)

Although this did not appear to be of as much concern to the other three REF2014 main panels, at least in their overview reports (REF2014 Main Panel B, 2015; REF2014 Main Panel C, 2015; REF2014 Main Panel D, 2015), a recent book exploring the views of impact assessors involved in REF also suggests caution about how public engagement is assessed in REF impact case studies. Derrick's interviews with REF2014 impact assessors identified a tension between the view, among at least some assessors, that public engagement *should* be valued, and their sense that the REF2014's definition of impact made this difficult in the context of the specific demand for evidence of a 'change or benefit' (Derrick, 2018: 71). This view accords with those of our interviewees in the sciences, as discussed in Chapter 5, for whom public engagement often appeared to be viewed as a form of 'outreach' activity deemed relatively separate from efforts to achieve impact (in industry or policy). This again reflects Chubb's (2017) findings, in which she reports that academics from 'the physical sciences, maths and engineering referred to working with schools (and activities that those representing other disciplines might call public engagement), as 'outreach' and that this work was motivated by a sense of duty to communicate science rather than a sense that it had much to do with impact.

These perceptions of the contrasting value of outward-facing academic work were attributed, at least in part, to a sense that a fundamental driver of the research impact agenda in the UK is a national government attempt to achieve demonstrable (initially economic) returns on investment (a perception which is supported by a wealth of policy documents, as discussed in Chapter 1, and shared by many of those writing about the impact agenda, e.g. Penfield et al, 2014; Donovan, 2011). The government-funded research councils were, in turn, positioned as competing for government investment in this climate:

> 'I think each of the research councils wants a bigger cut of the pie and I think, at the very, very highest level of the research councils, they have to go into a room, make the argument, and it eases the difficulty for them to make those arguments. I think it's very rare that anyone in government actually cares [...] about what the actual science is. They want to get re-elected and what will get them re-elected is people with a decent economy and things. Occasionally there's a nice buzz factor – [...] I think it's overrated but the discovery of the Higgs boson went down very well. It had a huge public perception and maybe the government at the time got a tiny, tiny, tiny little increment because of it but that's not at all why they funded it. They're looking for, ultimately, they're looking for economic results and I think they're not even looking for societal benefit [...] [or] the societal benefit that they're looking for is generated because of the economic impact.' (Academic, particle physics)

> 'Well in economic terms, I think it's just the funding bodies of government to try to basically get some return on the investments into the research. [...] We are talking about money but at the end of the day it creates employment, it increases the health and well-being of the society. So, I think that's the agenda.' (Academic, chemistry)

The few, notable exceptions in our research tended to be based in the humanities and arts, areas more likely to be funded by the Arts and Humanities Research Council (AHRC), such as the following historian, who depicted a hierarchy of impact operating within history that was in direct contrast to the accounts given by many other interviewees, particularly those working in the natural sciences (including the two quoted above):

'For us, commerce and politics are probably the lesser end. It would be society in the wider sense, influencing how people view certain things [that we would prioritise]. I mean we talk a lot about ancient democracy, talking about this from the basis of our research [...] with members of the general public would hopefully make them reflect about their own democracy [...] and what they think is good about it or bad.' (Academic, history)

Interestingly, the published literature gives the sense that it is academics writing from a humanities perspective who are particularly likely to link the impact agenda to a neoliberal economising of the academic sphere (Belfiore, 2015; Bulaitis, 2017), often making connections with earlier pressures for arts and cultural organisations to demonstrate their economic contribution from the 1980s onwards. Analysis of research council websites does suggest that the economic benefits of the research they fund are more often emphasised than societal ones. The AHRC, in particular, details an extensive programme of work to assess specifically the economic impacts of the research it funds (AHRC, 2009a), culminating in the *Leading the World* report which aims 'to show just how effectively arts and humanities research, including that funded by the AHRC, does produce economic impact on British society and the economy' (AHRC, 2009b). Likewise, a 2017 press release from the UKRI's predecessor, RCUK, celebrated 'the impacts' of investment in UK research in exclusively economic terms: 'This investment drives economic growth by helping to deliver the UK's Industrial Strategy of increasing productivity, creating high-value industry, jobs and a skilled workforce', reflecting that 'these are important stories to tell as they inform the public' (Research Councils UK, 2017). All of this evokes a sense in which, for research funders, 'public engagement' is often subsumed within a broader, economically oriented impact agenda; a means of helping to achieve economic impacts (via dissemination) rather than a form of dialogic engagement with the potential to challenge and alter academic practices and outputs.

Despite this, analyses of the REF2014 research impact case studies do not support the claim that economic impacts are prized above those likely to stem from public engagement work. The NCPPE's analysis of the 6,640 impact case studies submitted to REF2014 states that: 'We didn't discover any significant difference in the scores awarded to case studies featuring mentions of public engagement compared with those that don't' (Duncan and Manners, 2017: 8).[3] While perhaps reassuring, this is not a ringing endorsement (that is, there is no evidence that public engagement case studies do better) given the likelihood that public engagement work is both more complex and less predictable than some more contained and specifically directed forms of impact work (such as efforts to inform decisions among particular groups of policymakers or businesses). However, for researchers committed to working in this way, the NCPPE analysis broadly suggests that fears of penalising transformational, societally oriented research impact are unfounded. They also argue that public engagement is reasonably widespread, finding that 3,108 of 6,637 case studies specifically mention public engagement as part of their impact (Duncan and Manners, 2017).

Contrasting public engagement with other forms of research impact

Our participants also suggested that public engagement was less appealing to researchers, and often less well rewarded by funders and assessors, because achieving genuine dialogue with publics, and/or documenting impact, is harder:

> 'It is about the difference that we can actually capture. […] I think there is a lot of [public] engagement that probably won't have impact, or won't have any clear outcomes […] I think there is probably a lot of public engagement activities that the university does, and should do, that may not be captured in the way that we need for this [i.e. that 'counts' in terms of research impact].' (University professional services, knowledge exchange)

> 'If you want to engage with the public then organising events takes time. Doing it well, anyway, takes time. It's time consuming, and it's kind of brain space consuming. You need to think quite carefully about how to organise something. It isn't just standing up and talking to people but is actually generating some sort of conversation.' (Academic, social science)

There are likely at least three reasons for this, one relatively easily addressed, and two rather more complex. The first is simply that 'the public' is a more diffuse actor, and therefore less easily evidenced by statements from individuals (as noted in an earlier interviewee quotation). In response, both the NCPPE and Wellcome Trust guidance advises that researchers 'segment' their understanding of publics in order to effectively target their activity at more coherent and identifiable actors. While this seems feasible for most academic work it may, in itself, require considerable investment and learning. Reflecting this, one focus group participant who had recently undertaken some public engagement work, noted that the main contribution had been their own learning about how to engage with a particular (marginalised) group:

'We did some work with people [...] who were alcohol addicted, and we then did some work around their environment and how they engaged with the environment. [...] What it told us most was about how to engage with that group of people, and how other people might engage with that group of people in the future. So now the bigger impact from that study is really in that learning.' (Academic, nursing)

The second obstacle relates to the relative ability of publics to effect demonstrable impact, when compared to, for example, a senior civil servant who has been influenced by a research project. The nature of public 'power' is more diffuse, and therefore attempting to change a climate of public opinion may not quickly or easily translate into the kinds of auditable changes that the REF impact case studies are perceived to demand:

'What makes a really good impact case is there's a clear bit of science that was done in the relatively recent past with a clear citation track to the member of staff and then clear engagement between probably the same member of staff, but maybe others here at the university, with a company that you can actually say this is Mars plc or Intel or something and then you want a letter from the company saying, "and because of this particular advance that you guys gave us, we have now been able to increase our profits by such and such". So, a good impact case has a very clear connection between the science paper that generated the advance and a dollar sign at the end of it of this is what it's delivered.' (Academic, particle physics)

'If you set it up right, the audit trail with impacts in public policy can be very easy to do, because ... if you're already working with someone if you ask them to cite your paper then that's it. [Interviewee then gives example of having taken this approach successfully with his/her own work.]' (Academic, mathematics)

The third issue, mentioned by several academics who had been involved in fairly substantial public engagement activities, is that these activities may be informed by bodies of work (e.g. a whole strand of scientific thinking or by artistic outputs) rather than specific pieces of research, making them unsuitable for REF impact case studies:

'You may have had an exhibition [...] that had impact and people were excited and you have good revelations and all that. But, actually, the exhibition wasn't based on research [...]. We had several cases like that, where you had somebody creating an exhibition for big galleries [...] [In some cases] you can show the link between academic research and publications, feeding into [the exhibition]. But if you just had the exhibition, so if they just created the exhibition but couldn't link that back to any research publications they'd done prior to that, then it would be more difficult.' (University professional services, knowledge exchange)

The response to this has often been to concentrate on processes of public engagement, rather than attempting to capture outcomes. Thus, impact case studies report proxies for impact, such as numbers of people at events. This is not an entirely satisfactory approach: the NCPPE (Duncan and Manners, 2017: 8) notes that 'Evidence provided of impact on public understanding and awareness is often weak: usually researchers limit their evidence to a list of the outlets they have used and the numbers of people engaged.' Funders are increasingly encouraging researchers to evaluate their public engagement activities more thoroughly (see, for example, Aggett et al, 2012), and priorities for the approach to REF2021 include providing additional guidance on impact arising from public engagement (HEFCE et al, 2017). This seems vital to avoid a vicious circle: if public engagement is a risky, difficult form of impact to evidence then it may be avoided by both researchers and institutions who lack the budgetary or job security to invest in necessary processes of evaluation and monitoring.

Even a shift to valuing (through measurement) processes of engagement rather than outcomes can sit at odds with understandings of public engagement advanced by some researchers highly committed to it. King and Rivett (2015) take this approach, arguing for a 'relational approach' to understanding the value of public engagement:

> [I]t is often the process of engagement that is inherently most valuable to those we engage with – the conversations, debates and exchanges of skills and ideas rather than the final impact or change. And indeed potential change may come at a much later date, when no measurement will be in place to capture it. (King and Rivett, 2015: 229)

Especially in the social sciences and humanities, public engagement has long roots in alternative understandings of the role and value of academic work. These sit at odds with audit exercises, which Power (1997) describes as 'rituals of verification', shallow data-collection exercises which squeeze out opportunities for more reflexive organisational learning. This tension creates dilemmas for researchers who both need to survive within the contemporary academy, and act in ways consistent with their beliefs.

Disciplinary differences in focus on public engagement

The NCCPE analysis of REF2014 makes useful distinction between the disciplines. Perhaps predictably, they found that arts and humanities researchers were particularly likely to list public engagement as a research impact (24 per cent of case studies in that panel, compared to 6 or 7 per cent in the other panels) (Duncan and Manners, 2017). They also emphasised that particular forms of public engagement, for example outreach, were prevalent in particular fields. They note that researchers in medicine and public health are particularly *un*likely to report public engagement as a component of their research impact case studies which seems at odds with the strong emphasis on public engagement from key health-related research funders like the Wellcome Trust, and the insistence on public and patient *involvement* in the design and conduct of research for key funders like the National Institute for Health Research (NIHR, undated). Perhaps this reflects a sense that researchers in these fields, who have a range of reasonably easily demonstrable impacts from their research – as Belfiore (2015: 100) puts it: 'in the shape of illnesses cured, vaccines created, tsunamis and natural disasters averted, or new inventions brought to market' – simply did not need to include impact from the more diffuse work of public engagement. By contrast, several humanities researchers emphasise their disciplines' feelings of vulnerability to demands for research impact,

Figure 5.1: The main external audiences described by different disciplines

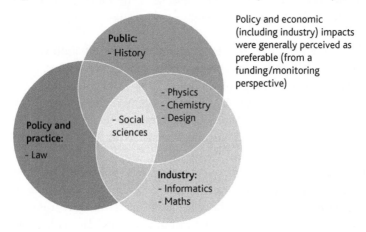

Public:
- History

Policy and economic (including industry) impacts were generally perceived as preferable (from a funding/monitoring perspective)

- Physics
- Chemistry
- Design

- Social sciences

Policy and practice:
- Law

Industry:
- Informatics
- Maths

despite having clear expertise in public engagement, while participants from the natural sciences described a clear distinction between research impact and public engagement work. In sum, the extent to which people think about public engagement work as being a part of, or connected to, impact work seems to vary by discipline, as summed up in Figure 5.1 (and as we began exploring in the previous chapter).

Conclusions

This chapter has explored the connections between public engagement and the research impact agenda in the context of contemporary UK academia and the increasing raft of funder requirements to commit to externally facing work. It has highlighted the ambivalences within usage of terminology, and the valuable work of the NCPPE in advancing a reflexive, considered definition of 'public engagement' which foregrounds the need for engagement to be a two-way process, not a didactic re-education of UK publics. It has explored the perceived difficulties and risks of public engagement in the current context of research impact, noting a clear belief that it is easier to demonstrate research impact focusing on policy and commercial (rather than public) audiences. Touching on disciplinary differences in approach, it has described the way that public engagement can appear as an 'impact of last resort' for disciplines, depending on the other measurable impacts available to them, and fundamentally rooted in the difficulties of evidencing the value of this work. And it has emphasised some of the discomforts of funnelling public engagement into audit processes for researchers for whom it is not a performance but an essential component of their understandings of their work.

In some ways, public engagement practices have the potential to serve as a source of solace, even inspiration, for critics of the UK's research impact agenda: both because definitions increasingly insist upon a two-way dialogue between researchers and publics, and because it directs researchers' efforts at relationship building, away from powerful elites and towards a wider range of actors. However, since most of our interviewees felt that public engagement results in impacts that are difficult to document for REF, we are left to conclude that the UK's current approach to research impact (or at least the way it is being understood by academics and institutions) is restricting this possibility. Much of the data for this chapter were analysed in 2017, and in the intervening period before publication, some of the key UK drivers of both public engagement and research impact have shifted with the creation of UKRI and the launch of the Industrial Strategy (Kagan and Diamond, 2019). If anything, these changes have de-emphasised the transformative social and cultural potential of academic research in favour of its economic role in fostering innovation:

> UKRI will have a nationwide remit to understand and maintain our research infrastructure and innovation landscape and use the research and innovation system to build on local strengths and deliver economic growth across the UK. (UKRI, undated)

This suggests that Watermeyer's (2012) initial hopes that the UK's research impact agenda would revitalise perceptions of, and support for, public engagement work may have been overly optimistic. Nonetheless, we suggest it remains true that an academic decision to undertaken upstream engagement work may provide 'a worthy rationalization for demonstrating the impact of their work, […] which moves beyond and improves the faceless, superficial and dispiriting mandate of top-down [research impact] evaluation perceived in the REF' (Watermeyer, 2012: 126). And we note that recent guidance for REF2021, which cites NCCPE guidance on public engagement, does at least suggest that public engagement is becoming a clearer part of REF guidance on research impact (REF, undated).

Notes

[1] Guidance was accessed and analysed in 2017. Where particular sources are known to have changed, we have updated references, but guidance in this field is rarely

stable, given its responsiveness to funder strategy and the REF cycle. The analysis in this chapter therefore inevitably represents something of a snapshot.

[2] The UK Department for Energy and Climate Change became part of a new Department for Business, Energy and Industrial Strategy in 2016.

[3] Note that while the text of submitted REF impact case studies is available but the individual scores attributed by REF panel members are not, the approach that Duncan and Manners (2017) took to this analysis involved identifying all case studies that mentioned public engagement (or similar) and then identifying case studies which must have scored highly, so 3★ or 4★, based on the number of case studies submitted by a particular institution to a specific unit of assessment and the overall institutional score for impact that was awarded in that unit of assessment. The approach is explained in full on page 42 of their report.

6

Public intellectualism and the impact agenda: international perspectives

Previous chapters have offered a critical review of the research impact agenda, situating it within international efforts to improve research utilisation for key groups including academics, research funders, 'knowledge brokers' and research users. This chapter considers where public intellectualism rests within these concerns. Specifically, the chapter explores the multiple public spheres that make up space between the academy and politics by focusing on: (i) three established academics working within the social sciences who engage outwardly in ways that might be described as 'public intellectualism'; and (ii) three established academics who work closely with external policy audiences on a range of recognised public policy 'problems', who we refer to as 'academic interlocutors'. These in-depth interview accounts from leading academics working in Australia, Canada, the USA and the UK allow us to continue the work of Chapter 5 in exploring the kinds of externally facing practices that are facilitated through the UK's approach to impact, compared to the kinds of practices being supported in other contexts with an established interest in knowledge exchange and research utilisation. Since the literature on public intellectualism is distinct from much of the literature on which this book has drawn so far, this chapter begins by briefly reviewing some of the key contributions to this literature. This allows us to situate the analysis in this chapter within these broader discussions, including by considering the elementary question of whether (and if so, how) notions of public intellectualism and impact are perceived to be complementary. The international perspectives included in the data in this chapter allow us to reflect on how developments in the UK are perceived by externally engaged academics elsewhere.

Which public and what intellectual?

In the opening sentence of his seminal essay on the relationship between social scientific inquiry and political positioning, the late Howard

Becker maintained that researchers will routinely 'find themselves caught in a crossfire. Some urge them not to take sides, to be neutral and do research that is technically correct and value free. Others tell them their work is shallow and useless if it does not express a deep commitment to a value position' (Becker, 1967: 239). How Becker resolved this in his own work is illustrated in some of the titles of his most well-known publications (e.g. *Radical Politics and Sociological Research: Observations on Methodology and Ideology*, co-authored with Horowitz and published in 1972, *Outsiders: Studies in the Sociology of Deviance*, published in 1973 and *Doing Things Together*, published in 1986). In this sense Becker did pick a side, but not in a straightforward way. His concern was with the framing and naming of social problems – their social construction rather than their self-evident character. This observation is of most relevance to our book when we recognise that, in the course of pursuing research impact, 'the academy is a participant and not just an observer' (Murji 2017: 59). For, as other chapters in this book demonstrate, very few advocates of utilising and translating their research deem such activity to be an armchair exercise. On the contrary, most actively aspire (in varying ways) to some kind of direct engagement that inevitably 'takes sides' in the most elementary sense: scholars of health inequalities advocate their reduction, researchers of gender discrimination seek to highlight these injustices, academics focusing on wealth disparities and poverty point to their harm, climate scientists demand action on climate change, and so forth.

In a recent assessment of this dynamic, focusing upon race scholarship in particular, Murji (2017: 57) has argued that research 'must always be a more than academic matter', not least by displaying a commitment to antiracism. At the same time, Murji recognises that what this may involve, practically, 'is itself an issue of contention and, usually, an intra-scholarly debate about the relationship between the academy and politics' (Murji, 2017: 57). Indeed, it is perhaps paradoxical that during the ascent of the impact agenda, a number of standard-bearers for the need for academics to better engage with society have pointed to a retreat of public intellectualism (Posner, 2003; Fuller, 2005; Meer, 2006; Said, 1994). This taps into a longstanding literature lamenting the decline of the public intellectual (Molnar, 1994), 'anti–intellectualism' (Hofstader, 1973; Johnson, 1989) and even 'philistinism' (Furedi, 2004); some of which is linked to the alleged malaise of 'dumbing down' (Jacoby, 2000) or indeed cultural populism (Eagleton, 1996).

Such complaints are interesting if for no other reason than that they operate with a relatively narrow conception of 'public intellectualism', often tacitly trading in, and reproducing, the vision of a white male 'who through intellectual command or charisma straddles and maintains credence' (Murji, 2017: 67). No less problematic is that such accounts also fail to recognise (or sometimes misrecognise) the multiple publics with which academia engages (or might engage). This chapter returns to this issue later on. For now, we reflect on what has been enveloped within the category of 'public intellectualism' by critically engaging with two such 'author priests' (Back, 2016: 62): Jean-Paul Sartre and Michel Foucault.

One formulation associated with Sartre (1974: 285) outlines a distinction between 'critical' and 'functional' public intellectuals. For Sartre, the distinction works by arguing that 'the duty of the [critical] intellectual is to denounce injustice wherever it occurs', as opposed to merely doing so 'functionally', according to party or factional interests. The implication is that public intellectuals should extrapolate outwards from a universal ethical standard on some issues, while conserving their independence by becoming publicly 'committed' intellectuals in order to comment freely and without known constraints that are either self and/or externally imposed. Complaining that Sartre's notion of a 'committed' intellectual represents a fictitious ideal of universality, fighting for universal truths and freedoms and assuming the task of speaking for humanity as a whole, Foucault (1977) instead advanced the idea of a more specific intellectual who would intervene on the side of the 'oppressed' over particular issues, while never claiming to 'speak' on the behalf of anybody. Foucault's general concern here was that an adoption of universal positions that necessitate speaking on the behalf of others actually functions to rob them of their already limited agency (since he viewed power as being exercised through discourse, such that those who produce discourse exercise the power to enforce its validity). To conceive of the intellectual solely in Foucauldian terms, however, may be no more helpful than Sartre's conception, since the intellectual 'interventions' conceived of by Foucault can surely not stand outside broader ethical and political considerations that bear down on university-based academics, and the research programmes they cultivate and are invested in. That is to say, academics pursuing this kind of public intellectualism cannot simply 'intervene' on specific issues as individual scholars, but would need to do so as facilitators and interlocutors if they are to avoid reproducing hierarchies between themselves and non-academics participating in the underlying research. Perhaps a better way to get a handle on the relationship between academic research and public intellectualism is to consider the institutional and cultural conditions under which academics labour and come into their fore as public intellectuals. As Modood (2018: 3) has argued, 'our starting-point here does have to be the fact that we are talking about intellectuals rooted in the ways of thinking, conserving, and researching that take place in and is distinctive of universities'. He continues:

> While this is the source of their intellectualism it can also be a constraint upon the ambition to be a [public intellectual]. For an academic to have any chance of success as a [public intellectual] … they must be influential within university circles first. They must influence fellow academics, their own discipline(s), students, and so on over a period of time and across the generations if they are to have any credibility beyond those circles. In that sense the university is not just a perch or the day job that pays the bills, it – meaning not of course just one's employer but the relevant academic communities and networks – is the workshop for forging ideas and conducting research for [public intellectuals] no less than for any other kind of academic. [Public intellectuals] must achieve a certain level of accomplishment within their discipline(s) and the reputational standing that goes with it. (Modood, 2018: 3)

The analogy of a workshop seems useful, as is the sense of the double bind: that the university sets direct and indirect parameters on intellectualism, precisely the tendency that Said (1994) characterised negatively as 'professionalism', which may feel in tension with public engagement work. Potential routes out centre not only on different, perhaps more engaged, 'intellectualism', but also on the very notion of the 'public' in categories of public intellectualism. How academics think about publics is likely to be informed not only by disciplinary training, and their own academic work, but also by normative values and beliefs. The idea (outlined in Chapter 5) that, if academics and universities are to look outwards to engage with and learn from broader publics (to have impact), then they should do so to serve public interests, not only governmental ones, has a normative dimension. It is also an ambition that necessarily registers the multi-scalar and dynamic quality of what the 'public' comprises (see Chapter 5). As Holmwood has argued:

> In contemporary discussions of the impact of research, much is made of the engagement with users and the development of 'pathways to impact' in which research is 'co-produced' with users or beneficiaries of it. However,

this takes the structure of associations as given, when the problem of publics is always the problem of consequences of associated actions for others. How are the 'publics' affected in the knowledge process to be protected and brought into a responsible share in the direction of activities? (Holmwood, 2011b: 240)

The notion of 'public' can be used to refer not only to populations of people, but also informed by the ideas of philosophers from Kant to Habermas (1974), specifically on the idea of a public sphere. For Habermas (1974), the public sphere is something that simultaneously sits inside and outside state governance – it is not a direct function of the state, yet it is open to debate on the nature of public issues on which state policy might be exercised. He thus characterised it as:

[A] sphere which mediates between society and state, in which the public organises itself as the bearer of public opinion, accords with the principle of the public sphere – that principle of public information which once had to be fought for against the arcane politics of monarchies and which since that time has made possible the democratic control of state activities. (Habermas, 1974: 351)

There is, of course, both a descriptive and normative dimension to Habermas' account. The normative function conceives of the public sphere as based upon notions of public good as distinct from private interest and forms of private life (notably families) (see Calhoun, 2000: 533). This has been widely criticised by a variety of authors, including Fraser (1995) and Casonova (1994), on at least two grounds. The first is that Habermas ignores how matters of both private and public life, such as religion and politics, have historically played an important role in constituting notions of the public. The second is that is that it is normatively undesirable and empirically implausible to confine notions of the public to a single, overarching sphere. Certainly, the academics we interviewed were often acutely aware of the need to negotiate multiple publics (sometimes simultaneously) and of the need to employ different, bespoke approaches for engaging with different audiences, though there also appears to be some disciplinary variation in the kinds of 'publics' academics most commonly orientate themselves towards (see Chapters 4 and 5).

Multiple publics and multiple knowledge

If we were to translocate the notion of multiple publics to Modood's (2018) analogy of the university as a 'workshop', and foreground public and not only governmental interests (as Chapter 5 implies we should), then we might further be served by Burawoy's (2011: 33) descriptions of four functions of university-based labour in the production of knowledge: professional, policy, critical and public. 'At heart', he maintains, the first kind 'is professional knowledge' that is generated and assessed according to academic criteria. This can and has been applied to the more policy style second kind of knowledge but does not 'short circuit the academic world' in order to produce 'meaningful and durable knowledge on demand by clients' (Burawoy, 2011: 33). A continuing dialogue nonetheless remains between professional knowledge and policy-centred knowledge. Running parallel is a third kind of 'critical knowledge' that is produced and sustained by a community of scholars and an accompanying 'community of discourse that transcends disciplines' (Burawoy, 2011: 33). Fourth, there is a knowledge that seeks a public conversation 'about the broad direction of society'. Burawoy continues: 'Just as there is an interdependence of professional and policy knowledge, so the same is true of critical and public knowledge – each infuses others with a discussion of the values recognized by society'. The sting in the tail comes in his argument against the instrumentalisation of knowledge, by insisting that the university 'also has to counter policy definitions of the worth of knowledge and elaborate the longer-term interests, building society in the university and the university in society'. (Burawoy, 2011: 33). This perseverance on the virtue of what is distinctive about university-based intellectualism is also reflected in Back's (2016: 24) resolve that professional academics should 'stop being afraid of arguing for the vocation of thinking'. Indeed, and in his discussion of the influence that public intellectuals might seek to have, Modood (2018: 14) refers to James Q. Wilson, who he describes as 'one of the most prominent [public intellectuals] of recent years', and whose influence 'was not to be found in the details of policy'. On the contrary, argues Modood, 'intellectuals provided the conceptual language, the ruling paradigms, the empirical examples (note I say *examples* not evidence) that became the accepted assumptions for those in charge of making policy'.

As Modood infers, the question of evidence is important here, and is perhaps the new fulcrum of public intellectualism and its capacity for impact. For example, in their recent account of 'symphonic social science',[1] Halford and Savage (2017) present their own empirical study to argue that, 'Whereas in previous generations it was social theorists – often sociologists – such as Habermas, Giddens, Foucault and Beck who commanded public as well as academic debate, it is now social scientists of *data* – Piketty (2014), Putnam (2000) and Wilkinson and Pickett (2009) – who are at the fore' (Halford and Savage, 2017: 1134–5). There has, in this respect, been at least a perceived shift in the academic landscape on which moves to promote research impact are taking place. What it accentuates is a broader emphasis on data which, if Halford and Savage (2017) are correct, invites us to consider whether public intellectualism that is not linked to empirical data can have the kinds of impacts that it might previously have achieved.

Having considered some of the key ideas and discussions about public intellectualism within the literature, the next part of this chapter considers how academics working in a range of different contexts negotiate academic labour with outward-facing work and explores how they each view public intellectualism and the UK's research impact agenda. Our small set of six interviewees are all very senior figures in their respective fields; they are each considered international experts by others and they all see their research as having wider significance than just in the countries in which they are based.

We include, first, Michèle Lamont who is professor of sociology and of African and African American studies and the Robert I. Goldman professor of European studies at Harvard University. She has been president of the American Sociological Association. She is also the director of the Weatherhead Center for International Affairs at Harvard University and the co-director of the Successful Societies Program of the Canadian Institute for Advanced Research. A cultural sociologist, Lamont is the author of a research which include studies of group boundaries, class and ethnoracial dynamics in the USA and France, cultures of excellence in higher education, social resilience and neoliberalism, and comparative cultural repertoires and the evaluation of qualitative social science research.

Second, Alison Phipps is UNESCO Chair in Refugee Integration through Languages and the Arts, professor of languages and intercultural studies and co-convener of the Glasgow Refugee, Asylum and Migration Network (GRAMNET) at the University of Glasgow. Her multilingual research takes place in settings which are often marked by extremes; in detention centres, campaign offices, reporting centres for UKBA (UK Border Agency) and during diasporic celebrations and holidays, in community halls, churches and mosques, as well as in domestic settings. She is presently chair of the Scottish government's New Scots Integration Program, and from 1999 to 2004 she was chair of the International Association for Languages and Intercultural Communication, and an advisor to the World Council of Churches' International Ecumenical Peace Convocation from 2007 to 2011.

Third, we have Les Back who is professor of sociology at Goldsmiths College, London. Back's work is ethnographically informed, based largely in the hinterlands of south London where he was born. His research began in the 1980s when he started a PhD emerging out of his experiences of being a youth worker. Since then he has conducted a wide range of empirical work largely based in Britain, although also including fieldwork in northern Alabama in the southern United States. In addition to social theory and research methodology, he has researched the topics of racism, popular culture and, especially, music and digital culture and city life. He describes his work as aspiring to create a sensuous or live sociology committed to searching for new modes of sociological writing and representation.

Then we have three senior academics interviewed by Smith who, due to the consent arrangements in place for the interviews, remain anonymous. These three individuals have all focused on trying to improve relations between academic research and public policy and practice. One is based in Canada and has focused mainly on health-related issues. The other two are based in Australia and the UK and they have both worked to improve research use across a wide range of public policy issues. All three have worked closely with policymakers, all have experience of working in settings beyond academia and all are strongly committed to the idea that academic research should be useful to policy and practice audiences. These are then, at least on the face of it, not 'public intellectuals' but precisely the kinds of academics whom the architects of the UK's REF agenda appear to have been aiming to support – we call them 'academic interlocutors'. By placing these two sets of interviews side by side, this chapter allows us to consider the extent to which variations in perspectives on external engagement, and associated incentives, map on to more fundamental epistemologies and modes of working.

What does successful impact involve and what motivates efforts to engage external audiences?

An obvious question to begin with is to ask: what does successful impact resemble, in the minds of our respondents, and what are the implications for their academic lives and for public intellectualism?

For Lamont, there is a clear disciplinary role in an answer to this question, which implies that competition for external influence can occur between disciplines and that this, in itself, may be a motivation for undertaking outward-facing work:

> 'They [economists] are really good at self-promotion and they are competitive with each other in terms of putting their hands on resources, influencing policymakers and making sure that their work comes out in outlets where it will have an impact. In contrast, many sociologists behave like kindergarteners when it comes to increasing our impact. There are a number of younger sociologists who are getting impressive contracts from publishers, and there are several books on inequality that are likely to have a big impact on the public discourse. This is really important. As a profession, we need to be much more attuned to the hegemonic discourse that economists produce on themselves, and their corporate spirit when it comes to promoting their discipline as a whole. Again, what we do matters a lot for the diffusion of less individualistic frameworks for interpreting societies. We have to be more present in the public sphere because of what our work can empower politically or otherwise.' (Lamont, interview with Meer)

It is striking that, in this extract, Lamont suggests that the course of successful impact is necessarily couched in a wider public salience, through 'hegemonic discourse' *outside* the mechanics of public administration (which marks a contrast with how the UK's impact agenda appears to have been interpreted – see Chapter 5). Then, towards the end of the above quotation, in addition to a sense of the need to compete with discourses produced by economists, Lamont appears to draw on a normative, almost ethical framework in making the case for sociologists to get more involved in the public sphere, stressing the possibilities for empowerment and (later on in the interview) dialogue. In different ways both Back and Phipps advocate a similar ethical sentiment, but one that is practised through community engagement as much as intellectual intervention. Elsewhere, in the same interview, Lamont says:

> 'I think that we elude our social and political responsibilities if we are not taking on the challenges of influencing the

public sphere. […] I think we play a very important role in maintaining or fostering pluralism in the public sphere. There are a lot of perspectives and types of questions that are not being asked now and we, as well as anthropologists and political philosophers, among others, have the intellectual equipment needed to bring these questions to the fore. Our political duty is fostering a richer democracy and generating greater social inclusion, if you will, especially given the challenge that the United States has been facing with the ascent of Donald Trump.' (Lamont, interview with Meer)

The above quotation outlines an overtly normative, even political, rationale for engaging with the public sphere. In contrast, our 'academic interlocutors' appeared to have more pragmatic motivations for engaging in external-facing work. Our Canadian interviewee, for example, recalled joining an institution around the same time that a colleague who was known for external-facing work left, leaving a gap that presented career opportunities. Similarly, the UK academic interlocutor described this as an area of intellectual fascination, in which productive collaborations had informed a subsequent career pathway. Only our Australian interviewee hinted at a more normative motivation, via suggestions that publicly funded academics had a responsibility to try to improve policies and practice.

In many respects, each set of interviewees outlined the kinds of motivations that we might anticipate based on our categorisation of public intellectual versus academic interlocutor. Lamont's account, for example, is consistent with kinds of public intellectualism that might be forged in Modood's (2018) allegorical 'workshop' discussed earlier. How sensitive, however, is this framing to the different scales and constituencies of the multiple publics outlined in Chapter 5? Lamont certainly appears aware of this challenge, but frames it as much as a vernacular challenge as an ideological one:

'I think, if you want to have social impact you have to use a language that can travel and that is often quite incompatible with writing that is more innovative theoretically. So, it falls upon us to provide different versions of the same argument that are suited for different publics.' (Lamont, interview with Meer)

Here we see a clear acknowledgement of the idea the multiple publics exist and a belief that these different publics require different languages.

Another of our 'public intellectuals', Les Back, placed a similar emphasis on the importance of tailoring communication to different audiences, though focused more on variations in mediums (as opposed to languages), emphasising the importance of the 'digital sharing of ideas and writing'. Here, there was more consistency across our two categories of academics, with each interviewee identifying multiple different kinds of audiences and the need to engage and communicate differently with each.

In Phipps' account, it can be the role of academics not only to engage with policy discourses, in the ways alluded to by Lamont, but to help provide (or create) a language for ideas that are currently not part of the lexicon. What emerges in Phipps' account is the importance of what has been termed the 'strategic role of ignorance' (McGoey, 2012). With the example of the 'refugee crisis', she elaborates:

> 'Some of the policy spaces are saying that we don't know how to know this. And some of it is about saying there's a lot of research but none of it is in this area. There's a lot to be said for saying that peacetime Europe hasn't known how to ask these questions or needed to ask these questions, and the answers to these questions aren't present in our normal ways of framing things. And I think increasingly, certainly for my work, I'm seeing that, and it's a much more philosophical role than "I have data, I have stuff that I can give you".' (Phipps, interview with Meer)

It is an interesting observation set against the discussion earlier, namely that there is a perception of an empirical shift, coterminous with the impact agenda, in which academics are positioned as a source of data and empirical findings, rather more than conceptual work. Yet, as Smith (2013) has previously argued, the way in which academics and others 'translate' empirical research 'findings' for non-academic audiences often involves decoupling the key ideas and stories from the underpinning data, and it is these (more malleable) ideas or 'data stories' (rather than the data themselves) that then travel. Phipps continues:

> 'It's the narrative, and the interpretation. I mean I have got, you know, I have what we can call data. But these days I tend to try not to, because I think we've got such a data fetish, particularly in the social sciences. And my training was in literature and the arts. And I actually see the literature and the arts being what makes the difference.

[...] But when there is a crisis that's when I get phoned up by policymakers to say, "look we need to know what's going on". [...] It's more about actually giving people the confidence to ask questions about things they don't know than trying to find stuff that is absolutely actually concrete. [...] You know the focus on policy as being the silver bullet – I actually think people make it up in messy ways themselves in communities. And it's where I think I am ... actually giving people the experience of that is more use than the facts and figures that we pull out of extractivist models of data collection.' (Phipps, interview with Meer)

Here, again, though perhaps more unexpectedly, there are some interesting consistencies across our two groups, with all three of our academic interlocutors noting a concern about any initiatives that place too much emphasis on 'data' and emphasising the importance of persuasive stories and narratives. For example:

'Research data are dry as dust. They don't speak for themselves. They are not life changing or not influential in and of themselves – they need advocates. Now whether that advocate should be the researcher or whether it needs to be some kind of intermediary or broker is a different matter but there's growing literature around things like engaged scholarship for example that suggests that academics should be passionate and engage with the work that they do and can have values and can be explicit about those values and therefore can act as advocates.' (UK-based 'academic interlocutor', interview with Smith)

Likewise, both the Australian and Canadian academics emphasised the limitations of evidence-based outputs and the importance of more relational spaces and 'soft' skills. Data, statistics, articles and briefings, it seems, were consistently understood to be of limited interest or value to anyone beyond academia unless they were situated within narratives and accompanied by some relational, even promotional, work. Linked to this, there was evident concern among both groups of interviewees about knowledge exchange/dissemination efforts that become overly focused on 'data'. However, as we shall see, this shared perspective did not translate into similar perspectives on the UK's approach to research impact.

Is there a 'public role' for engaged scholarship?

In different ways, our 'public intellectuals', Lamont, Phipps and Back, all appear to take a broad view of the role and function of academics within public policy debates. These remain macro challenges that return us to the question of whether, and how, scholars can simultaneously engage in different publics but also, á la Foucault, 'intervene' on particular issues. For Back, this 'in practice is a very delicate art' that tends to overlook the nuances, interpersonal encounters and perhaps also ethics of public engagement. He elaborates:

> 'My quibble is, what about the fine grain practicalities? How to know you are making the best judgements in any given situation. That seems to me like something we do not talk enough about ... I have learned so much from doing sociology in public, including making sure you involve the participants as well as you can, acknowledge them as peers and sometimes to stop and think – what is it that the participants want from us?' (Back, interview with Meer)

In this quotation, Back positions the role of academics as being about more than listening and repeating, or even helping people to have their voices heard (work Carlisle, 2000, calls 'facilitational advocacy'). This is a challenging set of observations that dovetails with an acceptance of limitations of interventions described by Phipps below:

> 'Middle-class advocacy is not what's going to change stuff. But that doesn't mean you shouldn't do it. But that you do need to be able to live in a state of permanent, hopefully temporary, knowledge of your failure: that you're on the losing side. It may well be that things are getting worse a little tiny bit less quickly than had you not engaged in the journey, but that this may well be something for which any hope of liberation that you may be working towards, which I think is part of the motivation, will happen after your lifetime.' (Phipps, interview with Meer)

Ultimately, both Back and Phipps converge on the sentiment that instrumentality is not the same as engagement, for 'failure' too is a feature of successful engagement, but in ways that fall outside the standard parameters of the impact agenda. This challenges the idea that the 'critical knowledge' dimension to Burawoy's (2011: 33) taxonomy can be compartmentalised or separated from other forms of knowledge. There is something in these comments that resembles a theory of action, and which makes a virtue of engagement in and of itself (rather than as a means to an end). Lamont, too, makes a similar point, arguing that academics "play a very important role in maintaining or fostering pluralism in the public sphere". The point is to foster and sustain a space in which scholars are not circumscribed by the parameters of measures against which universities are audited.

This, then, seems almost oppositional to the kinds of approaches to research impact currently being pursued in the UK, Australia and Canada, each of which involves some form of auditing and which either seem to sideline or separate public engagement from impact (see Chapter 5). Indeed, our Australian academic interlocutor said he felt there was "almost zero" consideration of public engagement in the context of the research impact assessment discussions he had been involved in.

Community connections

This previous set of observations connects to an elementary priority – the relationship with those whom research is being conducted with (or on), and the ethical implications this carries (an ethical dimension that so far appears lacking in most discussions of impact, as we examine in Chapter 3). Back discusses this as follows:

> 'I think it is very difficult to find the right kind of voice when it comes to both our proximity to the struggles that are unfolding in people's lives, and our capacity and need to speak to them. I often think the only way to navigate a space between hyper-political posturing or credentialism and committed public engagement is a kind of rigorous contextualisation and humility in terms of our capacity to speak to those kinds of questions.' (Back, interview with Meer).

This is a concern that ought to be central to objectives such as co-production, collaboration and partnership, but which can become lost or, perhaps worse, serve as instrumental relationships in research and dissemination processes. Phipps discusses her journey in forging these relationships and how they have shaped her subsequent research agenda:

'I basically volunteered with Scottish Detaining Visitors. I applied to go and visit the detention centres, and that then started me on a very different journey, and I haven't so much done research in detention centres as used some of the issues that I've noticed from there to start to structure research questions and projects, ways of thinking. And yeah, I mean that just then meant I was experiencing once a week for several years what people were facing in detention. And obviously you experience that as a volunteer, you experience that as a human being speaking to people. But you also, if you are a researcher and you don't believe in detachment, and you think subjective elements have a place in your research as I do, then those things start to inform how you think and what you read. Then I started to get involved in more of the activism as well as more of the research. So I think from that point of view it's quite an organic story that one thing just led to another.' (Phipps, interview with Meer)

What is immediately apparent here are the similarities between forging relationships through social justice commitments as much as for any reasons that may motivate this. This is precisely the argument that Holmwood (2011b: 25) makes about university-based research acting in *the service of the public* (original emphasis), but also recognising the boundaries that come with particular notions of 'the public', where only some communities are recognised, while others are excluded. In the case of Phipps, it is people designated with a migration status through which the state would seek to remove them from the 'public' in a very literal and physical sense. In the example below, Back describes the importance of community to ensure researchers to do not overlook another, more discursive, kind of removal:

'We have just passed the 35th anniversary of the New Cross Fire in which thirteen young people had their futures stolen from them. Another was added to the death toll of victims two years later when a young person who was at the fire committed suicide, unable to live with its memory. In 1981, I walked past the fire-scorched building at 439 New Cross Road every day. The victims weren't what the journalists and sociologists referred to distantly as 'West Indian youngsters'. No, they were people who you lived next door to and went to school with, and their absence was haunting. Confronting that experience meant trying to understand the complex, unfolding cultural history of race, class and gender in the urban fabric: these things are what I am trying to make sense of in classic Millsian terms.' (Back, interview with Meer)

To invoke C. Wright Mills, as Back does here, is also to invoke his most famous maxim of 'private troubles' connecting to 'public issues' (Mills, 1959). This returns us to the discussion of public intellectualism in which, if academics are looking outwards and speaking to broader publics (trying to have impact), there appears to be a belief among our 'public intellectuals' that they should do so only if they are committed to serving public interests (which is clearly distinct from governmental interests): an ambition that must necessarily register the multiscaler and dynamic quality of what the 'public' comprises.

Here, our academic interlocutors provided a very different perspective. For a start, it is noticeable that they rarely mentioned community, members of the public or civil society organisations. Indeed, the following extract provides an illustrative response to a question specifically about engagement with this sector:

'We have dealt directly with government and directly with the research community, and really just missed everything in between. [...] There are a few exceptions [...] but never, ever have we been approached by a community-based organisation, even the incredibly well-resourced ones [...] But nor have we, to our shame I think, ever really meaningfully engaged them outside various specific examples like [health issue], where I was doing volunteer work.' (Canada-based 'academic interlocutor', interview with Smith)

When pushed about the lack of focus on this sector, all three academic interlocutors provided pragmatic, instrumental rationales to help explain this lack of engagement. In the UK and Australia, this is related to the sense that it was easier to achieve the kind of impact that is being audited by engaging directly with policy organisations. In Canada, our interviewee emphasised the legal restrictions facing charitable organisations in receipt of government funds, which limited any 'advocacy' work that might be deemed 'political':

'Those organisations face a very difficult position because we have incredibly rigid rules about organisations that receive money from government not engaging in advocacy roles, or they would lose their charitable status. So community-based organisations in Canada live in fear that they will make a statement, which could be an evidence-based statement, but it's interpreted as advocacy and consequently they lose their charitable status, which would kill them in this country. So I think [...] that's created a real chill on those organisations' willingness to engage.' (Canada-based 'academic interlocutor', interview with Smith)

This explanation for the limited engagement with community organisations belies a far more instrumentalist sense of how this relationship might, ideally (in the absence of such legal restrictions) function; with community organisations working to advocate particular evidence-informed policy positions/proposals. In other words, community organisations are positioned as useful (or not) based on their ability to act as evidence mobilisers or brokers. This stands in stark contrast to the engaged and personalised accounts provided by two of our public intellectuals, Phipps and Back.

Double binds and drawbacks: perspectives on the UK's research impact agenda

One of the limitations on the idea of public intellectualism for university career academics is the double bind discussed earlier, in which academics 'must influence fellow academics, their own discipline(s), students, and so on over a period of time and across the generations if they are to have any credibility beyond those circles' (Modood, 2018: 3). In this way the university can set direct and indirect parameters on intellectualism, precisely the tendency that Said (1994) characterised negatively as 'professionalism', but also in terms of a parallel 'narrowing' detected by Back:

'[T]he university is narrowing and being limited by the audit culture and the injunction to prove that we are useful and worth our salt ... there is a kind of quiet victory for those modes of assertion and measurement. [...] As much as we have timidly accepted the corrosive competitiveness of this system, metrics are no measure of intellectual vitality. You can't tell if a person has interesting ideas by their H-Index or whether a place contains intellectually interesting people by their department's REF score.' (Back, interview with Meer)

On this issue of audit culture, all three academic interlocutors expressed similar concerns, but academics in Canada and Australia, where 'impact' is assessed differently, felt that links into policy and practice were still seen as very firmly secondary to academic expertise in terms of prestige (albeit with some variation by institution and discipline). In Canada, the sense was that there has been a deliberate effort to avoid investing resources in trying to retrospectively measure something which is innately complex. In Australia, the direction of developments is clearly much closer to the UK (as we set out in Chapter 2), and here our academic interlocutor suggested that stronger accountability mechanisms are a deliberate response to perceptions among some bureaucrats that the university sector is "fat and lazy, soft and self-indulgent". In other words, he suggested that part of the point of the impact agenda in Australia is to increase the sense of there being a stronger audit culture in academia.

In addition, as we discussed in Chapters 4 and 5, REF impact case studies, in particular, are often perceived by academics to favour narratives of policy or commercial impacts, since these are often easier to write up as 'demonstrable impact' than more diffuse or public-oriented impact activities. Phipps (in her interview with Meer) pointed to the dangers of academics conceiving of impact purely in these ways, with research being undertaken to address particular policy problems, since, "I think if you were needed all the time by the policy world, you'd actually just become a civil servant." This is neither recent nor unique to the UK, as Lamont describes of sociology in the USA:

> 'I am a little concerned that if the discipline becomes too applied or problem focused, we may lose the intellectual depth that comes with more conceptual approaches. At the same time, I think that the discipline of sociology in the United States has benefited greatly from focusing on perennial social problems (poverty, racism, immigration) and influencing policy. We just don't want to become slaves to it, or measure our worth solely or primarily in terms of "impact" or contribution to social or economic innovation.'
> (Lamont, interview with Meer)

These concerns relate to the perennial questions (discussed earlier, notably in Chapter 3) of criticality and autonomy, which Back sums up as follows: "It seems to me that we are increasingly cast in a reformist role, tinkering with minor changes in order to claim quantifiable value and 'impact'." Here, again, we can see some clear areas of agreement across our two groups of interviewees, with all three academic interlocutors raising similar concerns:

> 'I think there's a risk then that researchers might start to reshape their research down directions which mean they can then produce findings that are more likely to have demonstrable impacts, rather than doing stuff that is more diffuse and is likely to have a slow burn dialogical set of changes. So I worry about that. [...] I worry that the impact agenda will be used to choke off funding in certain areas.' (UK-based 'academic interlocutor', interview with Smith)

Indeed, despite welcoming aspects of the impact agenda, notably the increased support for academics who choose to work in externally engaged ways and an increased consideration of the fundamental purposes of university-based, publicly funded research, our academic interlocutors raised multiple concerns about the approach to research impact in the UK and Australia. In addition to concerns about the fate of some types of research and the potential for politicisation of research or the co-option of researchers by external interests, our academic interlocutors raised concerns about the unrealistic way in which research impact was being articulated and the lack of connectivity between impact guidance and available scholarly literature on the topic:

> 'Pathways to impact and the REF impact as originally envisaged the initial consultation document on impact that came out of HEFCE were kind of heroic in the set of assumptions they made about [impact] pathways. Rational linear models and steps to impacts; that you do a piece of research, someone picks it up, they cite it, they change their policy and everyone gets better. That's not how it works and it was disappointing to see such naïve and unsophisticated understandings of how research inferences are still being talked about [despite the wealth of work on this topic].' (UK-based 'academic interlocutor', interview with Smith)

Here, our Canadian academic felt Canada's approach was in some ways more reflexive and sophisticated than current UK efforts, having shifted away from earlier attempts to encourage all research funding applicants to set out their approach to knowledge translation (much like pathways to impact in the UK) to a model of making knowledge translation funding available to applicants via follow-on applications, once the research findings are clearer:

'For many years we faced this crazy incentive that every researcher thought they needed a [knowledge translation] section. They'd come to us, we'd help them with the one pager, but none of them would ever do it. [...] [I]t's like gambling, why would you gamble on the idea that you're going to have a result that is ready for prime time? And if it is, you can't predict, if you don't know the message how do you know what the mechanism is and all these other things? So it makes sense that it be a separate supplement after.' (Canada-based 'academic interlocutor', interview with Smith)

Two further concerns raised by our academic interlocutors about the UK's approach to research impact were, first, the cost of trying to assess research impact via case studies (and the associated trade-offs) and, second, the potential for the UK's emphasis on demonstrable impact to play a role in further reifying and supporting quantitative research over qualitative:

'Is this a good use of very intensive labour? Do we have any idea of the opportunity costs? For example, what if the cost is equivalent to funding 100,000 PhDs? Is it worth it? My view is the jury's out on that. [...] I suspect that it's overkill – that would be my view.' (Australia-based 'academic interlocutor', interview with Smith)

'I worry the impact agenda will be used as cover for other sorts of debates and contestations to drive. It will see researchers have the qualitative/quantitative debates, for example, which have been so unproductive in the past, on the grounds that quantitative research is the stuff that really has impact and therefore we shouldn't be investing in qualitative.' (UK-based 'academic interlocutor', interview with Smith)

These various concerns seemed to inform a consistent preference among our academic interlocutors for incentive structures to promote academic engagement with external audiences, creating opportunities for influence and conversations, rather than efforts to incentivise and assess 'impact':

'My personal preference is that engagement is a far more sensible thing to promote than impact which can be quite forced and artificial and looks so different across different examples that it almost doesn't make a lot of sense.' (Australia-based 'academic interlocutor', interview with Smith)

'Impact conveys such a physical analogy isn't it? It's of something hurtling through space, hitting a target and bing! You get a prize out at the end of it. I think that's not how these things happen so I tend to use terms as you've probably noticed, I tend to use 'influence' rather than 'impact' because all these different things are going on at once.' (UK-based 'academic interlocutor', interview with Smith)

'We have started to create a space [in Canada] in which people can come along and say, let's mostly leave the researchers doing their things and the policymakers doing their things, but figure out how do we create mechanisms that allow for more immediate linkages by people who are positioned to move back and forth.' (Canada-based 'academic interlocutor', interview with Smith)

Overall, while there are clear differences in the views, experiences and preferences of our six interviewees, their views about the UK's approach to research impact, and what better alternatives might look like, are surprisingly similar.

Conclusions

This chapter considers the longstanding idea that academics should 'intervene' and 'speak up' in public life by revisiting the concept of 'public intellectuals', and it has reflected on whether this vision of academia is enhanced or diminished by the UK's 'impact agenda'. "Middle-class advocacy is not what's going to change stuff. But that doesn't mean you shouldn't do it", Alison Phipps reminds us. In this chapter, we argue is that we, as academics, can and do (indeed must) 'take sides', but deciding what the implications of this are will vary depending on the issue and kind of 'public' we are working with. This is a more complex set of considerations than it may at first appear, and can perhaps be traced to the very idea of the 'public', and the argument that Holmwood (2011b: 25) makes about university-based research acting in *the service of the public* (original emphasis). Some of this, as

Michèle Lamont argues, is a vernacular challenge insofar as different publics require different languages, while some of this challenges us to register different mediums, including what Back characterises as the 'digital sharing of ideas and writing'.

Impact is not just of one kind and what, precisely, academics are seeking to achieve when they engage externally clearly varies, as the contrast between our public intellectuals and academic interlocutors bears out (and as the disciplinary distinctions explored in Chapter 4 also make clear). For the academic interlocutors in this chapter, it seems that it is the relatability of research to potential research users, such as communities of policy and practice, that is key. Whereas, for our public intellectuals, externally facing work was framed as something that ought to be more holistic, publicly engaged and overtly political (at least in the sense of 'taking sides'). Reflecting this, some forms of external engagement, including activities we might consider to be 'public intellectualism', may cohere with, and benefit from, 'impact agendas'. However, it is also clear that efforts to engage with external audiences can diverge from, and may potentially feel limited by, the kind of impact agenda that is prevailing in the UK and Australia (e.g. where engagement involves critiquing government or commercial interests or perhaps even where the intention is to facilitate dialogue, rather than impact).

Finally, it is important to emphasise that academics, of course, never have all the answers, even at the end of research projects (when there is at least a little less guesswork involved than at the grant application stage). With this in mind, we suggest efforts to promote and assess impact ought to be receptive to the 'strategic role of ignorance' (McGoey, 2012), where meaningful questions are as necessary as policy prescriptions. Whether there has indeed been a shift coterminous with the impact agenda, in which 'findings' can be communicated as repeated 'refrains', and as such are prevailing more than conceptual work, remains an open question. As Smith (2013) has previously argued, an analytically richer way to think about this dynamic is not in terms of data delivery per se, but the translation of research 'findings', including how these may well be uncoupled from the kinds of 'data stories' that characterise Halford and Savage's (2017) 'refrain' discussed earlier. This is important where research advocacy is concerned, for (as we suggest in Chapter 5) there is virtue in engagement with communities in and of itself (rather than as a means to an end).

Note

1 Pointing to 'repeated "refrains"', just as classical music symphonies introduce and return to recurring themes, with subtle modifications, so that the symphony as a whole is more than its specific themes (Halford and Savage, 2017: 1135).

7

Academic life in the impact vanguard: the view from knowledge exchange organisations

As we have seen, there appears to be a basic assumption within the UK's approach to research impact (see Chapters 1, 2 and 3) that the incentives for the engagement between researchers and research users lead to an increase in research impact. Consequently, recent decades have witnessed the expansion of funding initiatives aimed at supporting and incentivising knowledge translation. One of the key UK research council strategies to address concerns about research utility and impact has been to fund knowledge broker initiatives aimed at bridging the gap between research and application and increasing engagement between academic and non-academic audiences. These organisations and posts are predominantly located at universities and have employed mainly academics, although their remit goes beyond what would traditionally be considered academic work and includes developing practices aimed at supporting evidence-based policy and practice.

This approach to increasing evidence uptake in policy and practice is, at least to a degree, reflected in the recommendations from research use literature (see Choi, 2005; Oliver et al, 2014; Cairney and Oliver, 2018). This strand of scholarship argues that one of the barriers to research uptake is the academic epistemic culture, which incentivises research that is decontextualised, theoretical and not necessarily relevant to practical problems (D'Este et al, 2018). From this perspective, the impact agenda might be viewed as offering a crucial opportunity to diminish key barriers to research use by promoting the activities that help ensure there is less of a gap between user preferences and research practices; in effect, promoting new priorities, incentives and values in UK academia. How the impact agenda is actually being experienced by those at the 'vanguard' of these changes is, however, underexplored.

In this chapter, we start to explore this gap by focusing on academics working in two specially designated and funded university-based knowledge exchange organisations that were focusing on policy and practice audiences (see Chapter 1 for a more detailed overview of the research data). These organisations have both been involved in work to promote knowledge exchange and achieve research impact for over a decade. We view these organisations as positioned at the forefront of the wider changes that the impact agenda is encouraging across academic institutions in the UK. As such, this chapter highlights the subtle interplay of science policy (of which the impact agenda is part, as we set out in Chapter 2) and 'science in policy' (Brooks, 1964), where changes in research funding and evaluation shape the availability and applicability of research for policymakers and practitioners. Knowledge brokers offer an ideal empirical setting for exploring the effects that the impact agenda has had on the emerging practices of knowledge translation and on the credibility and legitimacy of such practices (see Bandola-Gill, 2019). We conclude this chapter with a reflection on discrepancies between the experiences of impact work by knowledge brokers and their assessment with REF. The chapter argues that, even though the research impact agenda does appear to have enabled more knowledge translation and exchange work in academia, the model of impact employed within REF is failing to reflect the reality of such work.

Who are the knowledge brokers?

Knowledge brokers are one of the key elements of a strategy to support the uptake of research across different settings, for example health (Ellen et al, 2013; Yost et al, 2014), innovation (Howells, 2006), or policy (Owens and Rayner, 1999; Ward et al, 2012). The basic assumption underlying these entities is that there are important differences in epistemic practices between science and potential users (e.g. those working in policy or practice settings), which act as barriers to research uptake. One of the key conceptual approaches reflecting this assumption is Caplan's (1979) 'two communities' thesis, which highlights the cultural differences between scientists and policymakers. From this perspective, knowledge brokers are entities whose aim is to 'bridge' these two communities, by developing shared understandings, skills and practices on both sides (Caswill and Lyall, 2013). Others draw more heavily on social constructivist approaches to knowledge, claiming that there are no objective boundaries between science and policy/practice (Jasanoff, 2004). Rather, the division between the two is constructed through an active process of negotiation, called 'boundary work', intended to protect and promote the value of 'science' (Gieryn, 1983). According to this approach, knowledge brokers are seen as facilitators of the boundary between science and non-science. As argued by Meyer, 'knowledge brokers are people or organizations that move knowledge around and create connections between researchers and their various audiences' (2010: 118). As such, knowledge brokers are charged with mediation between science and more practical contexts (Grundmann, 2017).

Regardless of the approach to understanding the relationship between science and policy and practice, the literature on evidence use consistently finds that research alone very rarely influences decision making (Nutley et al, 2007). Knowledge brokers are entities involved in the work necessary for research evidence to be understood, contextualised and taken up by the decision makers. These roles might entail a broad scope of activities, for example informing, consulting, matchmaking, engaging, collaborating and capacity building (Michaels, 2009; Bandola-Gill and Lyall, 2017). Knowledge brokers ideally possess the skills needed to understand the needs and preferences of both research producers and research users (Dobbins et al, 2009; Hering, 2016). In this sense, knowledge brokers are often portrayed as separate from academics or research producers and located 'in between' different organisational settings (Meyer, 2010). Some scholars conceive of knowledge brokers as a specific, emerging professional group (e.g. Waring et al, 2013). Others discuss knowledge brokering as a broader role of science or science communication that is occurring within a changing paradigm of wider science-society relationships (Bielak et al, 2008; Turnhout et al, 2013). In this broader sense, knowledge brokers are viewed as emblematic of a larger move towards blurring boundaries between science and society and increasing the participation of a diverse stakeholders in knowledge production. As such, the knowledge brokers might be seen as emblematic of the wide-ranging changes in the regimes of knowledge production, such as the emergence of post-normal science (Funtowicz and Ravetz, 1993) or Mode 2 science (Gibbons et al, 1994; Nowotny et al, 2001).

Knowledge brokers and research funding in the UK

Debates about knowledge brokers are more than conceptual; since the early 2000s, the vast majority of research councils in the UK began developing and promoting ideas about research translation across different settings, including via collaboration and partnership working. This has included offering a variety of funding schemes specifically focusing on knowledge exchange and brokering. At the same time, the implementation of the concept of a knowledge broker in a science funding context has resulted in the creation of specific forms of brokering entities. The knowledge brokers funded by the research councils consisted mostly of academics and were located at universities, and hence were still embedded in academic discourses and practices, rather than being truly 'in between' (Meyer, 2010) the two communities or spheres.

The rationale for funding knowledge brokers was explicitly linked to the generation of impact stemming from research. For example, an ESRC review entitled 'Taking Stock: A Summary of ESRC's Work to Evaluate the Impact of Research on Policy and Practice' (2009) explicitly discussed knowledge brokers as one of the initiatives supporting the achievement of impact, describing them as 'translators, amplifiers, network providers' (ESRC, 2009: 14). These posts were seen as entities that 'can and do facilitate impact on behalf of individual researchers who would not otherwise have access to the necessary resources and infrastructure' (ESRC, 2009: 14). This conceptualisation of knowledge brokerage has resulted in funding provided for a variety of initiatives at both individual and organisational levels, aimed at navigating and translating research in different social settings.

As the skills initially assigned to knowledge brokers (e.g. engagement with external actors and production of research impact) have become increasingly identified as central to academia in general, funding opportunities have evolved accordingly (see Chapter 2 and Watermeyer and Lewis, 2017). The conceptualisation of intermediary organisations has moved away from the idea of organisations that translate data, ideas and evidence between academia and potential research users to organisations that help facilitate the collaborative production of research. Hence, new forms of intermediary organisation are explicitly charged not only with translating research but also with helping to produce relevant research. Reflecting this shift, the concept of knowledge/research brokers is being progressively replaced by notions of 'partnership working', 'co-production' and 'co-creation', as Table 7.1 illustrates. There are now multiple funding schemes that promote these ways of working, both at the organisational level (for example Centres of Excellence[1] or What Works Centres)[2] and at individual levels (for example in a form of policy placements).[3]

One of the characteristics of these types of funding initiatives is the expectation placed on those involved to simultaneously promote research excellence *and* engagement with non-academic audiences. Balancing these goals is not unproblematic since the two are often seen as contradictory and linked to diverse sets of academic practices (D'Este et al, 2018). As we discuss in the following sections, this tension was central to the experiences of academics associated with knowledge

Table 7.1: Stakeholder engagement in strategic priorities of the UK research councils

Research council	Strategic priorities
Arts and Humanities Research Council (AHRC)	'To fulfil our mission, our objectives are to ... establish research partnerships across all regions of the UK, in Europe and across the world with other funding agencies, with museums, galleries and other cultural and heritage institutions, with the third sector in the UK and the Global South, and with government departments ... promote knowledge exchange between arts and humanities research and a range of other sectors, including the creative industries, the heritage sector and health services' (AHRC Delivery Plan, 2019: 5)
Biotechnology and Biological Sciences Research Council (BBSRC)	'Long-term ambitions: Foster approaches that facilitate collaboration and the exchange of people and ideas, between disciplines, between academia and industry, and between countries. Develop and sustain a range of models to support industry/academic partnership, knowledge exchange and translation which meet the needs of the diverse sectors that bioscience underpins. ... Identify and build mutually beneficial partnerships for UK bioscience and opportunities for it to help address international research priorities' (BBSRC Delivery Plan, 2019: 21)
Engineering and Physical Sciences Research Council (EPSRC)	'We will use our partnerships with universities, other innovation funders, business and government to embed timely, appropriate support for impact activities across all our investments. ... We believe they are key to supporting researchers to exploit their research outcomes and developing the beginning of the pipeline through to economic impact in emergent and rapidly developing new science areas' (EPSRC Delivery Plan, 2019: 17)
Economic and Social Research Council (ESRC)	'To increase the ability of social science research to deliver improved outcomes, we will invest in deepening our partnerships with research users ... We are committed to driving innovation and maximising the impact of the work we support, and have taken an international lead in progressing the impact agenda. From these strong foundations, we are now moving forward to achieve a step-change improvement in the impact of social science research. This involves moving the impact agenda on from influencing policy and practice to working more closely with research users so that research helps improve outcomes' (ESRC Delivery Plan 2019: 30)
Medical Research Council (MRC)	'Our partnerships with R&D activities in industry are vital to achieving a major impact on health. Many important changes need three-way alignment across industry, the health systems and the research base. We also achieve our objectives via strong international partnerships ... We will continue to work closely with health departments and charities to explore future research needs, develop strategy and assess the impacts of our research' (MRC Delivery Plan, 2019: 30)

Research council	Strategic priorities
Natural Environment Research Council (NERC)	'It has always been important to us and our community to ensure science reaches beyond scientists. Environmental science provides the ideas and understanding to open entirely new businesses and improve the resilience and productivity of existing industries. We work with our stakeholders in research and business, encouraging partnerships that stimulate ideas and nurture understanding between them' (NERC Delivery Plan, 2019: 3)
Science and Technology Facilities Council (STFC)	'Collaboration underpins everything we do and is vital to accomplishing our science and innovation goals and those of our partners. We work with thousands of stakeholders within the UK and across the world to deliver our programme. We build long-term relationships with a variety of industrial partners to enable UK business to leverage the capabilities and expertise developed to meet our science goals to address challenges in their business' (STFC Delivery Plan, 2019: 32)

broker organisations. In what follows, we will explore the ways in which actors charged explicitly with knowledge exchange and impact have perceived the changes ignited by the research impact agenda and its influence on knowledge exchange practices. In particular, we discuss the impact agenda as an enabler of knowledge exchange by providing resources (both in terms of funding and building the knowledge base) but also supporting cultural change in academia. On the other hand, we show that the research impact agenda was perceived to stymie some knowledge exchange work by promoting a narrow idea of impact and deepening the contradictions facing applied researchers.

The impact agenda as an enabler of knowledge exchange

Building expertise in knowledge brokering

One of the key positive changes triggered by the research impact agenda that was discussed by interviewees was a significant increase in the availability of resources for conducting knowledge translation activities. A majority of interviewees discussed impact agenda as the raison d'être of their publicly funded knowledge broker organisations. In this way, the increasing focus of research funders on the social and economic benefits of science has been a key instigator of the development of vast – theoretical and practical – expertise in methods for supporting research-informed changes in policy and practice.

Developing such expertise has not been a straightforward task, but one that appears to have been aided by some of the early investments in knowledge exchange made by research councils (particularly the ESRC).

Consequently, interviewees across both organisations reported that they initially (in the 2000s) struggled with the operationalisation of their knowledge exchange remit in terms of identifying and settling on specific practices. The interviewees from both organisations recalled that, even though their bids for knowledge broker funding were successful, putting these programmes into practice was demanding, as these organisations were among the first UK-wide knowledge exchange initiatives, meaning that there were few, if any, benchmarks available. For example:

'I think we put up a good case on paper for being different, I still think that the behaviours and the skills needed to do things differently, were not there at the beginning. I don't think people realised what was involved in doing research differently, in a co-produced way, where the questions might emerge with the interactions with the practitioners and policy people, rather than having them pre-defined, whereby you are working in a very messy, complex environment, which is constantly changing.' (Senior academic 1, public health)

'It took [us] a while to work out, it was one of the useful things to work out – could we represent on one sheet of paper what the task of the [organisation] was? Not to write it down, but to draw it in some way. It's easy to think of a research centre. But what does a research centre look like that doesn't even do research, that does this knowledge exchange, who takes social science research, but whose main audience is not social science?' (Senior academic 2, genomics and social science)

Interviewees' accounts suggest that establishing knowledge exchange programmes was a challenging task that required experimenting with various dissemination formats. A number of interviewees pointed out that this process obliged them to change their frame of thinking about research production and dissemination from a purely academic frame to one that would fit the needs of policymakers and practitioners. One common example used by interviewees was a process of trialling and refining different seminar formats in order to attract a larger policymaking (as opposed to academic) audience.

Following years of experimentation and adaptation, both organisations appeared to have developed an approach that strove to combine academic excellence with responsiveness to policy and practice. This resulted in a number of innovations in the offers made by knowledge broker organisations as they adapted their practices to better fit the needs of decision makers (e.g. in terms of timeliness, scope, structure and processes). The vast majority of interviewees acknowledged that the effectiveness of various knowledge-brokering projects carried out by their organisations increased over the years. However, the early research council funding was positioned as having been crucial to this early experimentation and in terms of capacity building among the researchers, allowing each organisation to develop a reputation for knowledge exchange expertise. For example:

> 'We have a very good track record of methodology around [public patient involvement], around stakeholder engagement, about co-creation. So, I think we are most likely to create a research solution that's actually solving people's problems.' (Senior academic 3, public health)

The availability of funding for knowledge-brokering activities appeared to have led to the emergence of specific 'communities of practice' (Wenger, 1999), who had developed expertise in research use, dissemination and (more recently) the co-production of research. Furthermore, the practical experience of knowledge brokering was translated by many of the interviewees into academic research, leading to a burgeoning area of research on research use (for a review of this area of research, see Boaz and Davies, 2019). In general, then, the interviewees from the knowledge broker organisations perceived the recent moves towards incentivising impact within the UK as informing a development of expertise – both practical and theoretical – in the area of knowledge translation.

'Spaces for impact' and scaling up knowledge translation

In many ways, the academics working in knowledge broker organisations (and the knowledge translation area more broadly) can be seen as beneficiaries of the UK's impact agenda, as it has both led to the greater availability of resources for this type of work and impacted on the visibility and legitimacy of knowledge exchange within academia. In some cases, interviewees' posts (past or present) had been directly supported by new knowledge exchange funding initiatives. Reflecting this, interviewees generally acknowledged that the impact agenda was, to a large degree, aligned with their organisational goals. One senior academic pointed out that the impact agenda "played into [our] commitment to get evidence into practice". In this section, we explore this sense of alignment in more detail. It is important to note, however (as we discuss later on in the chapter), that many interviewees were nonetheless critical of elements of the UK's impact agenda, notably the REF's approach to assessing impact.

One of the central ways in which the research impact agenda has incentivised the knowledge translation activities of academics has been through expanding hybrid spaces that exist between traditional science and policy/practice (Miller, 2001; Pohl, 2008). The interviewees for this chapter tended to frame knowledge broker organisations as spaces in which opportunities to work at the science–policy boundary could be explored and spaces which encouraged the development and promotion of approaches to knowledge exchange work, including via hybrid methods of research production (see also Bandola-Gill, 2019). Many interviewees perceived themselves to be 'non-traditional' academics, who focused not only on producing academic research but also on prioritising its relevance to solving practical problems. This type of research was seen as a collaborative, rather than traditionally academic activity, inherently requiring them to work across the science–policy/ practice boundary:

> 'I always came from a background where it was about the relevance of research. So, I would say it's something that I do with all of the different pieces of research I'm involved in, but clearly some are more applied than others. So, I've never seen the research I do as just about getting an academic paper published, and I've always tried to sort of see how ... what the wider relevance of that may be. And I work with a lot of collaborators outside of the university, so local government, the voluntary sector. So, inevitably, I'm working with them in order to do research.' (Senior academic 5, public health)

Even though the idea of researchers striving to achieve impact on policy and practice was not necessarily new in academic life for all the interviewees (especially for those working in applied disciplines, such as the one above, as we discuss in Chapters 4 and 8), interviewees pointed out that the developments in the impact agenda have supported a more systematic and widespread approach to both incentivising and legitimising such practices, as illustrated by the following quote:

'I think that there is now an acknowledgement or in fact an imperative or need for people in academia to engage in different activities [...] to do a number of different things and that engagement and impact is now recognised as much more legitimate activity. I think a lot of people, particularly working in public health did it anyway, but we did it under the radar.' (Senior academic 4, public health)

However, interviewees suggested that the impact agenda has allowed previously atomised sets of activities to gain momentum within dedicated knowledge brokerage spaces, where groups of non-traditional academics have been able to work together. The impact agenda has, in effect, enabled a process of joining-up thinking and scaling-up practices in this hybrid area, which interviewees consistently positioned as inherently distinct from traditional academic knowledge production. As one interviewee put it:

'I suppose having an organisation means you've got an environment and a setting where people can develop together and share and exchange views. Whereas inconceivably if you were in a particular institution you might be isolated or working on your own. Not necessarily, but there could be an issue of being a bit different to your peers, whereas when you are in a collective like [a knowledge broker organisation], you are among kindred spirits of people who are talking about the same issues and the same agendas.' (Senior academic 1, public health)

Furthermore, these brokering spaces were characterised by epistemic diversity and different types of knowledge production practices, including early efforts to undertake research in a co-produced way (Durose et al, 2017; Holmes et al, 2017) and through collaborative projects, co-sponsored by potential users in policy and practice settings. Interviewees suggested that the impact agenda has endowed these new approaches to doing research with greater legitimacy and stimulated more interest, partly through the sheer number of people engaged in these activities. As the following interviewee reflected, knowledge broker organisations can be viewed as offering relevant expertise for academics who are taking research impact seriously:

'I think some academics just want to continue as traditional academics. I wouldn't say everyone has been changed or touched by [our organisation] but I think people acknowledge that there is a major role there and that [our organisation] has built up credibility and expertise in that area. That for people who want to engage with that agenda, [a knowledge broker organisation] is a good channel and a good way of doing that.' (Senior academic 1, public health)

Yet, while interviewees suggested that knowledge broker organisations offered an opportunity for people who were interested in this type of work to receive advice, support and inspiration, some interviewees acknowledged that being part of a knowledge exchange organisation did not necessarily resolve the tensions between knowledge exchange and more traditional academic practices.

'A move towards a good direction': changing the organisational and resource environment for knowledge brokering

The introduction of the REF has influenced the way universities approach and strategise knowledge exchange activities (as reflected for example in their hiring practices, structural changes and even their missions and official strategies – Manville et al, 2015), which has inevitably affected the operations of knowledge brokers. Indeed, this shift in university management priorities was one of the changes that interviewees for this chapter, who were working on research impact, most commonly emphasised. As recalled by a senior academic working in public health:

'In the past, and I go back probably 10–12 years now, senior people have said to me: "You do this work with schools or you do this work with public health teams in X, Y and Z. Don't do that. Stop doing that." And essentially to focus on doing a piece of research and writing. That has changed because now universities see the engagement as a big part of what they do. But a big part of that was a change in Research Assessment Exercise and impact. So the very people who said: "Stop doing that", were the people who were knocking on my door when they realised they needed impact cases. So I think that there is now an acknowledgement or in fact an imperative or need for

> people in academia to engage in different activities and that engagement and impact are now recognised as much more legitimate activity.' (Senior academic 4, public health)

Several interviewees reported similar experiences. One interviewee even claimed that it is only because of the REF's inclusion of impact that they are allowed to conduct translational research, which they felt would previously have been impossible within their department.

One way of tracing the changes in the perception of impact work as a legitimate academic activity is by looking at the career impacts of involvement in knowledge-brokering organisations. The two such organisations explored in this chapter were both developed in mid-2000. And, in fact, interviewees who had joined these organisations at different times (earlier versus later in their lifespan) reported diametrically different experiences in terms of career cost or benefit. In the early years of the knowledge broker organisations, the data suggest it was difficult for academics to build a career within universities based on the kind of (impact-oriented) work they were expected to do in these knowledge broker settings. As recalled by an academic employed by a knowledge broker organisation in the mid-2000s to early 2010s:

> 'I do think that our academic reputation suffered. And I think I could say that quite categorically … so maybe not all of us, but many of us who were there who held PhDs and who have returned to academic careers afterwards, our reputation suffered … and for myself I definitely felt like I was perceived differently from other staff at the same grade, even though my job title included "research fellow". When you go into knowledge exchange work as an academic, all of a sudden you are not taken as seriously, which is a problem, given especially that now we are all supposed to be doing knowledge exchange work.' (Mid-career academic 6, genomics and social science)

One of the interviewees who worked for one of the knowledge-brokering organisations in the early 2000s even reported having left the organisation in order to protect their career prospects, feeling that it was not 'academic work' (mid-career researcher, genomics and social science). An interviewee involved in the management of one of the organisations also recalled that, when hiring early-career academics, they were transparent about what they saw as the career risks associated with joining the organisation (and there are parallels here with early-career researchers getting 'lost in the third space' of public engagement work – see Watermeyer, 2015). One of the directors even reported that they would make a point of letting the early-career researchers know that if the person planned on pursuing a traditional academic career, s/he should be sure not to stay in the organisation "for too long" (Senior academic, genomics and social science) (again, this is akin to Watermeyer's 2015 findings regarding the career development of academics involved in public engagement work).

By contrast, interviewees who had only become associated with the two knowledge broker organisations more recently tended to describe their experiences very differently. These academics reported that being affiliated with the knowledge broker organisations seemed beneficial to their academic careers as it opened up opportunities for developing a network of relevant external contacts with policymakers and practitioners. For example:

'I mean, from my point of view, my career, I think the impact work I've done has been very positive towards my career. It's certainly done a lot of good things for me, so I've just applied for a promotion to a Reader,[4] and I think if I didn't have the impact, I wouldn't have been in a position to apply for that.' (Mid-career academic, public health)

This change in the perceived career consequences of undertaking knowledge exchange and impact work seemed to be strongly linked to the development of REF impact case studies and UK Research Council requirements around impact (see Chapters 1 and 2). For example, collaborations with policymakers and practitioners which were developed while working with the knowledge broker organisations were positioned by interviewees as leading to the production of potential REF impact case studies (informing the distribution of higher education block grant funding) and/or helping to secure external grant research funding.

The perceived increase in the legitimacy of impact work brought about by the research impact agenda was, in turn, perceived to have had a positive influence on the processes of knowledge exchange being carried out by the knowledge broker organisations. For example, the data suggest that this shift helped to ameliorate problems with organisation- and resource-type barriers to undertaking knowledge exchange work (see Oliver et al, 2014), improving managerial support for conducting this kind of work and increasing the availability of resources (which, in turn, sometimes increased the accessibility of this work for potential beneficiaries, externally). Interviewees also suggested that incentives to undertake a more diverse portfolio of research activity (e.g. contracted research, evaluations and co-produced research) had also increased. Consequently, the impact agenda appeared to have increased the availability of research tailored to policymakers' and practitioners' needs, which was generally viewed positively from the perspective of individuals working in knowledge broker organisations. At the same time, even though the legitimacy of impact practices was perceived to have increased, it was clear that tensions between traditional academic work and impact-oriented work remained, as we explore in the remaining sections of this chapter.

The impact agenda as a challenge to knowledge exchange

Constructing contradictory incentives

Looking across the data for this chapter, the tension between producing research that is both publishable in the top academic journals and applicable to the task of solving policy and practice problems remained one of the central problems for individuals working in knowledge broker organisations. As argued elsewhere (Bandola-Gill, 2019), this tension is grounded in the epistemic differences between these contrasting types of research practices, which are exacerbated by academic institutions' tendency to separate practices of impact and academic research (see also Chapter 4). This reflects the fact that the UK's impact agenda has been introduced in a way that is aligned with what Flinders (2010) called 'splintered logic', whereby a new set of priorities and values is implemented on top of the existing system of practices and standards.

It seems that this tension is not only central to the work of knowledge brokers but, as the impact agenda develops, that it is increasingly becoming an tension facing academics working in the UK (see Chapters 4 and 8). The contradictory set of expectations placed on academics has led some to argue for a 'division of labour' which would more fully decouple impact from academic research. This idea was evident in the early incarnations of the two knowledge broker organisations that this chapter focuses on and, while most of our interviewees suggested there had been a move away from this separation, the idea has received further traction with the emergence of hybrid posts (Knight and Lightowler, 2010) and academic positions specifically premised upon research impact expertise (see Chapter 4).

The basic assumption behind these initiatives is that, in order to deal with the contradictory expectations of research impact and more traditional academic work, the roles responsible for these respective types of activities ought to be separated. Hence, the impact work should be delegated either to a specific group of applied academics or to dedicated positions. This proposition was put forward by the following interviewee, along with a suggestion that the emphasis place on impact in REF should increase substantially:

> 'REF was based, and still is based, primarily, on number of academic publications in high-ranking journals. They say that impact is taken into account, and yet there are these impact case studies. But the universities still give 80 per cent of their priority to the high-level impact in academic referee journals. So long as that's the case, the other kind of impact is going to take secondary role. It was upped a bit in the last REF that the role of impact and these impact case studies. Hopefully, it's going to be emphasised even more in the next REF, but we don't know yet.[5] That might make a difference in the long run, but it's not yet been managed in a way that will let it make a difference. What we need to do is make the impact be 50 per cent of the REF outcome, not 20 per cent, and for individual academics to be able to focus themselves 100 per cent on impact, or maybe 80 per cent on impact, 20 per cent on academic journals, so that everybody is not expected to be 20 per cent on impact and 80 per cent on hard and fast academic outcomes.' (Senior academic 7, genomics and social science)

The attraction of this kind of separation seems to be the idea that it could protect spaces for theoretical and basic research from the requirement to achieve impact, while rewarding those who were more inclined to undertake this kind of work (effectively relieving the pressure across academia to balance these competing demands). However, the data from the two knowledge broker organisations studied in this chapter suggest that implementing this kind of division of labour is likely to be challenging in practice, even if deemed desirable (and not all interviewees suggested that it was). There are two main causes of this: the incentive and reporting systems in academia, and the socialising process of academic education.

The first barrier to the implementation of the division of labour idea is the institutionalised incentive system in academia. Despite the increasing pressure on academics to achieve impact with their work, conducting research is still seen as central academic practice and this assumption is strongly reflected in the incentive and reporting structures. The academics working in the knowledge broker organisations highlighted time and again that they felt (from a career development perspective) they needed to ensure they were satisfying REF research outputs criteria by publishing a sufficient number of papers. Academics in knowledge broker positions were employed as research staff and as such were subject to assessment of their REF research outputs. This poses a challenge, as highlighted by one of the interviewees:

'[When] it was set up it wasn't supposed to do research [but knowledge exchange], and yet all the people who were appointed to work in it were expected to demonstrate that they were research active and REFable. That was an enormous tension. [...] It was a lack of realisation and understanding that stretched back even to the appointment of the directors of the [knowledge broker organisation] at various points in its life. Because of the pressures at the university level, they appointed the kind of director that was REFable, not the kind of director that would help other people to deliver their impact.' (Senior academic 8, genomics and social science)

Consequently, the system of academic incentives resulting from the impact agenda has become difficult to navigate. Many interviewees pointed out that there is a need to achieve balance between publishing and impact activities; however, the exact expectations did not appear to be transparent but malleable and fluid, depending on individual priorities, the types of institutions academics worked for and the level of academic esteem accorded the academics. While a clearer separation might help resolve this tension to a degree, it seems unlikely to resolve it completely, at least if traditional markers of academic success (such as publishing) remain dominant; these markers operate, in effect, as a passport to new academic opportunities and roles and so are likely to continue to feel necessary for anyone in an academic position, even if their current role has a clear impact focus.

The second barrier to division of labour is the way the process of education and socialisation for academic positions operates. Many of the academics whose role entailed more classic knowledge brokering – facilitating interactions between stakeholders, rather than being charged with conducting research – reported feeling frustrated by the lack of research activity, as this is what they felt they had been trained for.

> 'My role is really to instigate the research, to develop the connections with the policy and practice partners, and to develop a proposal to the point where they're ready to go and there's funding available. And then I step back and leave them to it, which is kind of frustrating, in a way, because I'm a researcher by training and I enjoy doing research, and I'm not doing, really, research at the moment.' (Knowledge broker 10, public health)

One of the perceived difficulties had to do with the fact that, because of their role, these individuals were immersed in academic discourse and involved in some aspects of the research process, without fully engaging in such a process. This particular group of interviewees reported being stigmatised as non-academic staff, which they found difficult, especially as they all held PhDs. In response, some of these academics said they worked on publications out of normal working hours in order to maintain what they felt was a core part of their academic CV.

These tensions highlight how difficult it is to genuinely take a division of labour route to supporting impact work when research publications function as such a defining feature of academic identity. Added to this, we can see (especially from some of the comments made by interviewees in Chapter 4) that the impact agenda has posed a challenge to academics, prompting reflection on what constitutes academic work. Some of the responses to this challenge can be understood in terms of Gieryn's (1983) notion of 'boundary work', which involves constructing and highlighting differences between what is considered to be 'science' and what is not, in order to protect scientific resources and authority. Support for division of impact labour might be understood as a form of boundary work, differentiating impact from research and stratifying roles accordingly. The experiences of the academics involved in the knowledge broker organisation seem to suggest that this kind of response is likely to be difficult to sustain, at least in a context that continues to prize markers of more traditional academic work (for details, see: Bandola-Gill, 2019). Research, and even more distinctly the publishing process, are still the main ways in which academics working in the UK seem to feel they can gain academic standing. The academics involved in the knowledge broker organisations studied for this chapter reported being treated differently when their positions did not involve production of publishable research.

Their accounts suggest that the current academic context in the UK is allowing academic careers to develop without an obvious 'impact penalty', but that there is a clear 'no-publishing penalty'. So, although impact work does appear to have become more legitimate, this kind of work still appears to be supplementary to, rather than interchangeable with, academic publishing.

An evidence-based impact agenda?

If we compare the findings of this chapter to those presented in Chapters 3, 4 and 6, it suggests that the academics working in knowledge broker organisations were generally more positive about the impact agenda than the general academic population, at least in principle. Despite this, interviewees working in knowledge broker organisations remained critical of the specific format of impact and its assessment within the REF. The key issue highlighted by the interviewees was the inability of the current REF approach to capture important aspects of the knowledge translation process. Knowledge brokers with considerable expertise in knowledge translation strategies were critical of the REF model, claiming that it was "too simplistic" (senior academic 4, public health), and positing that, although implementation of REF impact case studies ignited academic discussion over impact, "it's not very sophisticated debate yet" (senior academic 1, public health).

The majority of interviewees associated with the knowledge broker organisations argued that REF measures are focused on potentially immeasurable outcomes of knowledge exchange work, while ignoring key aspects of translation processes that are central to successful knowledge exchange and – consequently – to research-based policy and practice change. Looking across the data, interviewees pointed to four areas in which REF measurement of impact differed from their knowledge and experience of knowledge translation: type of evidence underpinning impact, institutional set-up of impact, definition of impact and understanding of knowledge exchange. The contrasts that interviewees made on each of these are summarised in Table 7.2.

Type of evidence

One of the most common critiques of the REF model of impact discussed by the academics involved in knowledge exchange initiatives was its narrow view of evidence, which they felt focused exclusively on research evidence produced within mono-disciplinary units of

Table 7.2: Knowledge brokers' perceived differences between impact in practice and impact as assessed in REF

	Impact based on knowledge-brokering experience	Impact within the REF model
Type of evidence	Multiple types of evidence	Academic research-based evidence
Institutional setting	Network based	Single institution
Definition of impact	Process centred	Outcome centred
Knowledge translation	Complex and adaptive	Linear

assessment. In contrast with this model, interviewees recalled how a much broader use of evidence types often underpinned their knowledge translation work. For example:

'What that [evidence-based policy] exactly means depends on the individual question, but it's often a very complex combination of local evidence, of international [scientific] evidence and how we bring them together to make a decision around a local problem.' (Senior academic 10, public health)

A number of interviewees pointed to the importance of interdisciplinary work (indeed, both of the organisations studied in this chapter collaborated with academics spanning multiple disciplines, including medical sciences, natural sciences and social sciences). Furthermore, the interviewees discussed supporting evidence that went beyond academic knowledge production: for example, practice-based knowledge (Freeman, 2007; Glasby, 2011) and experiential knowledge (Fleming and Rhodes, 2018; Meriluoto, 2018). Examples of such work included enabling and supporting patients, service users and practitioners not only to participate in knowledge production but even to act as the sole producers of evidence for the decision-making process. This approach is aligned with existing literature on evidence use which, for example, highlights the importance of having multiple forms of evidence to make up the 'evidence jigsaw' (Whitehead et al, 2004) that is used by policymakers and practitioners. Several interviewees contrasted this with their sense that the UK's current approach to research impact is encouraging academics to try to inform decision making solely with academic research produced in single disciplines and institutions.

Institutional set-up of impact

Interviewees specifically questioned the REF assumption of impact being traceable to a single unit of assessment within one institution. They framed knowledge-brokering activities as occurring in collaborative settings, across different universities and policy and practice organisations. From this perspective, the context in which knowledge was produced, translated and used had a diffused, network-like structure (Holmes et al, 2017). This marked a stark contrast with the single-institution outlook which interviewees felt was employed in the REF. The REF approach was positioned by interviewees as ignoring the background work necessary for achieving impact, such as developing and nourishing relationships with policymakers and practitioners, creating networks and communities of practice, and – consequently – establishing a pool of expertise which policymakers can draw upon. For example:

> You should be asking academics every time a policy or industry person comes to you and asks for advice, you should record that. It happens all the time. REF says that can't be regarded as an impact unless you know that they actually went away and did something different as a result of consulting you. Now, I think that's too extreme. I think if you're well known enough in an area that people are coming to you to ask your advice about how they should deal with some question that they've got, that should be impact in itself. That's your idea is having an impact out there in the policy world because policy people know about you, they read what you do, and we would welcome your advice, but they're not going to tell you what they did as a result of the advice you gave them. That's really impossible, that's over-expectation. (Mid-career academic 11, genomics)

Establishing close and positive relationships between academics and policymakers was described by the interviewees as the core activity of knowledge broker organisations (akin to descriptions in the literature: Oliver et al, 2014; van de Goor et al, 2017). This type of work was necessary to bridge different understandings of research and the research process, to navigate timeliness issues, to increase responsiveness and to maintain focus on the emerging issues. And yet, this type of activity, even though crucial for achieving impact, was believed to be virtually non-existent in REF monitoring.

Definition of impact

Another criticism of the REF approach to research impact made by several interviewees working in knowledge broker organisations focused on what they perceived to be an excessive attention on the final outcome of the activity, as opposed to the process. A number of interviewees pointed out that only a small minority of projects result in direct, concrete impact, particularly within the timeline required by REF (which several interviewees suggested was overly short). Instead, interviewees suggested that the setting up of a process that might support learning and effective uptake of evidence as a more realistic goal of knowledge brokering. For example:

> 'I wonder if some of the impacts from [our organisation] will be more about process that might be existing. One of our impacts from some of our work might be ... While people are taking up a particular set of methodologies that should make their work better, REF would probably want to know if it actually made work better, but it would be too difficult to tell. It would be virtually impossible to tell, to show around what the independent effect is that a change in the way of working by public health practitioners as a result of, say, [our] activities. It would be virtually impossible to tell, to show around what the independent effect is that a change in the way of working by public health practitioners as a result of, say, [brokering] activities.' (Senior academic 3, public health)

For some interviewees, a focus on process rather than outcome was seen as a more effective approach to the goal of research-based change in a complex policy and practice setting (see also Chapter 4):

> 'So, rather than do the research, present the research and say, "Hey, we think this is important, we think this should change", I think [our organisation] can engage people from the very beginning and we can work in partnership to develop the right research questions, to then influence change. I think that's a really strategic value of [our organisation], and I think certainly we should look to develop that further. That's really important.' (Mid-career academic 12, public health)

As highlighted in the quote above, the change in the process was perceived as imperative to achieving research impact. And yet, this aspect of the knowledge broker organisation's activity was deemed unlikely to be sufficient to count as impact in the REF's framework since the interviewee suggested that it would be difficult to document a specific change that resulted from this process.

Understanding of knowledge translation

A vast majority of the interviewees seemed to be signed up to the notion that academics should increase their engagement with non-academic audiences. Nevertheless, they also challenged the notion that policy and practice change occurs in ways that are initiated by specific pieces of research. As explained by one of the interviewees working in public health:

> 'I think impact itself as a concept is hugely problematic. I think I said earlier about what do you mean by impact, impact for who when, what's the scale and the reach of the impact, how do you make discriminations between that's a better impact than that one, how do you control or predict or plan for an impact? It's bonkers. And I think it's possible to stand here and create impact going backwards and see what led to it. But I just think the way the whole system works, certainly within the public health, I think the complex system that we work in and live in makes it really difficult for that agenda to be shoved into those neat boxes of "I did this, that led to this, that led to this" as a very simple causal chain.' (Senior academic 13, public health)

The linear format of REF impact case studies, in which narratives tend to start with research that is positioned as leading to impact, was frequently described as inadequate for capturing the multifaceted process of knowledge exchange in practice. Contrary to this model, interviewees generally seemed to conceptualise knowledge translation as prolonged and adaptive process, where multiple dissemination strategies and types of evidence interplay with the political and pragmatic reality of decision making in policy and practice settings. Furthermore, many of the interviewees pointed to policy change as a complex system, requiring a consideration of multiple changing elements, beyond specific pieces of academic research (which reflects the academic literature on policy change – see Smith and Katikireddi, 2013).

Conclusions

This chapter has explored the perceptions and experiences of the research impact agenda among academics affiliated with knowledge broker organisations. This group of academics might be seen as pioneering the research impact agenda since they have been involved in developing impact practices and expertise over the last 10–15 years, before the agenda had achieved the current, much more widespread awareness. The exploration of experiences of academics affiliated with knowledge broker organisations provides significant insights into the way research impact practices have progressively become institutionalised and legitimate in UK academia. As highlighted by the interviewees, the introduction of the REF and of pathways to impact statements among UK research councils led to much greater and widespread engagement of UK universities in research impact practices. This has helped to legitimise (or at least partially legitimise) these practices.

The institutionalisation of research impact within universities appears to have supported knowledge brokerage work in two key ways: at the individual level, it has made it more feasible to build an academic career on impact work; at the organisational level, it has supported the scaling up and institutionalisation of knowledge translation activities, ideas and resources within the universities. At the same time, the impact agenda has escalated epistemic and cultural tensions within academia, as it requires conducting practices which are not well aligned with either the dominant system of values and incentives in academia or with the academic research on research use, policy change, etc. Consequently, the academics working in the knowledge exchange organisations described trying to balance these multiple tensions: working to engage policymakers and practitioners while publishing in top academic journals, and contributing to the growing academic expertise on the complexity of knowledge translation, while also contributing to overly simplified accounts of impact in REF case studies.

In some ways, these individuals might be considered the primary beneficiaries of the impact agenda. As might be expected, therefore, they tended to be more positive about the impact agenda than academics more generally (see Chapters 3, 4 and 6), and clearly saw this agenda as an enabler of their work and as a set of changes that were helping ensure their work carried greater legitimacy. Nevertheless, many of those working in knowledge-brokering roles have concerns about the way the current research impact agenda is operating. The academics interviewed for this chapter pointed out the shortcomings of the REF approach to impact, highlighting what they felt was an insufficient focus on processes of knowledge exchange (as distinct from REF's more restrictive focus on outputs), REF's overly narrow definition of evidence and the implicit assumption that impacts can be linked, in a fairly linear way, with research occurring in single disciplines and institutions. Consequently, interviewees argued that the UK's current approach to research impact inherently incentivises practices that are not deemed to be effective, based on their experiences and expertise.

Overall, the experiences of knowledge brokers point to an important distinction between the UK's impact agenda as a programme of cultural change in academia and the impact agenda as a specific form of impact evaluation. Building on the analysis presented in Chapter 2, we argue that the research impact agenda should be viewed through a broader historical lens of changes in the incentive systems within UK academia. As reflected in the experiences of knowledge brokers, this process is far from simple; even though the general direction of the impact agenda might be welcomed by translation-oriented academics, the approach to the measurement of the impact remains an object of critique.

Notes

1   See for example: https://www.epsrc.ac.uk/research/centres/innovativemanufacturing/ or https://www.epsrc.ac.uk/research/centres/acecybersecurity/.
2   See: http://www.esrc.ac.uk/collaboration/collaboration-oportunities/what-works-centres/.
3   See for example: http://www.nerc.ac.uk/funding/available/schemes/placements/.
4   An academic position that, within UK universities, generally sits just below chair/ professor.
5   As we discuss in Chapter 2, the percentage of the overall REF score stemming from impact case studies was (subsequent to this interview) confirmed to increase from 20 per cent in 2014 to 25 per cent in 2021.

8

Looking back: evolving public health perspectives on research impact

As we have seen, for some academics, commitments to research impact represent a disturbing set of practices designed to draw boundaries around what constitutes 'legitimate' academic work in ways that reify apolitical, policy-driven research while silencing more critical voices (e.g. Slater, 2012). This, in turn, has fuelled concerns that efforts to promote research impact in the UK are, in effect, directing researchers towards the production of 'policy-based evidence' (Cohen, 2000; Hammersley, 2005; Slater, 2012). These concerns have, however, been less evident in public health than many other areas of academia, with senior public health researchers often arguing (as we saw in Chapter 4 and 7) that a stronger relationship between research and policy is desirable and that this is likely to be achieved through closer working relationships between researchers and policymakers (e.g. Hunter, 2009; Whitehead et al, 2004; Wimbush et al, 2005). However, the failure to achieve key public health goals in the UK, such as a substantial reduction in health inequalities, despite efforts by researchers and policymakers to work more closely together, has prompted questions about this relationship and about the quality, focus and/or utility of available research (Mackenbach, 2011).

In this chapter, we begin by briefly reviewing two key studies exploring the relationship between evidence and policy for the longstanding public health concern with the cross-cutting challenge of reducing health inequalities in the UK, both of which included policymakers as research participants. These papers suggest that policymakers concerned with public health and health inequalities in the UK put forward relatively consistent proposals for improving the use of research in policy across both studies, despite a publication gap of nearly a decade. Next, the chapter compares the views of public health academics interviewed in 2003–7, the run-up to the RAE in 2008 (before the emergence of research impact) with the views of academics working in the same field in 2011–15, who experienced REF2014 and the first attempt to assess impact case studies (additionally making brief reference to the perspective of interviewees based in policy organisations). This comparison shows that, in this relatively applied research field, an initial scepticism about the likely influence of efforts to promote and reward research impact gave way to a diversity of views, stretching from enthusiastic support (for academics who feel far more enabled to undertake external-facing work than they once did) to pragmatic acceptance. In between these two poles lies a more complex perspective: academics who are creatively adapting opportunities presented by the impact agenda to undertake more political, advocacy and publicly oriented work in public health, much of which appears to be inspired by the successes of tobacco control. The conclusion of the chapter reflects on the implications of these findings for the UK's evolving research impact agenda, especially in the context of the growing emphasis that is being placed on private sector engagement.

Existing policy recommendations for improving the use of public health evidence in policy

Previous studies exploring policy actors' perceptions of health inequalities research, and their advice on improving the relationship between research and policy, have largely focused on the views of actors directly involved in the construction of national policies – often working in a policy 'silo' of 'health inequalities' research, looking primarily to the Department of Health (e.g. Petticrew et al, 2004; Whitehead et al, 2004). At least two existing studies explicitly assessed policy actors' perceptions of health inequalities evidence in the UK (Petticrew et al, 2004; Smith, 2013), and both of these focused on the views of 'core' policy advisors (mainly individuals working in the civil service). The first was based on the findings of a two-day workshop involving seven 'senior policy advisors' which sought to explore how research evidence on health inequalities influences policymaking and 'how its relevance and utility could be improved' (Petticrew et al, 2004: 811). The second (Smith, 2013), involved 112 interviews, forty-three of which were with individuals who might be defined as 'policy actors' (twenty-three working in policy settings – largely civil servants, policy advisors and politicians, but also including four policy campaigners working in third-sector organisations). Given this focus, it is perhaps not surprising that the main recommendations for improving the use and impact of health inequalities research on policy, made by participants in both studies, are in line with recommendations emerging from major reviews of the knowledge exchange/diffusion literature (e.g. Contandriopoulos et al, 2010; Innvær et al, 2002; Mitton et al, 2007; Nutley et al, 2007; Walter et al, 2005). Box 8.1

Box 8.1 Summary of participant suggestions for improving the use and impact of health inequalities research in the UK that are consistent across two studies (Petticrew et al, 2004; Smith, 2013)

• Produce more evidence evaluating existing interventions/policies and include analysis of distributional impacts.
• Undertake more cost and cost-effectiveness evaluation (and the costs of inaction).
• Produce more solution-oriented research (e.g. modelling).
• Ensure research is 'timely' and 'relevant' to ongoing policy trajectories.
• Acknowledge contrasting research needs at different policy levels (e.g. local versus national).
• Undertake more work to better understand the policy process.
• Work collaboratively with policymakers.

---

summarises the recommendations that emerged from participants across both studies.

As Smith (2013) notes, although senior policy officials participating in studies about the relationship between evidence and policy frequently emphasise that policy development is political, and often serendipitous, the kinds of suggestions they make for improving the use of public health evidence in policy nonetheless tend to reflect an instrumental vision of the role that evidence can play. Hence, an emphasis is placed (as Box 8.1 illustrates) on the need for research concerning feasible policy interventions, in which the impacts, including and costs (and cost-savings), are clearly estimated.

This way of thinking about the role of research in policy sits comfortably with the UK's research impact agenda (Rogers et al, 2014). Yet it is also an approach that has, as earlier chapters outline, attracted criticism for threatening academic autonomy (Rogers et al, 2014; Slater, 2012) and redefining the value of academic outputs by their policy (rather than intellectual) worth. Reflecting some of these concerns, the more recent of the two studies (Smith, 2013) included some participants who recommended a rather different approach to effecting policy change, involving working with far broader audiences (e.g. campaigners, advocates, politicians and journalists rather than focusing on civil servants and ministers) and moving beyond evaluations of what has happened in the past to develop clear visions of alternative future scenarios that might come to exist.

These kinds of suggestions do not sit quite so comfortably with research impact guidance but are supported (and in some cases, directly informed) by popular, empirically informed theories of policy change within political science and the sociology of science/ knowledge. Political science tends to suggest that normative positions, institutions, ideas and external interests are all central to understanding the evolution of policy (for an overview, see Smith and Katikireddi, 2012). Sabatier and Jenkins Smith's (1999) widely employed 'advocacy coalition framework', for example, highlights the influential role of value-based coalitions of actors from multiple sectors, while Kingdon's (1995 [1984]) equally popular theory of 'policy streams' foregrounds various kinds of 'policy entrepreneurs', who are constantly working to influence policy debates. Work in the sociology of science, meanwhile, calls attention to the subjective and political nature of 'evidence' itself (e.g. Gieryn, 1983). This suggests that researchers seeking to achieve substantial policy change need to work with a broad range of policy actors, stretching well beyond the corridors of Whitehall and the devolved administrations. Our findings here suggest that this more political, advocacy-oriented approach to achieving research-informed change in public health appears to be gaining traction and benefitting from funding and institutional changes stemming from the research impact agenda, despite the apparent contrast with research impact guidance. However, as we discuss in the concluding section, it remains unclear how this approach will fare if, as some recent developments suggest, the UK's impact agenda and funding initiatives evolve to emphasise private sector beneficiaries.

Preliminary public health perceptions of the UK's impact agenda: from scepticism to celebration and concern

As we discussed in Chapter 4, there has been some suggestion that academics within disciplines that are overtly 'applied', such as public health, tend to support institutional shifts towards research utility and impact, while academics in more traditional subjects (e.g. the humanities) resist it (Nowotny et al, 2003). In this context, it is perhaps surprising that only a quarter of the academic interviewees interviewed in 2003–7 articulated an aspiration to produce research that would be *directly* useful to policymakers. Those who did express this view, however, often had strong views about the matter, often suggesting they believed academics had a *responsibility* to produce this kind of work. For example: 'I think it's important for universities and for academic research generally ... to make the links in with the Department [of

Health]. [...] I think ... academics have got a responsibility to help ... inform' (senior academic, public health)

The preference for this kind of academic role closely mirrors the view of academia that is idealised in much of the UK's official guidance for achieving research impact, positioning academics as individuals who approach research from a policy perspective and who are keen to work collaboratively and constructively with policymakers to address the questions and challenges on which policymakers are focusing (e.g. Blunkett, 2000; Cabinet Office, 1999). Perhaps less surprisingly, this was also the preferred role for academics that was articulated by most of the civil servants who were interviewed in the wider study (Smith, 2013). Yet, despite this convergence, few of the academic interviewees interviewed in 2003–7 felt academic working environments supported this way of working. For example:

> 'I think the incentives are ... almost all in the opposite direction, to have as little to do with practical policymaking as possible ... get on with your own research and impress your own peers. Certainly [...] two or three years spent in government seems to do nothing for your career.' (Senior academic, public health)

> 'Academics are academics because they are interested in research and scholarship and communicating with the next generation of students and peers and so on ... and although I think academics hope that research will have some influence on policy, most academics don't spend a lot of time trying to get their research impacting on policy. [...] In order [for your] research to impact policy, you have to spend a lot of time doing it. [...] There are lots of ... factors which militate against that because if you're gonna spend your time trying to talk to policymakers and write things in newspapers or write things in, you know, the sort of ... quick, easy things which policymakers might read [...] that actually takes time away from doing other things. [...] It's a real trade-off. [...] The sorts of ... criteria by which academics are judged are not really ... the [things that] impact on policymakers – it's much more kind of peer-reviewed articles and ... those sorts of things, research grants and so on [...] I think [...] the incentive structure doesn't ... encourage that so ... if people want to have their research taken up by policymakers then they themselves would have to, I think, need to kind of try

and promote it much more strongly [than they currently do].' (Senior academic, public health)

'Several of us do try and [work at the interface of research and policy] but we do it ... at risk to our own professional lives. Except, I don't find it a risk really 'cause I enjoy doing it so [laughs]. But ... you don't get promoted so much, [...] your university isn't quite so thrilled with you for doing that sort of work ... as it is for ... people who just write more papers or get more grants.' (Senior academic, public health)

Findings from studies in Australia suggest academic concerns about the lack of career incentives or rewards for engaging in policy-relevant work are not restricted to the UK (e.g. Haynes et al, 2011). However, it is worth noting that, while the above interviewees said they felt academia was not supportive of their desire to work with policymakers, the first and third academics quoted here indicated that they had nevertheless been able to undertake this kind of work and both were successful in academic terms, having secured chair-level posts in research-oriented universities (the middle quotation came from an academic who seemed less personally committed to achieving policy impact and who appeared to have focused on more traditional academic activities). This was a consistent trend: all of the interviewees who said they felt public health researchers should be working closely with policymakers indicated that they had themselves been able to work in this manner. For some, this was achieved through holding official and/or unofficial advisory positions. Others had contributed to policy inquiries, policy reviews or cross-party committees, while others had undertaken research that had been commissioned by policymakers. The data do not, therefore, suggest that academics interviewed in 2003–7 felt completely unable to work with policymakers, but they imply this kind of work was neither encouraged nor rewarded as much as those who aspired to this kind of role felt it should be.

As might be expected, these interviewees were generally supportive of the UK's research impact agenda and were supportive of early indications that the impact of research beyond academia was beginning to be better acknowledged:

'I think if you could show some research actually resulted in a [policy] change, if you put that in the RAE [Research Assessment Exercise – which did not include formal research impact assessment] submission, if there's evidence of esteem or impact ... I think it would, at the margins, be taken seriously.' (Senior academic, public health)

However, few of these interviewees believed that efforts to create institutional incentives to promote and reward research impact would make a significant difference in achieving research impact. For some interviewees, this view was grounded in a belief that the career incentives (e.g. RAE assessments) were unlikely to change substantially, despite claims to the contrary:

'I can't imagine there's anybody who really likes the RAE so, I mean I've never met anybody who does [laughs]. [...] I mean it says it's going to be different this year, now – the one that's coming up in 2008 [in terms of research impact] but I don't know – I don't know to what extent it is. All the things that I've had to submit so far for trial runs and things have been exactly the same as I did last time, you know, your four best papers, your grants, that sort of thing ... where you last gave a lecture. I mean, is this really what changes the world? If I go out to Hawaii and give a lecture, it doesn't really seem that that's likely to change a great deal.' (Senior academic, public health)

For others, however, the view that research impact was unlikely to become a core dimension of academic work related at least as much to a fundamental concern with protecting academic autonomy, combined with a perception that UK policymakers are not actually very interested in using academic evidence:

'It's difficult for academics to do policy-relevant research, in a nutshell, because the RAE doesn't really recognise it, unless it leads directly to publishable, journal-publishable products. I guess there's a view in parts of academia that dabbling too much with policy and practice is getting your hands a bit dirty [...] and I guess there's also a view on the part of academics that it's engaging with less rigorous research, so compromises are made if you get into this kind of collaboration. [...] I think there's probably a pragmatic view that ... you are ... losing autonomy over what happens to your research if you take it outside of the academic community of peers. [...] I'm sure there's a pretty sizeable group of academics, including senior academics, who are keen to do this kind of policy focused research but who would then be very nervous about what happens to it and ... would probably have low expectations about it being used wisely by the policymakers and practitioners, if used at all. [...] Government is perceived to listen less to academia than would have been true in the sixties and seventies [...] I think there's a kind of powerful default position in government where ... either civil servants find ways to ... not act upon the evidence, or not provide guidance to ministers on the evidence, or ministers and politicians find ways to ignore it because it is politically ... inconvenient.' (Senior academic, public health)

Despite these kinds of concerns, which were evident across multiple interviews in 2003–7, in the more recent batch of interviews, undertaken in 2010–14, there did appear to have been a clear shift in the extent to which academic interviewees felt supported in undertaking, and rewarded for, policy engagement, with some interviewees, such as the following academic, openly celebrating this shift:

'Once the impact agenda came in I honestly was like, "yippee!" Because now all the stuff that I've been doing or trying to do with local authorities and whatever has suddenly been legitimised within the university; it's not just something you do as an added extra, but a core part of your job, and so now you get ... praise and reward for doing what you're already doing. And public health is a discipline that is policy facing, be it helping in clinical trials in the NHS for example or be it the sort of stuff we've been talking about at a more kind of macro level, so it's not actually kind of a difficult adjustment I think for us to make as opposed to say arts and humanities or whatever.' (Senior academic, public health)

However, as with the interviewees working in knowledge broker settings in Chapter 7, this is not to say that academic interviewees were uncritical of the UK's impact agenda. Indeed, as might be expected, many interviewees (particularly those with social science training or those who had substantial experience of engaging in the policy world) criticised the attempt to capture, assess and reward research impact via the REF as naïve and simplistic. For example:

'It's such bollocks, it's such bollocks. [...] We were involved in the pilot for REF and the impact stuff, and I don't know whether they've changed the guidelines since the pilot but it was just insane: "please provide examples that explicitly trace the path from your odds ratio you show in your paper through to changing clinical practice or policy" – I mean that's just insane because [...] that's not how it works.' (Senior academic, public health)

In sum, the interview data suggest that public health academics in the UK were initially sceptical about the prospect that changes to academic incentive and reward frameworks would alter academic approaches to engaging with policy. Certainly, those who were committed to collaborating with policymakers and practitioners did not expect to feel substantially more supported as a result of the changes being discussed in 2003–7. Yet, as the UK's impact agenda emerged, accompanied by new sources of funding and new institutional rewards for outward-facing work, public health academics who wanted to undertake policy-oriented work generally did appear to feel better supported to undertake this kind of outward-facing work.

Public health academics' responses to the UK's impact agenda: three clusters

This section argues that, as the UK's impact agenda has deepened and evolved, perspectives within public health appear to be clustering around three distinct perspectives that can be situated across a spectrum stretching from enthusiastic support to pragmatic acceptance. Interestingly, as might be anticipated for such an applied area of research, none of the academics participating in the interviews for this chapter expressed anything close to the level of concern about the consequences of the impact agenda for academic autonomy evident within broader debates (as discussed in Chapter 3). Nonetheless, most academic interviewees expressed at least some concern about the potential consequences of the impact agenda.

Cluster 1: enthusiastic supporters

The first group were explicit, often very active, supporters of the research impact agenda. Indeed, many already had strong policy links well in advance of clearer incentives emerging:

'I happen to work in a university where certainly amongst the social scientists, many of us naturally do work which is at the interface between academia and policy, and we feel therefore that from a university side that having that impact agenda is beneficial to us because we do that kind of work anyway. It's not a strange thing for us to have to say that the work we've done has had some impact outside academic publishing.' (Senior academic, public health)

The support of this cluster for the UK's approach to research impact often appeared to be grounded in a belief that differences between public health research, policy and practice are largely a consequence of divisions between those involved in *producing research* and those *constructing and implementing policies* (a view that is also evident within existing literature about the science–policy relationship, e.g. Caplan, 1979; Innvær et al, 2002; Mitton et al, 2007). This, in turn, informed interviewee support for 'knowledge broker' posts and organisations, for exchange/secondment schemes between academia and policy settings, and for the provision of appropriate incentive structures for cross-sector career paths:

'It's a mode two type thinking where you sit down with decision makers, practitioners, others, and decide what their problems are and help them articulate what those research questions might be, rather than going and saying here's a research question, we've got funding, let us have access, which is what happens now.' (Senior academic, public health)

Perhaps unsurprisingly, this perspective was evident among the small number of academic interviewees who self-identified as knowledge brokers (as it was for the interviewees working in knowledge broker settings whose views were discussed in Chapter 7):

'For a start [a knowledge broker organisation] understand both sides of the coin. I think that's one of the main things is that [...] they can broker relationships with people that are public health professionals, people that work in public health, for example, and policymakers. So people that actually understand the research and have a background in that and get them to go and work in these environments so that they've got a really good understanding of what each of them need. [...] I think longer term you need to keep those relationships going and they're the ideal people to do it because they can see what the needs are from both sides.' (Knowledge broker working in an academic setting)

It was also a perspective commonly shared among interviewees working in policy settings, especially those working in government. For example: 'It's really helpful if you have people who [have] seen things from both sides' (senior civil servant, UK/English government).

For many of these interviewees, the optimal approach (which was generally perceived to be supported by the UK's impact agenda and which was outlined by interviewees in academia and government) involved partnership working and/or co-production, with academics and potential research users working closely together throughout the research process (Martin, 2010):

'We've been talking about infused, must more of a co-production model where the whole model of research has to change. [...] And that kind of continuous relationship from the beginning of the research process right through to the end just doesn't occur systematically.' (Senior academic, public health)

'[There are] developments around jointly developing research in groups comprising both policymakers and academics – I hope that trend continues so that policies are developed and tested more effectively.' (Senior civil servant, Scottish government)

These suggestions reflect available evidence regarding factors facilitating the use of research evidence in decision making (Contandriopoulos et al, 2010; Innvær et al, 2002; Mitton et al, 2007; Nutley et al, 2007; Walter et al, 2005) and are broadly in line with the kinds of suggestions being made in the UK's evolving impact agenda (Rogers et al, 2014). Ongoing, collaborative relationships between researchers and potential users are thought to increase levels of trust and dialogue around the definition of policy problems, the prioritisation of particular policy issues and the criteria against which potential solutions are assessed. All this informed some vocal expressions of support for the UK's approach to research impact, such as the following:

'I think it's the right way to go. I think we can't sit in our ivory towers and do research that pleases us. We're not here to do this for our own pleasure. There is a serious purpose to it and I see what we do as a form of service in the sense of we serve society and our job is to do our best to come up with solutions to big societal problems, and in our case in the field of public health and that's our duty, that's what we're here for and so the question of impact is central to that duty. There's no point in doing something that's not going to have an impact.' (Senior academic, public health)

Despite this evidence of support for the UK's current approach to research impact, these interviewees often indicated that they still felt relatively unusual within academia, acknowledging that their approach was not one that all academics were comfortable with:

'A lot of academics hate the impact agenda – they think that academia is academia and we get on with our research and we publish it wherever we publish it to get the respect of our peers and that's that.' (Senior academic, public health)

'Over time, it becomes evident […] who are the people who will be … comfortable working with policy and more useful to policymakers and who are the people who are much happier working in a purely academic environment.' (Senior academic and policy advisor, public health)

Some of these interviewees expressed hope that the impact agenda would encourage more of their peers to feel comfortable with this working style, or indicated that they felt this was already happening:

'I think there should be responsibility on academics to engage as much as possible in terms of trying to get their research to the people who might be able to make a difference, or influence policy. And I think increasingly the impact agenda is driving some people towards that.' (Senior academic, public health)

Others, however, indicated that they felt it was important for academia to maintain space for a range of different preferences and approaches. For example:

'I don't think we should be putting all our eggs in one basket – we should be allowing researchers to do all these roles. And some of them are better at some of those roles than others [...] I would say it's horses for courses and you want a mix of people.' (Senior academic, public health)

This suggestion is similar to the kind of division of responsibility that some interviewees in Chapter 7 put forward (while the broader data in Chapter 7 suggested that this kind of division would be difficult to maintain in practice).

Cluster 2: creative adapters

A second group of interviewees (the majority of the academics interviewed) put forward rather more complex perspectives. Interviewees in this category were generally keen to express basic support for the UK's decision to pursue, incentivise and reward research impact, but this support was balanced by evident concerns and reservations about some aspects of how this agenda was being pursued. The following extract is illustrative of this more reserved and conditional response to the UK's research impact agenda:

'I mean that's a good thing. But then it still raises questions about how it's measured, and what's measured as impact. So with all of these things ... what may sound good in theory or may sound neutral in theory, can always be applied in a certain way that isn't necessarily good or neutral.' (Senior academic, public health)

As Table 8.1 illustrates, five common risks of the UK's approach to research impact were identified by interviewees in this group (each of which maps on to concerns set out in Chapter 3). In contrast to some of the published literature, however, these concerns were often accompanied by accounts of creative responses that were designed to limit the impacts of these risks for the interviewee and their areas of research/policy interest (see the final column of Table 8.1).

Despite the fact that (as we discuss in earlier chapters, notably Chapters 2 and 7) guidance relating to the UK's research impact agenda, and many of the funding opportunities, promote close collaboration between researchers and potential research users (via co-production, etc.), many of the interviewees in this group described using opportunities arising from the UK's impact agenda to undertake work to influence policy via more external routes, including advocacy and, to a lesser degree, community/public engagement. For example:

Table 8.1: Creative adapters' concerns with, and management of, the UK's research impact agenda

Concern about the UK's approach to research impact	Illustrative extract	Creative adaptation in response
1. Encourages overly simplistic approaches to achieving and measuring research impact	Senior academic: 'I think we should be trying to do [research impact] but I'm very cautious about how you measure it. Because I think most of the impact many of us have is stopping stupid things being done. Now how do you trace that? [...] Often the most effective advocacy is the one that's not visible. Because you're doing things behind the scenes, and in a way it's almost a failure if you get into the public domain.'	Continue to undertake more complex or difficult-to-document approaches to achieving external change, using opportunities created by the impact agenda (e.g. institutional support to attend meetings with external actors, knowledge exchange funding), and either simplify the account for a REF impact case study or use alternative (simpler, easy-to-document) examples
2. Prioritises and rewards some research over others (e.g. that with short-term impacts over long-term impacts) and potentially shapes the research and engagement that academics do	Senior academic: 'I don't know about the most recent incarnation of REF but I think the previous REF was pretty biased towards certain kinds of research being given precedence over other kinds of research, impacts being measured in the short term rather than the long term. There's a whole issue around attribution of impact, which I think is seriously problematic. [...] So, you know, when you're having to attribute impact to your piece of research, then that by itself creates a bias in terms of what kind of research you're going to do. And also what kinds of policy and public engagement you're going to do. So there are huge limitations I think with the current formula.'	Continue to undertake work for other reasons (so avoid making choices about work that are driven by the research impact agenda) and, for longer-term, more challenging issues, work via external routes (e.g. collaborate with community groups and/or advocacy organisations, rather than with core policy actors, such as civil servants); document the impact of research on campaigns and communities (as opposed to substantive policy change)

Concern about the UK's approach to research impact	Illustrative extract	Creative adaptation in response
3. Limits the academic space for, and perceived value of, theoretical and 'blue skies' work	Senior academic: 'I do think that academics should be held to account on what they're doing and how it's related to the wider world and society but I'm not sure that that [the UK impact agenda] is a great idea on how to do it. I mean if, for example, you are a clinician and you've researched some new surgical procedure and actually that's gone into being used in hospitals and it's saved loads of people's lives. Then [...] that's absolutely fine, you could submit that as an example of the impact of your work. But if you are Bourdieu and you've written a coherent thesis on how it is that class is perpetuated, and that hasn't, surprise, surprise, ended up in the coalition [government's] White Paper on public health, that to me doesn't mean that the work of the theorist is of less value.'	Work to support the continued existence of research funders, and research funding streams, that are not focused on impact; create space for blue skies or theoretically oriented work within large grants/research-active institutions; work to broaden how research impact is assessed so that longer-term impacts (potentially arising from blue skies work) or theoretical work that contributes to public discussions 'count'
4. Promotes efforts to achieve single-project/academic impact, even if this is not desirable (rather than more gradual synthesised contributions)	Senior academic: 'The downside of [the impact] push ... is that I think again there's an implication that we should be pushing stuff all the time [...] and the down sides of that are that there isn't time, [...] that it's not thought through and that researchers then become, well not just advocates but sort of sales people for something for products. I do think that that's, there is a risk that that happens, because not everybody has something that's worth selling ... [...] Most research is not ... for people to do anything with, it's only very small building blocks.'	Celebrate and support academics and institutions undertaking synthesis work and attempt to persuade impact architects and assessors to reward synthesis

Concern about the UK's approach to research impact	Illustrative extract	Creative adaptation in response
5. Potentially restricts/compromises academic autonomy and independence	Academic: 'There's clear incentives for people to be more impactful, therefore there's clearer incentives for people to work with people that are active in policy discussions, but it's really important that independence is maintained. And as far as I know, universities haven't at this point done anything to try to ensure that that's the case. The emphasis is all "be impactful!" There are basically no regulations around making sure that you don't compromise yourself in any way in the effort to be impactful.'	Draw attention to the potential risks involved in academic collaboration (including via research) and contribute to efforts to develop guidance and regulation for engaging with external actors, especially where conflicts of interest may emerge

'[I]ncreasingly – it may be my age and stage of life – I've been much more trying to assemble the evidence but then promote its uptake [...] to advocate the importance of social justice and health equity.' (Senior academic, public health)

'I'm probably doing less basic research [than I used to] and much more writing and much more trying to explain things to a wider audience. [...] That's how my work's changing – it's much more talking to people who are not academics about academic work than doing so much academic work myself.' (Senior academic, public health)

It is worth noting that while several of these interviewees discussed working with local communities and undertaking public engagement (including both speakers quoted above), these accounts generally depicted academics as experts performing an educative function. With a couple of exceptions, the approaches to public engagement that were described fit relatively comfortably with the UK's research impact agenda and did not involve dialogical, participatory work (see Chapter 5 for further discussion of this distinction).

However, some of the other activities that this group described, especially in terms of managing any concerns about the agenda, were more creative and adaptive. For example, several of these interviewees described using opportunities afforded by the impact agenda to achieve changes via activities that might be understood as 'academic advocacy'

(Smith and Stewart, 2017). This included strategies to influence policy and society that map on to Chapman's (2007) account of public health advocacy, including the need to: develop clear policy proposals, be strategic and work with a wide range of actors. Additionally, some interviewees highlighted the importance of 'agenda setting', 'framing' and working to counter 'opposing' messages (e.g. from business interests involved in producing or marketing health-damaging products). Here, it is important to note, interviewees did not suggest that the impact agenda had been a driving force for undertaking these kinds of activities. Rather, this approach to effective change through advocacy appeared to be a response to frustrations about the pace and direction of social and policy change in the UK (Mackenbach, 2011). Indeed, the idea that advocacy is a core function of public health has much longer-standing roots (see, e.g., Virchow, 1985).

Overall, all of the interviewees in this group expressed some enthusiasm for the UK's impact agenda and most provided creative examples of how they felt public health was benefitting from impact-related opportunities, including in terms of developing better 'academic advocacy'. Nevertheless, several of these interviewees remained concerned about the potential for the UK's approach to research impact-shaping academic decisions about their work, both in terms of the substantive focus of research and in terms of external-facing activities:

> 'I think one of the problems is that if you're pushed to do more and more policy-relevant research and to align what you do ever more closely to needs of policymakers and practitioners, I think what's never really discussed or not often discussed is the fact that what you end up doing is losing, potentially losing some of your independence. Even if you think and try to be an independent researcher, inevitably you do give some of that up, because I think it's very difficult, it can be very difficult not to make compromises, so I think that's one of the costs that can be quite difficult to negotiate that territory.' (Senior academic, public health)

> 'Being able to feed directly into policymaking processes means researchers working with policymakers, which means you're less likely to get high breadth scores if in fact what you're doing is to challenge policy. So that creates an immediate bias. And then the ability of academics to impact on policy and practice indirectly is not taken into account. So working through the general public, working

through local community groups, the NGO sector, where you may not always fail to attribute impact directly to your work as an academic can cause certain academics to just say I'm not going to spend time doing this.' (Senior academic, public health)

It was also noticeable that few interviewees in this group seemed confident that the third concern could be overcome/managed, as the following interviewee's reflections on funding changes illustrates:

'The funders are obviously increasingly in charge with the impact agenda. If you think about the NIHR are very much about funding. Evaluations of whatever public health interventions and so on, I think there's recognition that research funding needs to be about addressing some sort of strategic priority set down by government, by policymakers and probably at the expense, despite what the ESRC might say, of sort of blue skies research, I guess people are finding it much harder to get funding in that sort of area.' (Senior academic, public health)

However, this concern rarely seemed very pressing to the interviewees in this group since it was not directly impacting on their own work, where the public health focus invariably meant they were not primarily focusing on 'blue skies' or theoretical work.

Cluster 3: pragmatic accommodators

A final, and significantly smaller, cluster of academics are what we describe as 'pragmatic accommodators'. This consisted of a small number of older (close-to-retirement) academics who indicated that they were not personally comfortable with outward-facing work but that they accepted key, underpinning rationales for the UK's research impact agenda. For this group, all of whom worked at Russell Group universities (i.e. institutions which were generally excelling in more traditional, research- and publication-focused markers of academic success), the impact agenda was depicted as contributing to a growing acceptability, within academia, of outward-facing, policy work:

'I was trained as an academic years ago, when you didn't do this kind of thing [promoting work beyond academia] and, if you did, it was actually considered rather vulgar

… It was sort of thought that people who did this kind of thing were people who didn't have much grey matter. Now I think that's an arrogant attitude and we are paid by public taxes and we should actually, our work should be made into a useable form for public debate or anything else that is necessary for democratic processes … but I'm afraid I'm not very good at it.' (Senior academic, public health)

The shift was generally talked about in equivocal terms and any enthusiasm was certainly not sufficient to encourage this group of interviewees to engage in more outward-facing work themselves, as the above extract illustrates. Indeed, some of these interviewees specifically noted that they welcomed the fact that the REF's approach to assessing impact via case studies did not require all academics to demonstrate research impact. Others reflected that they were glad these changes had only occurred as they were approaching retirement, which, they suggested, allowed them to abstain from any serious engagement with this kind of work. Here, it is perhaps worth noting that there were also academics who were close to retirement in each of the other clusters (i.e. although all of the interviewees in this cluster were at that career stage, several of their peers held substantively different views).

Conclusions: public health support for research impact (with reservations)

The academic interviewees discussed in this chapter capture an evident shift in opinion regarding the importance and consequences of UK efforts to incentivise and reward research impact. In the interviews undertaken in 2003–7, interviewees did not generally seem to believe that changes to support and promote outward-facing, policy-oriented work would make much of a difference to academic practices. Yet, the interviews undertaken in 2011–14 found that most interviewees thought that academic practices were changing as a result of the impact agenda. This reinforces the findings of other chapters in this book: the UK's research impact agenda is changing the experience of working as an academic in the UK and changing the types of work that it is considered legitimate for academics to do.

Interviewees' responses to this shift varied, though no one positioned themselves as actively opposed to the UK's research impact agenda (even though some were extremely disparaging about specific aspects of the agenda, especially around measurement and attribution). We categorised the most supportive interviewees as 'enthusiastic supporters' of the UK's approach and noted that most interviewees in this category had close links with policymakers prior to the emergence of the research impact agenda. The least supportive were perhaps the interviewees we called 'pragmatic accommodators'. These academics accepted the rationale for the impact agenda but were not actively engaging in impact-related work themselves. Finally, the largest, and perhaps most interesting, cluster were the 'creative adapters' – academics who described welcoming and benefitting from aspects of the UK's impact agenda, while also expressing concerns about some aspects of current approaches.

Within the 'creative adapters', a range of approaches to influencing policy were evident; we placed interviewees in this cluster if they described engaging in approaches to achieving societal or policy influence that did not fit comfortably with the UK's guidance on achieving research impact. This included several academics who clearly identified themselves as 'academic advocates' or who described undertaking 'advocacy'-type work.

Not everyone was comfortable with these kinds of approaches to achieving policy change though and some of the interviewees we categorised as 'enthusiastic supporters' were critical of some others within this 'creative adapters' group for being 'too political'. On the other hand, some of the 'creative adapters' criticised 'enthusiastic supporters' for becoming overly close to policymakers. In both cases, the fundamental basis of the criticism was around perceived incursions on academic autonomy and independence (see Pickett and Wilkinson, 2016 and Smith and Stewart, 2017 for further discussion of this tension within public health). The data do not suggest that the UK's approach to promoting and rewarding research impact have directly caused this tension (as noted above, the 'enthusiastic supporters' of research agenda tended to have longstanding policy links, while the 'creative adapters' who described engaging in advocacy work explained this choice with reference to perceived public health failures, rather than developments relating to the impact agenda). However, the fact that the research impact agenda is making external-facing work more feasible seemed to be increasing opportunities for both groups to undertake the kind of external-facing work they felt comfortable with. This, in turn, seemed to be increasing the visibility (and perhaps the extent) of this work and, therefore, the sense that there was a division/tension.

Overall, much like Chapter 7, this chapter draws attention to the fact that 'impact'-type work does not always sit comfortably with traditional academic work, even for those who are supportive of it. This reflects the often political and normative nature of impact and what

Kisby (2011) has referred to as the 'illusion' that the use of evidence in policy can be an essentially neutral, technical matter. This underlines the importance of examining not only how academics are engaging with 'impact' work (the focus of this chapter) but also how evidence of efforts to achieve research impact are being assessed, an issue that we focus on in Chapter 9.

9

Telling tales of impact: as seen through the eyes of user assessors

While news of impact as a new component of research performance evaluation appeared, in the late 2000s, to provoke much in the way of concern among large swathes of the UK's academic community (see Chapter 3), as we have also seen (particularly in Chapters 6 and 7), research impact, as featured in the UK's REF and research council funders, was not all bad news to all people. Nor, as Chapter 8 highlighted, was it a completely 'new' feature of university life – certainly, as will be argued in this chapter, in the context of the way it was responded to and ultimately co-opted by institutions as an instrument of self-promotion.

This chapter builds on some of the concerns outlined across the rest of the book and considers how academics' participation within the REF's impact audit regime produces contradictions that destabilise its rationalisation as a vehicle for enhanced scientific transparency and accountability. It discusses how the impact agenda has produced a variety of illusions and/or misassumptions related to transformational change on academic praxis. It also points to how the centralising and prioritising of impact as a performance expectation of academics is a false corrective that disregards and fails to acknowledge much of what many academics already do. This chapter is the book's most critical take on the research impact agenda, ultimately contending that, as a catalyst for cultural and behavioural change (leitmotifs of the era of new public management), the impact agenda no more ameliorates the nexus between science and society than it inauthenticates the potential for trustworthy, meaningful and sustainable relationships between scientists and their public patrons. Finally, it deals with the mythologies that have sprung from and courted an impact agenda for academic research in the UK.

Telling (one-sided) tales

In this chapter, we argue that the UK's approach to research impact specifically within the REF (which is the aspect of the impact agenda that appears to have prompted the most critique across the other chapters of this book) has affected and accentuated (and prospectively will continue to affect and accentuate) a cleft between academics and their public communities. This is because this approach to research impact 'demands' that academics invest resources in telling a good tale of themselves, and of themselves *only* at the expense and exclusion of their 'public partners', unless where called upon as corroborators. This is a profound and conspicuous irony. Such self-interested and reductionist accounts serve to separate, indeed isolate, academics in entirely contrived and artificial ways (which seem to run counter to efforts by UK research councils to promote co-created research endeavours). Such 'segregation for elevation' is especially peculiar where momentum in the conceptual organisation of knowledge has led to the reification of post-normal or post-academic science. The emergence of 'public' impact as a financially incentivised academic obligation, however, neglects such evolution and instead contrarily acts as a brace to the much-maligned edifice of the 'ivory tower'. So, despite discourse from the higher education policy community around scientific transparency, measures of accountability embodied in policy innovations like impact in the REF actually obfuscate the contributions of a more heterogeneous body of scientific producers (a point underlined by Smith and Stewart's 2017 assessment of the REF2014 impact case studies returned to the Social Work and Social Policy Unit of Assessment). This chapter is informed by several of the concerns about the research impact agenda that were outlined in Chapter 3. In addition to these, this chapter begins by outlining four further concerns with the approach to research impact assessment incorporated into REF.

Further concern 1: REF constructs a distinction between expert academics and passive beneficiaries

The first concern may seem paradoxical at first since, as we discussed in Chapter 8 in particular, a key approach to achieving research impact that is currently being advocated by research funders in the UK (and which is evident elsewhere) involves close collaboration and co-production between researchers and potential beneficiaries. Yet, impact in the REF appears to represent a reversion to, and veneration of, a paradigm of Mode-1 knowledge production, in which academics are positioned as the active research 'experts', while potential beneficiaries, such as policymakers, are demoted to the status of 'users'. This, we claim, occurs as their role changes – in the context of academics' enforced reporting through the REF – from being an active and essential cog in the machinery of scientific discovery to a passive receiver or beneficiary of academic triumphs.

Further concern 2: the non-portability of research impact for REF restricts academic freedom

In the REF rules, impact is not portable, which is to say that if an academic is to move institution, the impact from research s/he has generated stays with the institution s/he leaves behind. This is the opposite to research outputs, which in the guidelines of REF2021 can move with the researcher (though can also be double counted by previous and current host institutions). The intention of making impact non-portable may have been to limit the risk of institutional 'poaching' as a REF strategy, whereby institutions headhunt and appoint academics shortly before the REF cut-off date, with the specific intention of boosting their REF scores. The institutional ownership of impact raises questions about the extent of the contribution of universities in supporting academics in generating impact and not, as might be the typical expectation, in facilitating the generation of impact case studies. Moreover, the non-portability of impact in the REF says something about how impact is conceived by universities more as a 'positional' than 'public' good and primarily as a valuable item of academics' endeavours to be exploited and, crucially, retained for institutional gain.[1] Therein, impact may also be viewed as an aspect of scientific capital used against academics in their role as migratory knowledge workers. Where impact in the REF is predicated upon the porosity of knowledge communities (research producers and users), the confinement of impact to the claims of one institution appears to be a profound contradiction to the terms of knowledge creation and appropriation, limiting the freedoms of academics in negotiating and contributing to 'global knowledge flows' (Kennedy, 2014).

Further concern 3: REF impact requirements inform two distinct categories of academics – excellent and impactful

The REF rules also state that the research underpinning an impact case study must achieve a minimum threshold of 2★ quality. In the REF terms this means research that demonstrates: 'quality that is recognised internationally in terms of originality, significance and rigour' but falls short of 'quality that is internationally excellent in terms of originality, significance and rigour but which falls short of the highest standards of excellence' (3★) or 'quality that is world-leading in terms of originality, significance and rigour' (4★) (www.ref.ac.uk). However, crucially, in the world of the REF, only research of 4★ or 3★ quality receives remuneration by government in the form of QR research monies with a ratio of 4:1. Research deemed to be 2★, despite seeming to be quite decent, receives no return. Unsurprisingly, therefore, the vast majority of universities focus their attention on ensuring their academics produce research of 3★ and 4★ quality. The implication of the 2★ rating for impact is therefore a mixed bag and produces a strange corollary. Despite claims to the contrary (see Chapter 2), it implies that researchers can be impactful without producing the best kinds of research or that the best kinds of research may not always be the most impactful. Yet impact in the REF is significantly rewarded. Indeed, it has been shown to greatly exceed the return on QR achieved by outstanding (4★) research outputs (Watermeyer and Hedgecoe 2016).

The supposition that may be drawn, therefore, is that impact in the REF bifurcates researchers into two camps: those who may excel at producing impact and may be reasonable yet far from outstanding researchers, and those who may excel at research, yet whose efforts in translating such success into impact are more limited. This was a distinction that some academic interviewees in Chapters 4, 7 and 8 seemed to support, although this is also a distinction that the analysis in Chapter 7 suggests may be difficult to maintain. Moreover, in the context of what is known, at least anecdotally, of REF2014, the correlation between excellent research and excellent impact appears to have been relatively strong. In fact, a perusal of the REF2014 impact repository indicates multiple representations of impact built upon very good research. Notwithstanding, it would seem reasonable to assume that, given the associated premium of 4★ and 3★ research, universities in the run-up to REF2014 would privilege a focus on researchers capable of leveraging such scores from their outputs. Moving forwards towards REF2021 and more in the way of an impact consciousness within universities, a strategising of researchers into these kinds of categories would appear not wholly unrealistic (and, indeed, was somewhat evident in the accounts of academics presented in Chapters 7 and 8).

Further concern 4: the high monetary value associated with REF impact case studies has a potentially distortive effect

As already touched upon, there is a high economic value associated with impact case studies in the REF. Various calculations have reported a QR value of a 4★ impact case study to be anywhere near and beyond £350,000 (see, for example, Watermeyer and Hedgecoe, 2016). In comparative terms this has been translated as one 4* impact case study being of a commensurate value to seven 4* research outputs. The generation of just one 4* output in the REF is considered by many research-active academics to be quite some achievement. In fact, a return of seven such outputs may represent a strong aspiration for most medium sized departments. The extremely high value of the impact case study is thus unmistakable, increasing the pressure on institutions and academics to tell good impact tales.

In the REF marketplace, academics have been seen to operate as impact traders selling their impact wares in the form of highly stylised narratives in hope of inveigling REF academic and user assessor panellists as custodians of a QR war chest, calculated to be somewhere in the region of £2 billion. The financial return on the evidencing of 'excellent' impact is so significant that it dwarfs an investment in research as configured through the peer review (by the same assessors) of research outputs and the distribution of QR. Moreover, in the research game of 'competitive accountability', an ability to showcase impact provides significant spoils. With impact in REF2014 having a 20 per cent weighting, high-scoring impact case studies were instrumental to the overall institutional performance in REF league tables. Thus, it is easy to see how an impact agenda provides institutions with an incentive to overstate the significance of what they do.

Drawing value from tales told

To analyse the REF's impact agenda further, there is a need to burrow into the experiences of the assessors on REF disciplinary subpanels. It is especially illuminating to consider the views of those sitting on REF panels as 'user assessors' – in simple terms, individuals employed in non-academic (often practitioner or policy contexts) and how they understood the 'quality' of the accounts put forward. In discussing qualitative interviews with these individuals in this chapter, we see that they encountered their role rather differently to what we might typically associate with peer review. Crucially, assessments appear to have become bound up with arbitration regarding the indisputability, or conversely the fragility, of the claims.

The conversations with user assessors across arts and humanities and social sciences subpanels employed in this chapter allow us to revisit and reconsider the various concerns outlined in Chapter 3 and, additionally, at the start of this chapter. In so doing, it is important to acknowledge that interviewees reported undertaking REF related work in the context of limited time and capacity; user assessors are usually not afforded the same dedicated space to focus on REF that universities tend to allow participating academics. Of all the user assessors consulted, none were fully absolved from their day-to-day job responsibilities. In fact, the participation of many user assessors in the REF appeared to represent something of a juggling act. This in itself is a potential cause for concern; the arbitration of the score for an output as valuable as a REF impact case study could be argued to demand an undiluted and undistracted focus. Moreover, the accounts of user assessors point to a cultural perspective unlike their academic counterparts, which, perhaps surprisingly, champions theory. User assessors often bemoaned specifically the neglect of 'a theory of change' among academic panellists, rendering them far less sympathetic to the claims of impact presented by case study authors; though the relatively small number of user assessors would represent a minority of agnostics.

Beyond insight into the structural and organisational challenges faced by user assessors in REF2014, we can glean from their accounts a sense of frustration, intolerance and perhaps even indignation of impact case studies as disingenuous artefacts of public accountability. Accounts established within a series of interviews conducted with user assessors (see Watermeyer and Chubb 2018) reveal how a turn towards 'competitive accountability' through impact in the REF reveals the susceptibility and proclivity of academics to overstate and embellish, through such convention, their public contributions (see Chapter 3 and Future Concern 4 in the previous section). This fairy-tale phenomenon could perhaps be understood as the consequence of nervousness, naivety and uncertainty among academics in responding to a new performance paradigm. Concurrently, it may be understood as a reflection of the survivalist instinct of academics and/or their university employers and the associated need for affirmation and recognition in the face of the REF as a kind of public/moral inquest and the related pursuit of institutional funding. Detractors of the academic community may more pejoratively point to impact in the REF as a new 'soap-box' space for scientists to indulge in public pontification and self-valorisation. Yet perhaps most tellingly, where impact in the REF has signified the triumph of 'artifice over integrity' (Chubb and Watermeyer 2017), and the privileging of stylistic virtuosity over the empirical mundane, the frailty of the science and society nexus has been made explicit. Indeed, it may be argued that the public role of science has, through impact in the REF, become all the more ambiguous. It may even be the case that scientists' public persona has been debilitated by the looseness and inaccuracy of such historical record – certainly where viewed and assessed by their public arbitrators, REF user assessors.

This moves us to reflect on two striking accounts offered in the course of our discussions with REF2014 user assessors, of their job in determining the efficacy of academics' impact claims in REF2014. Our first assessor – who we will call 'Sarah' – had both significant experience as a jobbing academic and civil servant and spoke of the challenge of assessing impact case studies, in particular the challenge of unstitching the embroidery of the impact case study so as to reveal the 'true' if (intentionally) obfuscated fabric of historical truth. Given the uniqueness of her dual perspective as both an academic and policy person, she becomes the focus of our discussion.

'Sarah' discussed, as did many others we talked to, the prevalence of a particular journalistic trope for impact case studies and a sense of impact case studies as 'dressed to impress':

> 'I think one of the debates we had was between the kind of bid-writer phenomena, you know, people who got people in to write their impact case studies in a very kind of journalist way, and trying to unpick that to find out what the actual impact was underneath. I think the whole panel were very conscious of that.'

However, it was acknowledged that a 'bid-writer' presence within impact case studies had a twofold effect. First, it was felt that the eloquence and artistry of the interlocutor could have an excessive influence on impact deliberations. Where there was little time afforded to the interrogation of evidence, it was felt that the authority of an impact claim would be buttressed by the cogency of its rhetoric. A failure to engage with the evidence – reflected upon as a miscellany of everything and nothing – included within impact case studies was viewed by 'Sarah' as compromising the rigour of the evaluation process and multiplying the extent to which panellists would have to rely on or be led by the oratorical acuity of the narrator:

> 'There were lots of links to websites and links to … little videos and whatnot. And sometimes it was hard to judge the case study without looking at them. But we were told, "don't look at the corroborating evidence unless there's a problem" because you can't look at it all, so don't look at any of it unless there's a real issue and you can't agree on that case and you need more information. Because unless you look at everybody's and look at everything it's not really a fair process, which I'd agree with. I don't know how that

was presented. People seemed to be expecting you to look up all this stuff and of course you don't have time, all that you can look at is what they've written, and so the idea of having the corroborating evidence, I suppose it's important that it's there if there is a problem, but it's not read unless there … unless I thought there was … well I've written here, "It will only be accessed if there's considerable doubt about the claims made". So, really, we ignored it unless … we were really concerned about the link between the research and the impact.'

The flip side of the concern some assessors expressed with over-rewarding persuasively written but undersubstantiated tales of impact was a concern to ensure those whose power of persuasion in communicating the impact of their research was less pronounced (or, in some cases, sorely lacking) were not overly penalised. This might almost be thought of as mediation to, or means of stabilising, the bias caused by the perceived mellifluousness of some case study authors:

'It's difficult to judge whether something's just badly written or whether actually there's some very important impact being reported. And I think of one or two things that were pretty badly written and still got quite high ratings.'

Necessarily, a tendency – no matter how infrequent – to reward 'less accomplished' case studies ought to be couched in the terms of impact evaluation as a manifestly performative activity, shaped by cultural norms and social variables (cf. Lamont 2009). All REF panellists were necessarily involved in a process of curating and safeguarding their credibility as expert authorities. This was, perhaps, particularly true for academic panellists, whose invitation to be involved was predicated on recognition of their seniority, intellectual capital, connoisseurship and capacity to negotiate 'new modalities of scholarly distinction' (cf. Watermeyer and Chubb 2018). In the new world of impact in the REF, all panellists – whether academic or research user – appeared committed to avoiding anything that might infirm or challenge the definitiveness of their judgements. A need to appear non-partisan, objective and balanced would, in the account of 'Sarah', accordingly result in some poorly constructed case studies receiving high scores from REF panellists. 'Sarah' also, however, spoke candidly of her frustration in reviewing several badly written impact case studies and thus, albeit inadvertently, reinforced a correlation between the technical proficiency of a case study and the quality of the impact it reports:

> 'Some people had just done a shitty job of putting them together. And when you're confronted with a document that is just not very well written, it's quite hard to find evidence in it of things, and certainly I found myself thinking, "How has this got through someone's internal quality control?" when I was looking at some of these documents. So that bit was quite difficult.'

'Sarah' also talked about how her experience of working in both academic and research user contexts afforded her an ability to penetrate and/or isolate – in the evaluation process – the potential allure of the salesperson pitch, which seems to have characterised the more sophisticated and compelling impact narratives. She discussed being particularly sensitive to, and therefore critical of, 'window dressing' (perhaps not always readily discernible) and expressed some concern that gilded statements could camouflage vacuous impact claims. For 'Sarah', a "bullshit antenna" was essential hardware in the identification of REF impact narratives dressed in the "Emperor's new clothes". However, 'Sarah' intimated that this aspect of her forensic toolkit, seemingly so necessary to the process of impact evaluation, might not be available to all evaluators, due to differences in their professional experience/history:

> 'Something that's very well written can appear to be terribly important, and actually it's just rubbish, but … it's been incredibly well presented. And that kind of, excuse my language, but my bullshit antennae are very well developed because of six years in government and all the rest. I think that some people's antennae are not as much.'

The challenges of impact evaluation were further commented upon and reinforced by another user assessor we interviewed, a senior civil servant we'll call 'Jack'. 'Jack' made reference to how a pared down and more humble representation of impact made by some researchers in the REF placed a spotlight on their ideological investment in affecting positive change. In these stripped-back accounts, he felt the moral agency of researchers was far more prominent than in other, more decorated depositions in which the self-interest in impact as a lever for personal/ institutional recognition and gain seemed more apparent. In 'Jack's' account of being a user assessor of impact we see an identification with academics 'committing' to a version of public citizenship unfettered by the trappings and encumbrance of an instrumentalist and neoliberal rationale. In fact, for 'Jack', REF impact case studies showcased how some researchers were more interested and invested in *sharing* their experiences of critical engagement with user constituencies, rather than *selling* stories of impact with all the histrionics of journalism:

> 'I think the truthfulness rather than the gloss … I thought there was a greater commitment to it from some institutions, from some individuals, a greater commitment to, and […] even within the style of what was being written about, there was a more open, a more truthful, a more, thoughtful approach to it, rather than just … you're writing to try and persuade somebody to give you a four star out of this. There was something that actually said, "This is something that mattered to us, mattered to the community, that actually was genuinely having an impact on whatever element it was".'

'Jack' also made reference to the challenge faced by impact evaluators in being not only vigilant to the artifice of many impact case studies but the danger of being too easily won over by forms of supporting evidence (if such evidence was consulted in the context of limited time and capacity). In such a context, 'Jack' spoke of the fallibility of panellists who he felt were potentially wooed or blinded by the starriness of names associated with, or providing corroboration of, researchers' impact claims or the kinds of quantitative mesmerisation that might accompany the contextualisation of *hard* – or be that economic – impacts:

> 'It was a sense of not being impressed by certain types of partner, not being impressed by certain metrics which might be there to do with an income generation or to do with reach and actually thinking quite carefully about the clarity of the case, and the evidence provided, and the big challenge for me was that idea of the transformative as well and trying to understand actually what that meant.'

Conclusions

In this penultimate chapter, we have argued that impact as constituted in the REF is representative of a culture of 'competitive accountability' that is endemic in UK higher education. Building on the concerns outlined in Chapter 3 (many of which have been developed further in subsequent empirical chapters), this chapter began by outlining four additional concerns with the approach to research impact that is embedded within REF. We then explored the views of REF user assessors and the challenges they faced in REF2014 in making sense of case study claims of affecting impact. The testimony of 'Sarah' and 'Jack' reveals a profound sense of concern at the way with which they perceived academics to be embellishing impact case studies, and the difficulties they felt REF impact assessors faced in unpicking compelling rhetoric from evidence. Although the chapter only employed two interviews directly, these were selected to illustrate much broader findings within the data.

Their accounts suggest that 'competitive accountability' fosters a transition in the outlook and ideology of academics and the way academics make sense of themselves and what they do. From their perspective as case study evaluators, we perceive academics 'telling tales' of their public triumphs that may belie and greatly exceed the true nature of their role and contribution in public life. We also see a system of evaluation with organisational and infrastructural failings related to the inadequate handling of evidence (not helped by the limited time and capacity afforded to many non-academic assessors). At the same time, we are able to detect an attempt by academics to articulate (within impact case studies) a more authentic and meaningful version of their public interface and their 'commitment' through their research to achieving 'public' goods. Many, if not most, academics are said to walk a daily tightrope between practising the role of the independent and critically autonomous scholar and yet the scholar whose livelihood depends upon conforming to the standards and expectations of the host institution. We are many of us, the academic tribe, walking what Smith (2012) calls 'flexians'; complicit with, yet confrontational to, the form of our governance.

At first sight, therefore, impact in the REF exposes academics' complicity in telling tales of their various achievements and a profound sense of their self-importance. In so doing it also perhaps draws attention to the fragility of their self-concept when subject to new demands for professional justification, and under the intensified neoliberal spotlight they exaggerate and perhaps compensate for that which they are not. However, impact in the REF may also reflect a false vanity and simulated immodesty. Indeed, a startling finding from ongoing research into the effect of impact case studies on research praxis, reveals that a significant number of academic researchers detailed within REF2014 impact case studies were unaware of their inclusion (Watermeyer, 2019). Thus, impact in the REF indicates perhaps the further estrangement of academics from an authentic and self-derived version of *public* personhood; where the authorship of narratives that articulate what they do is decoupled from their own sense of what they do. All of this must lead us to question the reliability (and value) of REF impact case studies as a barometer of academics' social contract and their ability to meet public/policy expectations regarding impact.

Note

1   A question of portability in terms of research outputs and the economic/societal impacts which these underpin has featured prominently in discussions of *who* and/or *what* is the focus of research assessment – the individual academic or the institution to which s/he is affiliated. In the Stern review of REF2014, the emphasis appears to be upon the institution as a research environment acting as an impact catalyst and therefore an assessment of the infrastructure and conditions that may contribute to and scaffold researchers' impact generation.

10

Conclusion: what would an evidence-informed impact agenda involve?

Summing up our findings

This book has drawn on a wide range of qualitative data to explore how the UK's approach to research impact is playing out. It started by outlining the policy changes that had informed, and culminated in, the current approach to research impact (Chapter 2) and by outlining the various arguments for, and concerns about, the consequences of this approach (Chapters 1 and 3). In Chapter 3, we grouped issues raised in existing literature into ten key concerns. These ranged from the fundamental (is it possible to meaningfully demonstrate, measure and attribute research impact? What are the theoretical foundations of the UK's approach to research impact and how do these accord with relevant scholarly literature? Does the UK's approach to research impact restrict academic freedom/autonomy and/or misleadingly assume research impact to be always positive?) to the more prosaic and pragmatic (do incentives for academics to demonstrate research impact risk activities which will further overload external audiences with information? Is the seemingly arbitrary time limit appropriate or restrictive? What are the costs of assessing research impact and do these represent value for money? Does the current approach reify individual working and traditional elites?). Much of the literature informing this chapter sketched out theoretical concerns or identified issues in how research impact was affecting specific areas of scholarly work. This book builds on these existing contributions by taking an empirically grounded, in-depth exploration of how relevant groups (particularly academics working in the UK but also impact assessors, funders and academics working elsewhere) view the UK experiment with research impact. While our own social science grounding and outlook has inevitably informed the focus of our data and analysis (including, perhaps most notably, a recurrent focus on policy and practice as key 'targets' of research impact efforts), collectively our data map across a wide range of academic disciplines.

Our findings, like the existing literature, paint a complex and varied picture. There is no doubt that contrasting views exist about the UK's approach to research impact, within and beyond the UK, and that these are often strongly held. Many of the impact agenda's most enthusiastic supporters appear to be academics working in the UK who were already undertaking the kind of work that is perceived to be promoted and supported by the UK's approach to impact, many of whom have a background of working closely and collaboratively with external audiences. For these academics, the very fact of formally recognising and rewarding academic contributions to developments beyond academia has been liberating and affirming. The perceptions of most of the academics we spoke to are, however, more varied, even where we might have expected to find strong support for research impact: notably university-based knowledge exchange organisations (explored in Chapter 7) and the very applied discipline of public health (explored in Chapter 8). Indeed, elements of the empirical findings within the book lend support to each of the concerns laid out in Chapter 3 and add to this the following additional six:

1. Confusion about the relationship between public engagement, public intellectualism and efforts to promote, support and reward research impact, with evidence across a range of disciplines that public engagement activities are unlikely to score highly in REF given their greater unpredictability and resource demands (an issue discussed in Chapters 4 and 5 and also identified in the Stern Review). As Chapter 5 notes, the picture is more positive in relation to perceptions of research funders' interest in supporting public engagement and it is clear that the NCCPE is making efforts to shift the assessment approach to public engagement in REF2021, but it remains to be seen how effective this is in institutions that appear to have internalised a perceived preference for impacts on policy, practice and businesses.
2. A sense that work to synthesise and make research useful for external audiences is still not being adequately incentivised, recognised or rewarded (see Chapter 8). Within REF, this stems from a requirement to link case studies of research impact to underpinning research, undertaken by the same team who achieved the impact, combined with a perception that meta-analysis (including systematic reviews) is, on its own, unlikely to count as research within REF. This issue was also raised in the Stern Review but it is less clear that efforts are being made to address this issue (compared to the efforts

to enhance REF panel assessors' perceptions of public engagement) for REF2021.

3. There is a widely held (albeit not universal) perception in our data that academic appointments and promotions are now reflecting academics' ability to demonstrate research impact (particularly if those achievements are deemed likely to function as financially lucrative high-performing REF impact case studies). There are mixed views on whether this is desirable and some concern about the potential tension between impact-oriented work and what appeared to be a widely held consensus that research and teaching excellence should remain core to academic roles.

4. Perhaps somewhat paradoxically (and in contrast to a strategic push by research funders to support and encourage academic–beneficiary collaboration and co-production), we identified a concern (in Chapter 9) that the format of REF impact case studies affirms, perhaps even reinforces, the divide between research/knowledge producers and potential users/beneficiaries. This reflects the requirement of a narrative in which research/knowledge producers are required to demonstrate how they have had a distinct and demonstrable impact on the other. This concern is perhaps sharpened by contrasting the current REF approach with a potential alternative in which activities supporting dialogue, collaboration and knowledge exchange are assessed and rewarded.

5. A concern that non-academic user assessors of REF impact case studies are not being given adequate time for the work involved, leading to a limited capacity to interrogate evidence claims about impact (again, see Chapter 9).

6. A belief, expressed by some interviewees, that the REF approach to research impact is generating distinct types of academics (with a potential hierarchy of status – see Chapters 6 and 8 in particular). This is at least partly because of the distinction between what the REF deems to be excellence in the context of impact case studies (where research rated 2★ is deemed sufficient) and what it deems to be excellence in the context of research outputs (3★ and 4★ research) (as discussed in Chapter 9).

Underlying many of the concerns about the research impact agenda (both those discussed in Chapters 1–3 and the additional concerns, summarised above, that emerged from analysis of our interview data in Chapters 4–9) we can see at least two fundamental tensions. The first relates to varying beliefs about the core purpose of universities and the academics they employ. For some, the core purpose is to provide and occupy an intellectual space that enables and promotes autonomous, creative thinking and experimentation, with opportunities to construct entirely new ways of thinking, to make scientific discoveries and to critically challenging dominant discourses and accepted truths, through education and through research (see, e.g., Hofmeyr, 2008; Said, 1994). For others, the purpose is more overtly and directly related to the external benefits that the work of university-based academics provides (ranging from social and environmental goods to economic benefits). These positions effectively describe two ends of a spectrum and many of the academics we spoke to appeared to fall somewhere in the middle of this spectrum (in relation to their views on research and teaching). It is unsurprising that most academics expressed at least some concern about the consequences of shift so clearly and overtly intended to pull academics towards one end of the spectrum.

The second fundamental tension relates to varying perspectives on the expansion of audit culture into more and more domains of academic life. As one interviewee in Chapter 4 reflected, the knowledge exchange space was, until the emergence of the research impact agenda, distinctive within academia in the UK in being relatively unmonitored and unregulated. Indeed, Watermeyer (2019) compares the enhanced significance and accumulating 'weight' of an impact agenda in UK higher education to the tightening of a 'noose of competitive accountability'. The UK's approach to research impact effectively means that the accountability mechanisms and calculative practices operating in higher education more broadly, in relation to research and teaching (Shore, 2008), have been expanded and extended to regulate the spaces of knowledge exchange. Efforts to introduce technologies of audit to governance regimes are usually intended to increase trust, transparency and accountability in the work and performance of those being audited (see Boswell, 2018). The way in which the UK's approach to the research impact agenda has evolved certainly appears to have been driven by concerns about trust in science/academia, as well as concerns about the returns on investment (as we mapped out in Chapter 2). Yet it is far from clear that the UK's approach to research impact has achieved these ambitions or, indeed, that members of the public share the concerns about academic work that policymakers appear to have assumed (see Collini, 2012).

A generous analysis of the UK's research impact agenda might highlight that the vast majority of academics and universities appear to be submitting to the impact audit regimes that have been introduced.

This is, however, a low threshold for assessing the success of such wide-ranging changes. As multiple existing studies demonstrate, targets and performance measures can hold an irresistible allure, even when core actors doubt their validity (see, for example, Boswell, 2018; and Malito et al, 2018). This leads to ritualistic practices marked by a dualism, in which actors critique core tenets of audit regimes, while engaging in ways that enact and enable the regime's continuation (Boswell, 2018). This dualism is perhaps magnified within academia, which combines a culture of competitive performativity in which systems of classification are routinely constructed and employed, with an awareness of the flaws of audit regimes that is enhanced by the contributions of academics whose expertise centres on critically deconstructing statistics and performance indicators. This dualism was evident within many of our interviews and, again, a spectrum was evident; while most interviewees could identify flaws in the UK's approach to auditing impact, some were markedly more comfortable with the idea that research impact should be subject to performance assessment than others. As our interview data attests, the current spell of the impact agenda over the UK's academic research community is neither total nor impregnable.

In sum, the impact agenda's many detractors include people who object to research having to demonstrate a 'real-world' value, and those who are fiercely committed to that real-world value but feel it is cheapened through incorporation into an audit regime. The UK's current approach to auditing academia via the REF represents an uneasy compromise. The very idea of assessing the real-world contributions of academic work via impact case studies is premised on the notion that our discoveries and ideas can almost unilaterally change the world. Yet, the case studies are evidenced via narratives which, theoretically at least, provide space to acknowledge the complexities in this process. In the highly competitive practice of classifying and ranking impact case studies for financial return, there is, however, an inevitable pressure to tell rather simpler, more heroic tales of individual impacts.

What might an alternative, evidence-informed approach to research impact involve?

As the above summary makes clear, this book has assessed the current approach to research impact in the UK through a critical lens. Despite this, all of us are, like numerous other academics, deeply committed to making positive changes in the world. None of us aspire to an 'ivory tower' model of academia, with its connotations of elitism, distinction and separation. We recognise that some forms of external engagement, including activities we might consider to be 'public intellectualism' or 'advocacy', may cohere with, and benefit from, 'impact agendas' (see Chapters 5 and 7). To varying degrees, we also accept what seems, to us, to be a medium-term inevitability – that institutions of higher education will be subjected to audit regimes. However, we also agree that efforts to engage with external audiences can diverge from, and may potentially be limited by, the kind of impact agenda that is prevailing in the UK and Australia (e.g. where engagement involves critiquing government or commercial interests or where the intention is to facilitate dialogue, rather than impact). In this section, therefore, we attempt to sketch out ways of supporting academic contributions to the wider world that we feel are more informed by evidence, more productive and less likely to be restrictive than the path the UK and, to some degree, Australia have currently chosen.

Since we each bring with us our own experiences, preferences and convictions, it was not easy for us to identify a shared way forward. Nonetheless, the following, alternative approach to supporting academic contributions to the wider world was a collective effort. Our aim was to identify approaches that we felt would better reflect what is known (through existing empirical and theoretical work) about: (i) the complex relationship between academic endeavours and real-world change; and (ii) the consequences of audit regimes and performance measures:

1. *Reward impactful environments, rather than individual achievements.*
   Although guidance for REF2021 includes some focus on collaboration within the required environment statements (HEFCE et al, 2017), individualised case studies easily become detached from the environments in which they are produced. Fundamentally, the requirement of impact case studies to demonstrate and document change inevitably narrows the scope of impact activities and – consequently – outcomes. We should, instead, strengthen a focus on how universities create impactful environments; workplaces that are outward-looking, open and engaged with the world beyond academia. At a very basic level, this would involve workload allocations for outward-facing work, signalling an appreciation of the time required for, and value attributed to, this kind of work in and of itself. Such an approach might also encourage more innovation. For example, universities might invest in greater dialogue with external actors (including members of the public) about where we devote our efforts (thereby avoiding a situation in which we are responding to untested assumptions about public

preferences). Or universities might develop systems of recognition which acknowledge not only academic grant income, publication metrics and fortuitous examples of demonstrable impact but also academic efforts to engage with and to do good in the world. This would avoid the temptation for universities to invest in the requisite number of impact case studies without investing in an environment that makes externally facing work possible for everyone who wants to do it.

2. *Value a wider range of activities.* The NCPPE is leading the way in both supporting academics to do public engagement better and encouraging the research audit process to value it fairly. There is more work to do and, we suggest, it may be desirable to go further, recognising the impacts of the university's wider role as an 'anchor institution' (Birch et al, 2013) in its locality. In other words, universities would be recognised for their work in areas such as widening participation, lifelong learning and employee volunteering, as well as in more impact-oriented work. We could focus on being good employers in the community, and in creating open public spaces (against a backdrop of cities where private realms are in the ascendancy). We could celebrate our work in equipping young activists to change their worlds, or in supporting some of our most vulnerable students to benefit from a university education (e.g. University of the West of England, 2017). If the management mantra of 'research-led teaching' is taken to its natural conclusion, we should better reward the interconnections between these different strands of activity.

3. *Protect spaces and funding for critical and discovery-focused academic scholarship (without obvious impacts).* There are multiple examples of academic scholarship that is valuable for reasons other than impact. This includes critical, theoretical and experimental work (some of which, as several interviewees pointed out, contributed to major impacts at later dates but which would not have been supported if resources had been dependent on being able to articulate the likely impacts in advance). Even where projects had the intention of contributing to research impact, impact may not necessarily follow. Moreover, there can be multiple reasons why research does not always lead to the kinds of answers academics were anticipating when they first embarked on the project (since there is always some guesswork involved at the research design/grant application stage). All of this leads us to suggest that efforts to promote impact ought to be receptive to the 'strategic role of ignorance' (McGoey, 2012), which suggests that contributions to the development of meaningful

questions can be as necessary as contributions to research-informed answers. At the time of going to press, it seems unclear whether the UKRI's decision to drop the 'pathways to impact' and 'impact summary' sections of grant applications (UKRI, 2020) will enable flexibility here, though the suggestion that impact should now be considered throughout the application process suggests not.

4. *Reject crude and simplistic classifications of 'excellence' (which, e.g., denigrate the local).* The quality of research in REF is ranked crudely as being locally, nationally and internationally relevant, with deleterious effects. Here, we are put in mind of Massey's (2013) critique of 'disembodied, free-floating, generalizing science' and defence of the local as 'deprioritized and denigrated'. The most recent guidance notes that there is value in 'having a big impact on a small group of people', but our interview data reinforces our sense that the glory, the status of the 'impact superstar' (Back, 2015), will rarely be earned through transformative projects that are local. If we want universities to be active members of their local communities, this could, and should, be changed. This, of course, does not mean that we want to reverse the current classification system, to the denigration of international and global impacts. Impact is not just of one kind, and what precisely academics are seeking to achieve when they engage externally clearly varies, inevitably reflecting the focus of the work involved, academic networks and shifting windows of opportunity. Our argument here is that it should not be the proximity of external communities that is key to assessing excellence, but relatability to potential research users such as communities of policy and practice. Hence, we suggest that simple classification systems for what counts as 'excellence' in REF should be avoided in favour of thorough peer review and deliberation.

5. *Weaken the link between original research and impact to encourage knowledge synthesis and collaboration.* Both REF impact case studies and the articulation of impact ambitions within grant applications assume a clear causal chain between original research/scholarship and impacts. This was perceived to be wholly unrealistic by many of the interviewees (a perception strongly supported by the existing literature). Multiple activities that are valuable for achieving research impact are not recognised or valued by the current REF audit regime since they focus on pooling and synthesising knowledge that goes beyond a single individual's (or team's) research. We suggest, instead, that research funders and REF assessors are encouraged to value academic scholarship that focuses on knowledge synthesis and to

reject the notion of research as an activity conducted by individual superstars.

6. *Develop a conversation about the ethics of impact.* The approach to research impact being taken in the UK and elsewhere appears to assume that if research is 'excellent' then the impacts will inevitably be positive. There is, of course, no logical reason to assume that this would be the case. There are plenty of examples in which excellent research has had deleterious societal impacts (as Chapter 3 discusses). This is hard to predict, and there will of course be subjective variations in what is deemed to be a positive impact and what is deemed to be a negative impact (just as there are variations in what is deemed to be good research practice). In this context, it would be overly simplistic to try to categorise impacts as more or less positive. We should, however, be creating conversations and tools that allow us to meaningfully consider the ethics of research impact.

7. *Defend and promote academic rigour and autonomy.* There are plenty of non-academic research contexts in which professionals produce research outputs quickly and responsively (e.g. within governments, charities, private companies, think tanks, etc.). Some elements of the UK's current approach to research impact appear to be encouraging academics to move substantially towards these ways of working and this, we feel, has the potential to undervalue the 'unique selling point' of academic research and scholarship and to diminish the distinction between consultants and academics. What exactly is unique about academic research/scholarship will vary by discipline and field but, for the social sciences, we suggest this involves a rigorous approach to methodology, transparency (as a meta-standard which demarcates academic knowledge from other knowledge – see Buthe et al, 2015), a serious engagement with theoretical precepts and a willingness to engage in peer review.

8. *Create spaces in which valiant failures are celebrated and learned from.* While research funding guidance recognises that impact can be difficult to predict, the current form of assessment, and the high financial value of impact case studies, combine to prompt institutions to focus on tried-and-tested approaches to impact. This seems to be the opposite of what we might hope investments in knowledge exchange and research impact would achieve. Hence, we suggest that funders and universities should do more to promote innovation in engagement and knowledge exchange and to encourage contributions that are about learning from challenges and failures (as well as successes).

The above suggestions are not exhaustive but they are intended to be a starting point for discussing how we might move beyond the limitations of the current approach to research impact. Mindful of the 'looseness' that characterises impact as a new form of 'scholarly distinction' (Watermeyer and Chubb 2018), we suggest the academic community would do well to go beyond the REF (Watermeyer 2018) to find inspiration and momentum for a more meaningful and profitable science and society nexus. Ironically, impact in the REF may be keeping academics contained within the ivory tower and their communities well outside of it. Yet, the impact agenda, in research funding applications and in the REF, is not entirely beyond our control; we, as academics, are involved in constructing, enacting and reviewing impact's performance indicators and we therefore have an opportunity to reshape the current approach. The unexpected announcement by the UKRI, in January 2020, that grant applications would no longer include specific sections in which applicants have to outline impact plans underlines the fluid and malleable nature of the research impact agenda; this is, at least potentially, a 'window of opportunity' for those seeking to re-shape this agenda.

References

Aggett, S., Dunn, A. and Vincent, R. (2012). *Engaging with Impact: How Do We Know if We Have Made a Difference?* London: Wellcome Trust. URL: https://wellcome.ac.uk/sites/default/files/wtp052364_0.pdf (accessed 29 April 2019).

AHRC (2009a). *AHRC Economic Impact Reporting Framework.* URL: https://ahrc.ukri.org/documents/project-reports-and-reviews/ahrc-economic-impact-reporting-framework/2009/.

AHRC (2009b). *Leading the World: The Economic Impact of UK Arts and Humanities Research*, Bristol: AHRC. URL: https://ahrc.ukri.org/documents/publications/leading-the-world/.

AHRC (2014). *What We Do – Strengthen Research Impact.* http://www.ahrc.ac.uk/What-We-Do/Strengthen-research-impact/Pages/Strengthen-Research-Impact.aspx (accessed 10 January 2014).

AHRC (2019). *Delivery Plan 2019.* URL: https://ahrc.ukri.org/documents/strategy/ahrc-delivery-plan-2019/.

Back, L. (2015). On the side of the powerful: the 'impact agenda' and sociology in public. *The Sociological Review*, 23 September. URL: https://www.thesociologicalreview.com/blog/on-the-side-of-the-powerful-the-impact-agenda-sociology-in-public.html.

Back, L. (2016). *Academic Diary.* London: Goldsmiths University Press.

Ball, S.J. and Exley, S. (2010). Making policy with 'good ideas': policy networks and the 'intellectuals' of New Labour. *Journal of Education Policy*, 25(2), 151–69.

Bambra, C. (2013). The primacy of politics: the rise and fall of evidence-based public health policy? *Journal of Public Health*, 35, 486–7.

Bandola-Gill, J. (2019). Between relevance and excellence? Research impact agenda and the production of policy knowledge. *Science and Public Policy*, scz037.

Bandola-Gill, J. and Lyall, C. (2017). Knowledge brokers and policy advice in policy formulation. In M. Howlett and I. Mukherjee (eds), *Handbook of Policy Formulation*. Cheltenham: Edward Elgar.

Barnes, C. (1996). Disability and the myth of the independent researcher. *Disability & Society*, 11, 107–12.

Barnes, C. (2015). The use of altmetrics as a tool for measuring research impact. *Australian Academic & Research Libraries*, 46:2: 121–34.

BBSRC (2019). *Delivery Plan 2019.* URL: https://www.ukri.org/files/about/dps/bbsrc-dp-2019/.

Becher, T. (1989). *Academic Tribes and Territories: Intellectual Enquiry and the Cultures of Disciplines.* Buckingham: SRHE and Open University Press.

Becher, T. and Trowler, P. (2001). *Academic Tribes and Territories.* 2nd edn. Buckingham: SRHE and Open University Press.

Becker, H.S. (1967). Whose side are we on? *Social Problems*, 14(3), 239–47.

Becker, H.S. (1973). *Outsiders: Studies in the Sociology of Deviance*, 2nd edn. New York: Free Press.

Becker, H.S. (1986). *Doing Things Together: Selected Papers.* Evanston, IL: Northwestern University Press.

Becker, H.S. and Horowitz, I.L. (1972). Radical politics and sociological research: observations on methodology and ideology. *American Journal of Sociology*, 78(1), 48–66.

Bekker, M., van Egmond, S., Wehrens, R., Putters, K. and Bal, R. (2010). Linking research and policy in dutch healthcare: infrastructure, innovations and impacts. *Evidence & Policy*, 6(2), 237–53.

Belfiore, E. (2015). 'Impact', 'value' and 'bad economics': making sense of the problem of value in the arts and humanities. *Arts and Humanities in Higher Education*, 14(1), 95–110.

Berman, E.P. and Hirschman, D. (2018). The Sociology of Quantification: Where Are We Now? *Contemporary Sociology*, 47(3), 257–66.

Bero, L.A. (2005). Tobacco industry manipulation of research. *Public Health Reports*, 120, 200–8.

Bevan, G. and Hood, C. (2006). What's measured is what matters: targets and gaming in the English public health care system. *Public Administration*, 84(3), 517–38.

Bielak, A., Campbell, A., Pope, S., Schaefer, K. and Shaxson, L. (2008). From science communication to knowledge brokering: the shift from 'science push' to 'policy pull'. In D. Cheng, M. Claessens, N.R.J. Gasciogne, J. Metcalfe, B. Schiele and S. Shi (eds), *Communicating Science in Social Contexts: New Models, New Practices.* Dordrecht: Springer.

Birch, E., Perry, D.C. and Taylor, H.L. (2013). Universities as anchor institutions. *Journal of Higher Education Outreach and Engagement*, 17(3), 7.

Biri, D., Oliver, K.A. and Cooper, A. (2014). What is the impact of BEAMS research? An evaluation of REF impact case studies from UCL BEAMS. *STEaPP Working Paper.* London: Department of Science, Technology, Engineering, and Public Policy, University College London.

Black, N. (2001). Evidence based policy: proceed with care. *BMJ*, 323(7307), 275–80.

Blume, S. (1977). Policy as theory: a framework for understanding the contribution of social science to welfare policy. *Acia Sociologica*, 20, 47–62.

Blunkett, D. (2000). Influence or irrelevance: can social research improve government? *Research Intelligence, BERA*, 71.

Boaz, A. and Davies, H. (eds) (2019). *What works now? Evidence-informed policy and practice*. Bristol: Policy Press.

Bornmann, L. (2012). Measuring the societal impact of research. *Science & Society*, 13(8), 673–6.

Boswell, C. (2009). *The Political Uses of Expert Knowledge: Immigration Policy and Social Research*. Cambridge: Cambridge University Press.

Boswell, C. (2018). *Manufacturing Political Trust: Targets and Performance Measurement in Public Policy*. Cambridge: Cambridge University Press.

Boswell, C. and Smith, K.E. (2017). Rethinking policy 'impact': four models of research-policy relations. *Palgrave Communications*, 3(1), 44.

Boswell, C., Yearley, S., Fleming, C. and Spinardi, G. (2015). The effects of targets and indicators on policy formulation: narrowing down, crowding out and locking in. In A.J. Jordan and J.R. Turnpenny (eds), *The Tools of Policy Formulation : Actors, Capacities, Venues and Effects*. Cheltenham: Edward Elgar.

Braben, D. et al (2009). Modest revolt to save research from red tape (letter with 19 signatories). *Times Higher Education*, 12 February. URL: https://www.timeshighereducation.com/comment/letters/modest-revolt-to-save-research-from-red-tape/405335.article (accessed 6 January 2019).

Brereton, F., O'Neill, E. and Dunne, L. (2017). Towards measuring societal impact of research: insights from an Irish case study. *Irish Journal of Sociology*, 25(2) 150–73.

Brooks, H. (1964). The scientific adviser. *Scientists and National Policy-Making*, 76.

Bulaitis, Z. (2017). Measuring impact in the humanities: learning from accountability and economics in a contemporary history of cultural value. *Palgrave Communications*, 3(1), 7.

Bulmer, M. (ed.) (1987). *Social Science Research and Government: Comparative Essays on Britain and the Unites States*. Cambridge: Cambridge University Press.

Burawoy, M. (2005). 2004 American Sociological Association presidential address: for public sociology. *British Journal of Sociology*, 56(2), 259–94.

Burawoy, M. (2011). Redefining the public university: global and national contexts. In J. Holmwood (ed.), *A Manifesto for the Public University*. London: Bloomsbury Press.

Buthe, T., Jacobs, A.M., Bleich, E., Pekkanen, R., Trachtenberg, M., Cramer, K. and Fairfield, T. (2015). Transparency in qualitative and multi-method research: a symposium. *Qualitative and Multi-Method Research*, 13(1). URL: https://papers.ssrn.com/abstract=2652097.

Buxton, M. and Hanney, S. (1996). How can payback from health services research be assessed? *Journal of Health Services Research and Policy*, 1(1): 35–43.

Cabinet Office (1993). *Realising Our Potential: A Strategy for Science, Engineering and Technology*. London: Cabinet Office.

Cabinet Office (1999). *Modernising Government (White Paper)*. London: The Stationery Office.

Cabinet Office (2000). *Wiring it Up: Whitehall's Management of Cross-Cutting Policies and Services: A Performance and Innovation Unit Report*. London: Cabinet Office.

Cairney, P. and Oliver, K. (2018). How should academics engage in policymaking to achieve impact?. *Political Studies Review*. https://doi.org/10.1177/1478929918807714.

Calhoun, C. (2000). Social theory and the public sphere. In B.S. Turner (ed.), *The Blackwell Companion to Social Theory*. Oxford: Blackwell.

Caplan, N. (1979). The two-communities theory and knowledge utilization. *American Behavioral Scientist*, 22, 459–70.

Carlisle, S. (2000). Health promotion, advocacy and health inequalities: a conceptual framework. *Health Promotion International*, 15(4): 369–76.

Casanova, J. (1994). Public religions in the modern world. Chicago: University of Chicago Press.

Caswill, C. and Lyall, C. (2013). Knowledge brokers, entrepreneurs and markets. *Evidence & Policy: A Journal of Research, Debate and Practice*, 9(3), 353–69.

Chapman, S. (2007). *Public Health Advocacy and Tobacco Control: Making Smoking History*. Oxford: Blackwell.

Choi, B.C.K. (2005). Can scientists and policy makers work together? *Journal of Epidemiology & Community Health*, 59(8), 632–7.

Chowdhury, G., Koya, K. and Philipson, P. (2016). Measuring the impact of research: lessons from the UK's Research Excellence Framework 2014. *PLOS ONE*, 11(6), e0156978.

Chubb, J. (2017). *Instrumentalism and Epistemic Responsibility: Researchers and the Impact Agenda in the UK and Australia*. PhD thesis, University of York.

Chubb, J. and Watermeyer, R. (2017). Artifice or integrity in the marketization of research? Investigating the moral economy of impact statements within research funding proposals in the UK and Australia. *Studies in Higher Education*, 42(12), 2360–72.

Clarke, S. (2010). Pure science with a practical aim: the meanings of fundamental research in Britain, circa 1916–1950. *Isis*, 101(2), 285–311.

Collini, S. (2009). Commentary: impact on humanities. *The Times Literary Supplement*, 13 November, 18–19.

Collini, S. (2012). *What Are Universities For?* London: Penguin.

Collinson, J.A. (2004). Occupational identity on the edge: social science contract researchers in higher education. *Sociology*, 38(2), 313–329.

Commonwealth of Australia (2005). Research quality framework: assessing the quality and impact of research in Australia—final advice on the preferred RQF model, Canberra: Commonwealth of Australia.

Contandriopoulos, D., Lemire, M., Denis, J.-L. and Tremblay, É. (2010). Knowledge exchange processes in organizations and policy arenas: a narrative systematic review of the literature. *Milbank Quarterly*, 88, 444–83.

Cozzens, S.E. and Woodhouse, E.J. (1995). Science, government and the politics of knowledge. In S. Jasanoff, G.E. Markle, J.C. Petersen and T. Pinch (eds), *Handbook of Science and Technology Studies*. London: SAGE.

D'Este, P.D., Ramos-vielba, I., Woolley, R., Amara, N. and Vale, D. (2018). How do researchers generate scientific and societal impacts ? Toward an analytical and operational framework. *Science and Public Policy*, 45(6), 752–63.

Darby, S. (2017). Making space for co-produced research 'impact': learning from a participatory action research case study. Area, 49: 230–7.

Davey Smith, G., Ebrahim, S. and Frankel, S. (2001). How policy informs the evidence. *BMJ*, 322, 184–5.

Davies, H., Nutley, S. and Walter, I. (2005). Assessing the impact of social science research: conceptual, methodological and practical issues, a background discussion paper for ESRC Symposium on Assessing Non-Academic Impact of Research May 2005. URL: https://www.odi.org/sites/odi.org.uk/files/odi-assets/events-documents/4381.pdf (accessed 29 April 2019).

De Rijcke, S., Wouters, P.F., Rushforth, A.D., Franssen, T.P. and Hammarfelt, B. (2016). Evaluation practices and effects of indicator use: a literature review. *Research Evaluation*, 25(2), 161–9.

De Silva, P.U.K. and Vance, C.K. (2017). Assessing the societal impact of scientific research. In P.U.K. De Silva and C.K. Vance, *Scientific Scholarly Communication: The Changing Landscape*. Cham: Springer.

Derrick, G. (2018). The evaluator's eye: impact assessment and academic peer review. Basingstoke: Palgrave Macmillan.

Derrick, G. and Benneworth, P. (2019). Grimpact: time to acknowledge the dark side of the impact agenda, *LSE Impact Blog*. URL: https://blogs.lse.ac.uk/impactofsocialsciences/2019/05/28/grimpact-time-to-acknowledge-the-dark-side-of-the-impact-agenda/.

Dobbins, M., Hanna, S.E., Ciliska, D., Manske, S., Cameron, R., Mercer, S.L. and Robeson, P. (2009). A randomized controlled trial evaluating the impact of knowledge translation and exchange strategies. *Implementation Science*, 4(1), 61.

Donovan, C. (2011). State of the art in assessing research impact: introduction to a special issue. *Research Evaluation*, 20(3), 175–9.

Donovan, C. (2019) For ethical 'impactology'. *Journal of Responsible Innovation*, 6(1), 78–83.

Duncan, S. and Manners, P. (2017). *Engaging Publics with Research: Reviewing the REF 2014 Impact Case Studies and Templates*. Bristol: National Co-ordinating Centre for Public Engagement.

Dunleavy, P. (2011). Current thinking in assessing impact. Address given to the Investigating Academic Impact Conference, 13 June 13, London School of Economics.

Dunlop, C. (2018). The political economy of politics and international studies impact: REF2014 case analysis. *British Politics*, 13, 270.

Durose, C., Needham, C., Mangan, C. and Rees, J. (2017). Generating 'good enough' evidence for co-production. *Evidence and Policy*, 13(1), 135–51.

Eagleton, T. (1996). *The Illusions of Postmodernism*. Oxford: Blackwell Publishers.

Eakin, J. (2016). Educating critical qualitative health researchers in the land of the randomized controlled trial. *Qualitative Inquiry*, 22(2), 107–18.

Ellen, M.E., Léon, G., Bouchard, G., Lavis, J.N., Ouimet, M. and Grimshaw, J.M. (2013). What supports do health system organizations have in place to facilitate evidence-informed decision-making? A qualitative study. *Implementation Science*, 8(1), 84.

EPSRC (2019). *Delivery Plan 2019*. URL: https://epsrc.ukri.org/newsevents/pubs/deliveryplan2019/.

ERiC (2010). Evaluating the societal relevance of academic research: A guide. URL: https://pure.knaw.nl/portal/files/472346/ERiC_guide.pdf (accessed 29 April 2019).

ESRC (1994). *Building Partnerships: Enhancing the Quality of Management Research*. Swindon: Economic and Social Research Council.

ESRC (2005). *ESRC 2005 Delivery Plan*.

ESRC (2006). *ESRC 2006 Delivery Plan*.

ESRC (2009). *Taking Stock. A Summary of ESRC's Work to Evaluate the Impact of Research on Policy and Practice*. Swindon: Economic and Social Research Council.

ESRC (2014a). *How to Maximize Research Impact*. URL: http://www.esrc.ac.uk/funding-and-guidance/toolsand-resources/how-to-maximise-impact/ (Accessed 10 January 2014).

ESRC (2014b). *Impact Toolkit*. URL: http://www.esrc.ac.uk/funding-and-guidance/tools-andresources/impact-toolkit/ (accessed 10 January 2014).

ESRC (2014c). *What is Research Impact?* URL: http://www.esrc.ac.uk/research/evaluation-and-impact/what-is-research-impact/ (accessed 10 January 2014).

ESRC (2015). *Strategic Plan 2015*. Swindon: ESRC. URL: https://esrc.ukri.org/files/news-events-and-publications/publications/corporate-publications/strategic-plan/esrc-strategic-plan-2015/ (accessed 27 December 2019).

ESRC (2016). *Impact Prize Winners 2016*. URL: https://esrc.ukri.org/research/celebrating-impact-prize/previous-years-winners/impact-prize-winners-2016/ (accessed 27 December 2019).

ESRC (2019). *Delivery Plan 2019*. URL: https://www.ukri.org/files/about/dps/esrc-dp-2019/.

ESRC (undated). *Why Public Engagement is Important*. URL: https://esrc.ukri.org/public-engagement/public-engagement-guidance/why-public-engagement-is-important/ (accessed 30 April 2019).

European Commission (2017). *Reflection Paper on the Future of EU Finances*. Brussels: European Commission. URL: https://ec.europa.eu/commission/sites/beta-political/files/reflection-paper-eu-finances_en.pdf (accessed 29 April 2019).

European IPR Helpdesk (2018). *Making the Most of Your H2020 Project: Boosting the Impact of Your Project through Effective Communication, Dissemination and Exploitation*. European IPR Helpdesk. URL: https://cms.eurice.eu/storage/uploads/news/files/European_IPR_Helpdesk_Brochure_Boosting_Impact.pdf (accessed 29 April 2019).

Evans, Mary (2004). *Killing Thinking: The Death of the Universities*. London: Continuum.

Eynon, R. (2012). The challenges and possibilities of the impact agenda. *Learning, Media and Technology*, 37(March 2015), 1–3.

Felt, U. and Fochler, M. (2010). Machineries for making publics: inscribing and de-scribing publics in public engagement. *Minerva*, 48(3), 219–38.

Fielding, M. (2003). The impact of impact. *Cambridge Journal of Education*, 33(2), 289–95.

Fischer, F. and Miller, G.J. (2007). *Handbook of Public Policy Analysis: Theory, Politics, and Methods*. Boca Raton, FL: Taylor & Francis.

Fleming, J. and Rhodes, R. (2018). Can experience be evidence? Craft knowledge and evidence-based policing. *Policy and Politics*, 46(1), 3–26.

Flinders, M. (2010). Splintered logic and political debate. In G. Hodge, C. Greve and A. Boardman (eds), *Edward Elgar International Handbook on Public–Private Partnerships*. Cheltenham: Edward Elgar.

Foucault, M. (1977). *Language, Counter-Memory, Practise*. Ithaca, NY: Cornell University Press.

Fraser, N. (1995). *Feminist Contentions: A Philosophical Exchange*. New York: Routledge.

Freeman, R. (2007). Epistemological bricolage: how practitioners make sense of learning. *Administration & Society*, 39(4), 476–96.

Freudenberg, N., Picard Bradley, S. and Serrano, M. (2009). Public health campaigns to change industry practices that damage health: an analysis of 12 case studies. *Health Education & Behavior*, 36(2), 230–49.

Fuller, S. (2005). *The Intellectual*. Cambridge: Icon Books.

Funtowicz, S.O. and Ravetz, J.R. (1993). Science for the post-normal age. *Futures*, 25(7), 739–55.

Furedi, F. (2004). *Where Have All the Intellectuals Gone? Confronting 21st Century Philistinism*. London: Continuum.

Gibbons, M., Limoges, C., Nowotny, H., Schwartzman, S., Scott, P. and Trow, M. (1994). *The New Production of Knowledge: The Dynamics of Science and Research in Contemporary Societies*. London: SAGE.

Gieryn, T.F. (1983). Boundary-work and the demarcation of science from non-science: strains and interests in professional ideologies of scientists. *American Sociological Review*, 48(6), 781–95.

Giroux, H. and Myrsiades, K. (eds) (2001). *Beyond the Corporate University: Culture and Pedagogy in the New Millennium*. Lanham: Rowman & Littlefield.

Glasby, J. (2011). *Evidence, Policy and Practice Critical Perspectives in Health and Social Care (Why Evidence Doesn't Influence Policy, Why it Should and How it Might)*. Bristol: Policy Press.

Goffman, E. (1961). Role distance. In D. Brissett and C. Edgley (eds) *Life as Theater: A Dramaturgical Sourcebook*. Abingdon: Routledge, 101–11.

Grant, J., Brutscher, P.-B., Kirk, S.E., Butler, L. and Wooding, S. (2010). Capturing research impacts – a review of international practice. Prepared for the Higher Education Funding Council for England. RAND Corporation (RAND Europe).

Greenhalgh, T. and Fahy, N. (2015). Research impact in the community-based health sciences: an analysis of 162 case studies from the 2014 UK Research Excellence Framework. *BMC Medicine*, 13(1), 232.

Greenhalgh, T., Raftery, J., Hanney, S. and Glover, M. (2016). Research impact: a narrative review. *BMC Med*, 14, 78.

Greenhalgh, T., Glenn, R., Macfarlane, F., Bate, P. and Kyriakidou, O. (2004) Diffusion of innovations in service organizations: systematic review and recommendations. *Milbank Quarterly* 82(4), 581–629.

Greenhalgh, T., Fahy, N., Walshe, K., Davies, H., Glasziou, P., Altman, D. and Cattan, M. (2015). Research impact in the community-based health sciences: an analysis of 162 case studies from the 2014 UK Research Excellence Framework. *BMC Medicine*, 13(1), 232.

Grundmann, R. (2017). The problem of expertise in knowledge societies. *Minerva*, 55(1), 25–48.

Gunn, A. and Mintrom, M. (2017). Evaluating the non-academic impact of academic research: design considerations. *Journal of Higher Education Policy and Management*, 39(1), 20–30.

Guston, D.H. (2000). *Between Politics and Science: Assuring the Integrity and Productivity of Research*. Cambridge: Cambridge University Press.

Habermas, J. (1974). *The Structural Transformation of the Public Sphere*. Cambridge: Polity.

Halford, S. and Savage, M. (2017). Speaking sociologically with big data: symphonic social science and the future for big data research. *Sociology*, 1–18. DOI: 10.1177/0038038517698639.

Hallsworth, M. and Rutter, J. (2011). *Making Policy Better: Improving Whitehall's Business*. London: Institute for Government. URL: https://www.instituteforgovernment.org.uk/sites/default/files/publications/Making%20Policy%20Better.pdf.

Halpern, D. (2003). Evidence-based policy: 'build on' or 'spray on'. Does evidence matter? Overseas Development Institute. URL: http://www.odi.org.uk/sites/odi.org.uk/files/odi-assets/events-documents/2604.pdf.

Hammersley, M. (2005). Is the evidence-based practice movement doing more good than harm? Reflections on Iain Chalmers' case for research-based policy making and practice. *Evidence & Policy: A Journal of Research, Debate and Practice*, 1, 85–100.

Hammersley, M. (2014). The perils of 'impact' for academic social science. *Contemporary Social Science*, 9(3), 345–55.

Harris, S. (2005). Rethinking academic identities in neo-liberal times. *Teaching in Higher Education*, 10(4): 421–33.

Hastings, G. (2007). The diaspora has already begun. *Marketing Intelligence & Planning*, 25(2), 117–22.

Haustein, S. (2016). Grand challenges in altmetrics: heterogeneity, data quality and dependencies. *Scientometrics*, 108(1): 413–23.

Haux, T. (2018). What is impact? Learning from examples across the professional life course. In C. Needham, E. Heins and J. Rees (eds) *Social Policy Review 30: Analysis and Debate in Social Policy 2018*. Bristol: Policy Press.

Haux, T. (2019). *Dimensions of Impact in the Social Sciences: The Case of Social Policy, Sociology and Political Science Research*. Bristol: Policy Press.

Haynes, A. S., Derrick, G. E., Chapman, S., Redman, S., Hall, W.D., Gillespie, J. and Sturk, H. (2011). From 'our world' to the 'real world': exploring the views and behaviour of policy-influential Australian public health researchers. *Social Science & Medicine*, 72(7), 1047–55.

Heclo, H. (1974). *Modern Social Politics in Britain and Sweden*. New Haven: Yale University Press.

HEFCE (2009). *Research Excellence Framework: Second Consultation on the Assessment and Funding of Research*. Stoke Gifford: HEFCE.

HEFCE (2016a). *Higher Education in England. Key Facts. 2016*. Stoke Gifford: HEFCE.

HEFCE (2016b). *Publication patterns in research underpinning impact in REF2014. A report to HEFCE by Digital Science*. Stoke Gifford: HEFCE.

HEFCE, Scottish Funding Council, Higher Education Funding Council for Wales, and NI Department for the Economy (2017). *Initial decisions on the Research Excellence Framework 2021*. Bristol: Research Excellence Framework. URL: http://www.ref.ac.uk/media/ref,2021/downloads/REF2017_01.pdf.

Henderson, M. (2012). *The Geek Manifesto: Why Science Matters*. London: Corgi.

Hering, J.G. (2016). Do we need 'more research' or better implementation through knowledge brokering? *Sustainability Science*, 11(2), 363–9.

HM Treasury (2004). *Science and Innovation Investment Framework 2004–2014*. London: The Stationery Office.

Hodgkinson, P. (2000). Who wants to be a social engineer? A commentary on David Blunkett's speech to the ESRC. *Sociological Research Online*, 5.

Hofmeyr, A.B. (2008). Beyond the ivory tower: the public role of the intellectual today. *Phronimon*, 9(2), 73–91.

Hofstader, R. (1973). *Anti-Intellectualism in American Life*. London: Vintage.

Holbrook, J.B. and Frodeman, R. (2011). Peer review and the *ex ante* assessment of societal impacts. *Research Evaluation*, 20(3), 239–46.

Holmes, B.J., Best, A., Davies, H., Hunter, D., Kelly, M.P., Marshall, M. and Rycroft-Malone, J. (2017). Mobilising knowledge in complex health systems: a call to action. *Evidence and Policy*, 13(3), 539–60.

Holmwood, J. (2011a). The idea of a public university. In J. Holmwood (ed.), *A Manifesto for the Public University*. London: Bloomsbury Press.

Holmwood, J. (2011b). The impact of 'impact' on UK social science. *Methodological Innovation Online*, 6(1), 13–17.

Howells, J. (2006). Intermediation and the role of intermediaries in innovation. *Research Policy*, 35(5), 715–28.

Hughes, A. and Martin, B. (2012). *Enhancing Impact: The Value of Public Sector R&D*. UKIRC, CIHE and the Centre for Business Research at the University of Cambridge: Cambridge. URL: https://www.cbr.cam.ac.uk/fileadmin/user_upload/centre-for-business-research/downloads/special-reports/specialreport-enhancingimpact.pdf.

Hunter, D.J. (2009). Relationship between evidence and policy: a case of evidence-based policy or policy-based evidence? *Public Health*, 123(9), 583–6.

Husband, C. (2016). *Research and Policy in Ethnic Relations*. Bristol: Policy Press.

Hutchens, G. (2018). Universities baffled by coalition's 'national interest' test for public funding. *The Guardian*, 31 October. URL: https://www.theguardian.com/australia-news/2018/oct/31/academics-will-have-to-pass-national-interest-test-for-public-funding-coalition-says (accessed 29 April 2019).

Immergut, E.M. (1998). The theoretical core of the new institutionalism. *Politics and Society*, 26(1), 5–34.

Innvaer, S., Vist, G., Trommald, M. and Oxman, A. (2002). Health policymakers' perceptions of their use of evidence: a systematic review. *The Journal of Health Services Research & Policy*, 7(4), 239–44.

Irwin, A. (2006). The politics of talk: coming to terms with the 'new' scientific governance. *Social Studies of Science*, 36(2), 299–320.

Jacoby, R. (2000). *The Last Intellectuals*. London: Basic Books.

James, O. (2004). The UK core executive's use of public service agreements as a tool of governance. *Public Administration*, 82(2), 397–419.

Jasanoff, S. (1987). Contested boundaries in policy-relevant science. *Social Studies of Science*, 17(2), 195–230.

Jasanoff, S. (2004). *States of Knowledge: The Co-production of Science and Social Order*. London: Routledge.

Johnson, P. (1989). *Intellectuals*. London: Weidenfeld & Nicolson.

Kagan, C. and Diamond, J. (2019). From knowledge transfer to public engagement. In C. Kagan and J. Diamond, *University–Community Relations in the UK: Rethinking University–Community Policy Connections*. London: Palgrave Macmillan.

Karp, P. (2018). 'Knuckle-dragging philistines': Labor targets Liberals for blocking arts grants. *The Guardian*, 26 October. URL: https://www.theguardian.com/australia-news/2018/oct/26/knuckle-dragging-philistines-labor-targets-liberals-for-blocking-arts-grants (accessed 29 April 2019).

Katikireddi, S.V., Higgins, M., Bond, L., Bonell, C. and Macintyre, S. (2011). How evidence based is English public health policy? *BMJ*, 343: d7310.

Kay, A. (2005). A critique of the use of path dependency in policy studies. *Public Administration,* 83(3), 553–71.

Kelly, D., Kent, B., McMahon, A., Taylor, J. and Traynor, M. (2016). Impact case studies submitted to REF 2014: the hidden impact of nursing research. *Journal of Research in Nursing*, 21(4), 256–68.

Kennedy, M. (2014). *Globalizing Knowledge: Intellectuals, Universities and Publics in Transformation*. Stanford, CA: Stanford University Press.

King, L. and Rivett, G. (2015). Engaging people in making history: impact, public engagement and the world beyond the campus. *History Workshop Journal*, 80(1), 218–33.

King's College, London and Digital Science (2015). The nature, scale and beneficiaries of research impact: an initial analysis of Research Excellence Framework (REF) 2014 impact case studies, Research Report 2015/01. HEFCE, March.

Kingdon, J.W. (1995). [1984]). *Agendas, Alternatives, and Public Policies*, 2nd edn. New York: HarperCollins College Publishers.

Kisby, B. (2011). Interpreting facts, verifying interpretations: public policy, truth and evidence. *Public Policy and Administration*, 26(1), 107–27.

Knight, C. and Lightowler, C. (2010). Reflections of 'knowledge exchange professionals' in the social sciences: emerging opportunities and challenges for university-based knowledge brokers. *Evidence & Policy*, 6(4), 543–56.

Knorr-Cetina, K. (1981). *The Manufacture of Knowledge: An Essay in the Constructivist and Contextual Nature of Science*. Oxford: Pergamon.

Kogan, M. and Hanney, S. (2000). *Reforming Higher Education*. London: Jessica Kingsley.

Ladyman, J. (2009). Against impact. *Oxford Magazine*, 294: 4–5.

Lambert, R. (2003). *Lambert Review of Business-University Collaboration (Final Report)*. London: HMSO. URL: http://www.ncub.co.uk/index.php?option=com_docman&view=download&category_slug=publications&alias=81-lambert-review&Itemid=2728 (accessed 29 April 2019).

Lamont, M. (2009). *How Professors Think: Inside the Curious World of Academic Judgement*. Cambridge, MA: Harvard University Press.

Latour, B. and Woolgar, S. (1986). *Laboratory Life: The Construction of Scientific Facts*. Princeton, NJ: Princeton University Press.

Lavis, J.N., Posada, F.B., Haines, A. and Osei, E. (2004). Use of research to inform public policymaking. *Lancet*, 364, 1615–21.

Leathwood, C. and Read, B. (2012). Final report: assessing the impact of developments in research policy for research on higher education: an exploratory study. Society for Research into Higher Education (SRHE). UR: https://www.srhe.ac.uk/downloads/Leathwood_Read_Final_Report_16_July_2012.pdf (accessed 7 January 2019).

Lee, C.W. (2015). *Do-It-Yourself Democracy: The Rise of the Public Engagement Industry*. New York: Oxford University Press.

Lindblom, C. (1959). The science of muddling through. *Public Administration Review* 19: 79–88.

Lister, R. (2005). (2nd ed.) *The Inclusive Society? Social Inclusion and New Labour*. Basingstoke: Palgrave Macmillan.

Lomas, J. (2000). Using 'linkage and exchange' to move research into policy at a Canadian foundation. *Health Affairs*, 19, 236–40.

London School of Economics Public Policy Group (2011). *Maximising the Impacts of Your Research: A Handbook for Social Scientists*. London: LSE. URL: http://eprints.lse.ac.uk/35758/1/Handbook_PDF_for_the_LSE_impact_blog_April_2011.pdf.

LSE GV314 Group (2014). evaluation under contract: government pressure and the production of policy research. *Public Administration*, 92, 224–39.

Lundh, A., Sismondo, S., Lexchin, J., Busuioc, O.A. and Bero, L. (2012). Industry sponsorship and research outcome (review). Cochrane Database of Systematic Reviews, Cochrane Library.

MacDonald, R. (2017). 'Impact', research and slaying zombies: the pressures and possibilities of the REF. *International Journal of Sociology and Social Policy*, 37(11–12), 696–710.

MacDonald, R., Shildrick, T. and Furlong, A. (2013). In search of 'intergenerational cultures of worklessness': hunting yetis and shooting zombies. *Critical Social Policy*, 34(2), 199–220.

Macintyre, S., Chalmers, I., Horton, R. and Smith, R. (2001). Using evidence to inform health policy: case study. *BMJ*, 322(7280), 222–25.

Mackenbach, J.P. (2011). Can we reduce health inequalities? An analysis of the English strategy (1997–2010). *Journal of Epidemiology and Community Health*, 65, 568–75.

Malito, D.V., Umbach, G. and Bhuta, N. (2018). *The Palgrave Handbook of Indicators in Global Governance*. Cham: Palgrave Macmillan.

Manville, C., Guthrie, S., Henham, M.-L., Garrod, B., Sousa, S., Kirtley, A. et al (2015a). Assessing impact submissions for REF2014: An evaluation. RAND. URL: https://www.rand.org/pubs/research_reports/RR1032.html (accessed 11 May 2017).

Manville, C., Jones, M.M., Frearson, M., Castle-Clarke, S., Henham, M.L., Gunashekar, S. and Grant, J. (2015b). *Preparing Impact Submissions for REF 2014: An Evaluation*. Cambridge: RAND Europe:

Marcella, R., Lockerbie, H., Bloice, L., Hood, C. and Barton, F. (2018). The effects of the research excellence framework research impact agenda on early- and mid-career researchers in library and information science. *Journal of Information Science*, 44(5), 608–18.

Martin, B.R. (2011). The Research Excellence Framework and the 'impact agenda': are we creating a Frankenstein monster? *Research Evaluation*, 20(3), 247–54.

Martin, S. (2010). Co-production of social research: strategies for engaged scholarship. *Public Money & Management*, 30(4), 211–18.

Massey, D. (2013). *Space, Place and Gender*. Oxford: John Wiley & Sons.

Matthews, P., Rutherfoord, R., Connelly, S., Richardson, L., Durose, C. and Vanderhoven, D. (2018). Everyday stories of impact: interpreting knowledge exchange in the contemporary university. *Evidence & Policy*, 14(4), 665–82.

McCowan, T. (2018). Five perils of the impact agenda in higher education. *London Review of Education*, 16(2), 279–95.

McGoey, L. (2012). Strategic unknowns: Towards a sociology of ignorance. *Economy and Society*, 41(1), 1–16.

Meagher, L.R. and Martin, U. (2017). Slightly dirty maths: the richly textured mechanisms of impact. *Research Evaluation*, 26(1), 15–27.

Meer, N. (2006). 'Get off your knees': print media public intellectuals and Muslims in Britain. *Journalism Studies*, 7(1), 35–59.

Meriluoto, T. (2018). Neutral experts or passionate participants? Renegotiating expertise and the right to act in Finnish participatory social policy. *European Journal of Cultural and Political Sociology*, 81, 116–39.

Merton, R. (1942). *The Sociology of Science: Theoretical and Empirical Investigations*. Chicago: Chicago University Press.

Meyer, M. (2010). The rise of the knowledge broker. *Science Communication*, 32(1), 118–27.

Mhurchú, A.N., McLeod, L., Collins, S. and Siles-Brügge, G. (2017). The present and the future of the research excellence framework impact agenda in the UK academy: a reflection from politics and international studies. *Political Studies Review*, 15(1), 60–72.

Michaels, S. (2009). Matching knowledge brokering strategies to environmental policy problems and settings. *Environmental Science and Policy*, 12(7), 994–1011.

Miller, C. (2001). Hybrid management: boundary organizations, science policy, and environmental governance in the climate regime. *Science, Technology & Human Values*, 26(4), 478–500.

Mills, C.W. (1959). *The Sociological Imagination*. Oxford: Oxford University Press.

Mitton, C., Adair, C.E., McKenzie, E., Patten, S.B. and Waye Perry, B. (2007). Knowledge transfer and exchange: review and synthesis of the literature. *The Milbank Quarterly*, 85, 729–68.

Modood, T. (2018). Thinking about public intellectuals. *SCTIW Review*, February, 1–9.

Molnar, T. (1994). *The Decline of the Intellectual*. Piscataway: Transaction Publishers.

MRC (2013). *Handbook for Applicants and Grantholders 2013*. Swindon: MRC.

MRC (2016). Outputs, outcomes and impact of MRC research 2014/ 15 report. URL: https://mrc.ukri.org/publications/browse/outputs-report-2015-policy-and-engagement/ (accessed 29 April 2019).

Mroz, A. (2009). Leader: short-term outlook, no blue skies. *Times Higher Education*, 12 February 2009. URL: https://www.timeshighereducation.com/comment/leader/leader-short-term-outlook-no-blue-skies/405363.article (accessed 6 January 2019).

Murad, M.H., Asi, N., Alsawas, M. and Alahdab, F. (2016). New evidence pyramid. *BMJ Evidence-Based Medicine*, 21, 125–7.

Murji, K. (2017). *Racism, Policy and Politics*. Bristol: Policy Press.

Murphy, T. and Sage, D. (2014). Perceptions of the UK's Research Excellence Framework 2014: a media analysis, *Journal of Higher Education Policy and Management*, 36(6), 603–15.

Murray, K. and Harkin, D. (2017). Policing in cool and hot climates: legitimacy, power and the rise and fall of mass stop and search in Scotland. *The British Journal of Criminology*, 57(4). 885–905.

Naughton, M. (2005). 'Evidence-based policy' and the government of the criminal justice system – only if the evidence fits! *Critical Social Policy*, 25, 47–69.

Navarro, V. (2004). The politics of health inequalities research in the United States. *International Journal of Health Services*, 34(1), 87–99.

NERC (2019). *Delivery Plan 2019*. URL: https://www.ukri.org/files/about/dps/nerc-dp-2019/.

Newman, J. and Clarke, J. (2009). *Publics, Politics and Power: Remaking the Public in Public Services*. London and Thousand Oaks, CA: SAGE.

NIHR (undated). How we involve patients, carers and the public. URL: https://www.nihr.ac.uk/about-us/our-contribution-to-research/how-we-involve-patients-carers-and-the-public.htm.

Nixon, J., Marks, A., Rowland, A. and Walker, M. (2001). Towards a new academic professionalism: a manifesto of hope. *British Journal of Sociology of Education*, 22(2), 227–44.

Nowotny, H., Scott, P. and Gibbons, M. (2001). *Re-Thinking Science Knowledge in an Age of Uncertainty*. Cambridge: Polity Press.

Nowotny, H., Scott, P. and Gibbons, M. (2003). Introduction: 'Mode 2' revisited: the new production of knowledge. *Minerva*, 41(3), 179–94.

Nutley, S., Walter, I. and Davies, H. (2007). *Using Evidence: How Research Can Inform Public Services*. Bristol: Policy Press.

Oancea, A. (2013). Interpretations of research impact in seven disciplines. *European Educational Research Journal*, 12(2), 242–50.

Oliver, K. and Boaz, A. (2019). Transforming evidence for policy and practice: creating space for new conversations. *Palgrave Communications*, 5, 60.

Oliver, K. and Cairney, P. (2019). The dos and don'ts of influencing policy: a systematic review of advice to academics. *Palgrave Communications*, 5(21), 1–8.

Oliver, K., Innvar, S., Lorenc, T., Woodman, J. and Thomas, J. (2014). A systematic review of barriers to and facilitators of the use of evidence by policymakers. *BMC Health Services Research*, 14(1), 2.

Osborne, T. and Rose, N. (1999). Do the social sciences create phenomena? The example of public opinion research. *The British Journal of Sociology*, 50, 367–96.

Ovseiko, P., Greenhalgh, T., Adam, P. et al (2016). A global call for action to include gender in research impact assessment. *Health Research Policy and Systems*, 14(1), 50.

Owens, S. and Rayner, T.I.M. (1999). 'When knowledge matters': the role and influence of the Royal Commission on Environmental Pollution. *Journal of Environmental Policy & Planning*, 24(February), 7–24.

Pain, R. (2014). Impact: striking a blow or walking together? *Acme*, 13(1), 19–23.

Pain, R., Kesby, M. and Askins, K. (2011). Geographies of impact: power, participation and potential. *Area*, 43(2), 183–8.

Pain, R., Kesby, M. and Askins, K. (2012). The politics of social justice in neo-liberal times: a response to Slater. *Area*, 44(1), 120–3.

Panel on Return on Investment in Health Research (2009). *Making an Impact: A Preferred Framework and Indicators to Measure Returns on Investment in Health Research*. Ottawa: Canadian Academy of Health Sciences.

Payne-Gifford, S. (2014). What is the meaning of the impact agenda: is it repackaged or a new entity? Views from inside research councils. *Achieving Impact in Research*, 10–19. URL: https://doi.org/10.4135/9781473913950.n2.

Pedersen, D.B. (2017). IMPACT: Redskaber og metoder til måling af forskningens gennemslagskraft. Det Frie Forskningsråd (Danish Council for Independent Research). URL: https://dff.dk/aktuelt/publikationer/impact-redskaber-og-metoder-til-maling-af-forskningens-gennemslagskraft (accessed 29 April 2019).

Penfield, T., Baker, M.J., Scoble, R. and Wykes, M.C. (2014). Assessment, evaluations, and definitions of research impact: a review. *Research Evaluation*, 23(1), 21–32.

Petticrew, M., Whitehead, M., Macintyre, S.J., Graham, H. and Egan, M. (2004). Evidence for public health policy on inequalities: 1: the reality according to policymakers. *Journal of Epidemiology and Community Health*, 58(10), 811–16.

Pettigrew, A.M. (2011). Scholarship with impact. *British Journal of Management*, 22, 347–54.

Phillips, R. (2010). The impact agenda and geographies of curiosity. *Transactions of the Institute of British Geographers*, 35(4), 447–52.

Phipps, David (2011). A report detailing the development of a university-based knowledge mobilization unit that enhances research outreach and engagement. *Scholarly and Research Communication*, 2(2).

Pickett, K. and Wilkinson, R. (2016). Spirit level: a case study of the public dissemination of health inequalities research – Oxford Scholarship. In K.E. Smith, S.E. Hill and C. Bambra (eds), *Health Inequalities: Critical Perspectives*. Oxford: Oxford University Press.

Piketty, T. (2014). *Capital in the Twenty-First Century*. Cambridge, MA: Harvard University Press.

Pohl, C. (2008). From science to policy through transdisciplinary research. *Environmental Science and Policy*, 11(1), 46–53.

Posner, R. (2003). *Public Intellectuals: A Study of Decline*. Cambridge, MA: Harvard University Press.

Power, M. (1997). *The Audit Society: Rituals of Verification*. Oxford: Clarendon Press.

Putnam R.D. (2000). *Bowling Alone: The Collapse and Revival of American Community*. New York: Simon & Schuster.

RCUK. (2017). Pathways to impact. URL: http://www.rcuk.ac.uk/innovation/impacts/ (accessed 20 August 2017).

Reed, M. (2017). *How to write a winning impact summary and pathway to impact. Fast Track Impact Research Impact Guides.* URL: https://www.fasttrackimpact.com/single-post/2017/06/01/How-to-write-an-impact-summary-and-pathway-to-impact.

REF (2012). Panel criteria and working methods. URL: http://www.ref.ac.uk/media/ref/content/pub/panelcriteriaandworkingmethods/01_12.pdf> (accessed 26 October 2012).

REF (2019a). Guidance on submissions (2019/01). REF 2021. URL: https://www.ref.ac.uk/media/1092/ref-2019_01-guidance-on-submissions.pdf (accessed 29 April 2019).

REF (2019b). Panel criteria and working methods. REF 2019/02 January 2019. URL: https://www.ref.ac.uk/media/1084/ref-2019_02-panel-criteria-and-working-methods.pdf (accessed December 2019).

REF (undated). Developing further guidance on impact arising from public engagement in REF 2021. URL: https://www.ref.ac.uk/media/1037/ref-2021-impact-workshop-impact-arising-from-public-engagement.pdf (accessed 29 April 2019).

REF 2014 (2011). Assessment framework and guidance on submissions. URL: http://www.ref.ac.uk/media/ref/content/pub/assessmentframeworkandguidanceonsubmissions/GOS%20including%20addendum.pdf (accessed 15 May 2017).

REF 2014 (2014). Assessment criteria and level definitions. URL: http://www.ref.ac.uk/panels/assessmentcriteriaandleveldefinitions/ (accessed 11 May 2017).

REF (2011a). Decisions on assessing research impact. URL: http://www.ref.ac.uk/pubs/2011–01/.

REF (2011b). Research Excellence Framework: Assessment framework and guidance on submissions. URL: https://www.ref.ac.uk/2014/media/ref/content/pub/assessmentframeworkandguidanceonsubmissions/GOS%20including%20addendum.pdf.

REF2014 Main Panel A (2015). Research Excellence Framework 2014: overview report by Main Panel A and sub-panels 1 to 6. URL: https://www.ref.ac.uk/2014/media/ref/content/expanel/member/Main%20Panel%20A%20overview%20report.pdf (accessed 7 January 2019).

REF2014 Main Panel B (2015). Research Excellence Framework 2014: overview report by Main Panel B and sub-panels 7 to 15. URL: https://www.ref.ac.uk/2014/media/ref/content/expanel/member/Main%20Panel%20B%20overview%20report.pdf (accessed 7 January 2019).

REF2014 Main Panel C (2015). Research Excellence Framework 2014: overview report by Main Panel C and sub-panels 16 to 26. URL: https://www.ref.ac.uk/2014/media/ref/content/expanel/member/Main%20Panel%20C%20overview%20report.pdf (accessed 7 January 2019).

REF2014 Main Panel D (2015). Research Excellence Framework 2014: overview report by Main Panel D and sub-panels 27 to 36. URL: https://www.ref.ac.uk/2014/media/ref/content/expanel/member/Main%20Panel%20D%20overview%20report.pdf (accessed 7 January 2019).

Rein, M. (1980). Methodology for the study of the interplay between social science and social policy. *International Social Science Journal*, 22, 361–8.

Research Councils UK (2011). *RCUK Impact Requirements: Frequently Asked Questions*. Swindon: RCUK.

Research Councils UK (2014). *Joint Statement on Impact by HEFCE, RCUK and Universities UK*. URL: http://www.rcuk.ac.uk/RCUK-prod/assets/documents/innovation/JointStatementImpact.pdf (accessed 10 October 2015).

Research Councils UK (2017). Impact of £3.4Bn investment demonstrates the UK place as a global leader in research and innovation. 27 March. URL: http://www.rcuk.ac.uk/media/news/170327/ (accessed 24 November 2017).

Research Councils UK (undated). RCUK review of pathways to impact: summary. URL: http://www.rcuk.ac.uk/documents/documents/ptoiexecsummary-pdf/ (accessed 11 May 2017).

Robbins, P.T., Wield, D. and Wilson, G. (2017). Mapping engineering and development research excellence in the UK: an analysis of REF2014 impact case studies. *Journal of International Development*, 29(1), 89–105.

Rogers, A., Bear, C., Hunt, M., Mills, S. and Sandover, R. (2014). Intervention: the impact agenda and human geography in UK higher education. *ACME: An International E-Journal for Critical Geographies*, 13(1), 1–9.

Roll-Hansen, N. (2017). A historical perspective on the distinction between basic and applied science. *Journal for General Philosophy of Science*, 48(4), 535–51.

Royal Society (2006). *Survey of Factors Affecting Science Communication by Scientists and Engineers*. London: Royal Society.

Sabatier, P.A. and Jenkins-Smith, H.C. (1999). The Advocacy Coalition Framework: an assessment. In P.A. Sabatier (ed.), *Theories of the Policy Process*. Oxford: Westview Press.

Said, E. (1994). *Representations of the Intellectual: The 1993 Reith Lectures*. London: Vintage.

Salter, A., Tartari, V., D'Este, P. and Neely, A. (2010). *The Republic of Engagement: Exploring UK Academic Attitudes to Collaborating with Industry and Entrepreneurship*. Advanced Institute of Management Research (AIM) and UK–Innovation Research Centre UK.

Sanderson, I. (2009). Intelligent policy making for a complex world: pragmatism, evidence and learning. *Political Studies*, 57(4), 699–719. URL: https://doi.org/10.1111/j.1467-9248.2009.00791.x.

Sartre, J.-P. (1974). *The Writings of Jean-Paul Sartre*, M. Contat and M. Rybalka (eds). Evanston, IL: Northwestern University Press.

Sasse, T. and Hadden, C. (2018). *How Government Can Work with Academia*. London: Institute for Government.

Sayer, D. (2015). *Rank Hypocrisies: The Insult of the REF*. London: SAGE.

Schmidt, V.A. (2008). Discursive institutionalism: the explanatory power of ideas and discourse. *Annual Review of Political Science*, 11, 303–26.

Shildrick, T., MacDonald, R., Furlong, A., Roden, J. and Crow, R. (2012). *Are Cultures of Worklessness Passed Down the Generations?* York: Joseph Rowntree.

Shore, C. (2008). Audit culture and illiberal governance: universities and the politics of accountability. *Anthropological Theory*, 8(3), 278–98.

Shore, C. and Wright, S. (2015). Governing by numbers: audit culture, rankings and the new world order. *Social Anthropology*, 23(1), 22–2.

Slater, T. (2012). Impacted geographers: a response to Pain, Kesby and Askins, *Area*, 44(1), 117–19.

Smith, K. (2010). Research, policy and funding: academic treadmills and the squeeze on intellectual spaces. *The British Journal of Sociology*, 61, 176–95.

Smith, K. (2012). Fools, facilitators and flexians: academic identities in marketised environments. *Higher Education Quarterly*, 66(2), 155–73.

Smith, K.E. (2013). *Beyond Evidence Based Policy in Public Health: The Interplay of Ideas*. Basingstoke: Palgrave Macmillan.

Smith, K.E. and Joyce, K.E. (2012). Capturing complex realities: understanding efforts to achieve evidence-based policy and practice in public health. *Evidence & Policy*, 8(1), 59–80.

Smith, K.E. and Katikireddi, S.V. (2013). A glossary of theories for understanding policymaking. *Journal of Epidemiology & Community Health*, 67(2), 198–202.

Smith, K.E. and Stewart, E. (2017). We need to talk about impact: why social policy academics need to engage with the UK's research impact agenda. *Journal of Social Policy*, 46(1), 109–27.

Smith, S., Ward, V. and House, A. (2011). 'Impact' in the proposals for the UK's Research Excellence Framework: shifting the boundaries of academic autonomy. *Research Policy*, 40(10), 1369–79.

Spaapen, J. and van Drooge, L. et al (2011). SIAMPI final report. URL: http://www.siampi.eu/Pages/SIA/Content/SIAMPI_Final%20report.pdf (accessed 29 April 2019).

Stern, N. (2016). *Building on Success and Learning from Experience: An Independent Review of the Research Excellence Framework*. London: Department for Business, Energy and Industrial Strategy. URL: https://assets.publishing.service.gov.uk/government/uploads/system/uploads/attachment_data/file/541338/ind-16–9-ref-stern-review.pdf (accessed 29 April 2019).

STFC (2019). *Delivery Plan 2019*. URL: https://stfc.ukri.org/files/delivery-plan-2019/.

Terama, E., Smallman, M., Lock, S.J., Johnson, C. and Austwick, M.Z. (2016). Beyond academia: interrogating research impact in the research excellence framework. *PLOS ONE*, 11(12), e0168533.

Tetroe, J.M., Graham, I.D., Foy, R., Robinson, N., Eccles, M.P., Wensing, M., Durieux, P., Légaré, F., Nielson, C.P., Adily, A., Ward, J.E., Porter, C., Shea, B. and Grimshaw, J.M. (2008). Health research funding agencies' support and promotion of knowledge translation: an international study. *The Milbank Quarterly*, 86, 125–55.

Turnhout, E., Stuiver, M., Judith, J., Harms, B. and Leeuwis, C. (2013). New roles of science in society: different repertoires of knowledge brokering. *Science and Public Policy*, 40(3), 354–65.

UKRI (undated). Pathways to impact. URL: https://www.ukri.org/innovation/excellence-with-impact/pathways-to-impact/ (accessed 29 April 2019).

UKRI (2020) 'Pathways to Impact: Impact core to the UK Research and Innovation application process', UKRI News, 27th January 2020. URL: https://www.ukri.org/news/pathways-to-impact-impact-core-to-the-uk-research-and-innovation-application-process/ (accessed 6th February 2020).

University of the West of England (2017). *UWE Cares Policy.* Bristol: University of the West of England. URL: http://www1.uwe.ac.uk/students/feesandfunding/fundingandscholarships/uwebursary/uwecares.aspx.

Van de Goor, L., Hämäläinen, R.-M., Syed, A., Juel Lau, C., Sandu, P., Spitters, H. and Aro, A.R. (2017). Determinants of evidence use in public health policy making: results from a study across six EU countries. *Health Policy*, 121, 273–81.

Van Egmond, S., Bekker, M., Bal, R. and van der Grinten, T. (2011). Connecting evidence and policy: bringing researchers and policy makers together for effective evidence-based health policy in the Netherlands: a case study. *Evidence & Policy*, 7(1), 25–39.

Virchow, R. (1985). *Collected Essays on Public Health and Epidemiology.* Canton: Science History Publications.

Walter, I., Nutley, S. and Davis, H. (2005). What works to promote evidence-based practice? *Evidence & Policy*, 1, 335–63.

Ward, V., Smith, S., House, A. and Hamer, S. (2012). Exploring knowledge exchange: a useful framework for practice and policy. *Social Science & Medicine*, 74(3), 297–304.

Waring, J., Currie, G., Crompton, A. and Bishop, S. (2013). An exploratory study of knowledge brokering in hospital settings: facilitating knowledge sharing and learning for patient safety? *Social Science and Medicine*, 98, 79–86.

Watermeyer, R. (2012). From engagement to impact? Articulating the public value of academic research. *Tertiary Education and Management*, 18(2), 115–30.

Watermeyer, R. (2014). Issues in the articulation of 'impact': the responses of UK academics to 'impact' as a new measure of research assessment. *Studies in Higher Education*, 39(2), 359–77.

Watermeyer, R. (2015). Lost in the 'third space': the impact of public engagement in higher education on academic identity, research practice and career progression. *European Journal of Higher Education*, 5(3), 331–47.

Watermeyer, R. (2016). Impact in the REF: issues and obstacles. *Studies in Higher Education*, 41(2), 199–214.

Watermeyer, R. (2018). REF impact: a new mode of scholarly distinction? *Higher Education: Policy, People and Politics* (blog). URL: https://wonkhe.com/blogs/ref-impact-a-new-mode-of-scholarly-distinction/.

Watermeyer, R. (2019). *Competitive Accountability in Academic Life: The Struggle for Social Impact and Public Legitimacy*. Cheltenham: Edward Elgar.

Watermeyer, R. (2020) REF impact and the dispossession of academic identity: Haunted by the impact phantom. *Minerva* (forthcoming).

Watermeyer, R. and Chubb, J. (2018). Evaluating impact in the UK's Research Excellence Framework (REF): liminality, looseness and new modalities of scholarly distinction. *Studies in Higher Education*, 4(9), 1554–66.

Watermeyer, R. and Hedgecoe, A. (2016). Selling 'impact': peer reviewer projections of what counts and what is needed in REF impact case studies. A retrospective analysis. *Journal of Education Policy*, 31(5), 651–65.

Watermeyer, R. and Lewis, J. (2017). Why universities and academics should bother with public engagement. *The Conversation*. URL: http://theconversation.com/why-universities-and-academics-should-bother-with-public-engagement-72550.

Watermeyer, R. and Olssen, M. (2016). Exclusion and excellence: the individual costs of institutional competitiveness. *Minerva*, 54(2), 201–18.

Weber, M. (1995 [1906]). *The Russian Revolutions* (G.C. Wells and P. Baehr, Trans.). Ithaca, NY: Cornell University Press.

Weiss, C. (1977). Research for policy's sake: the enlightenment function of social research. *Policy Analysis*, 3, 531–47.

Weiss, C. (1979). The many meanings of research utilization. *Public Administration Review*, 39, 426–31.

Weiss, C. (1980). Knowledge creep and decision accretion. *Knowledge: Creation, Diffusion, Utilization*, 1(3), 381–404.

Wellcome Trust (2015). Evaluating public engagement in the Wellcome Trust's UK centres. UK Centres' Public Engagement Workshop, 6–8 May. London: Wellcome Trust. URL: https://wellcome.ac.uk/sites/default/files/wtp059889_0.pdf (accessed on 29 April 2019).

Wellcome Trust (2016). Factors affecting public engagement by UK researchers. URL: https://wellcome.ac.uk/news/what-are-barriers-uk-researchers-engaging-public.

Wellcome Trust (undated a). Wellcome Trust candidate information pack. URL: https://online.flippingbook.com/view/79931/8.

Wellcome Trust (undated b). Planning your public engagement. URL: https://wellcome.ac.uk/funding/guidance/planning-your-public-engagement.

Wenger, E. (1999). *Communities of Practice: Learning, Meaning, and Identity*. Cambridge: Cambridge University Press.

Whitehead, M., Petticrew, M., Graham, H., Macintyre, S., Bambra, C. and Egan, M. (2004). Evidence for public health policy on inequalities 2: assembling the evidence jigsaw. *Journal of Epidemiology and Community Health*, 58(10), 817–21.

Wilkie, T. (1991). *British Science and Politics since 1945*. Oxford: Basil Blackwell.

Wilkinson, C. (2019). Evidencing impact: a case study of UK academic perspectives on evidencing research impact. *Studies in Higher Education*, 44(1), 72–85.

Wilkinson, R. and Pickett, K. (2009). *The Spirit Level: Why More Equal Societies Almost Always Do Better*. London: Allen Lane.

Williams, G. (2012). The disciplining effects of impact evaluation practices: negotiating the pressures of impact within an ESRC–DFID project. *Transactions of the Institute of British Geographers*, 37, 489–95.

Williams, G. (2013). Researching with impact in the Global South? Impact-evaluation practices and the reproduction of 'development knowledge'. *Contemporary Social Science*, 8(3), 223–36.

Williams, K. and Grant, J. (2018). A comparative review of how the policy and procedures to assess research impact evolved in Australia and the UK. *Research Evaluation*, 27(2), 93–105.

Wilsdon, J., Allen, L., Belfiore, E. et al (2015). The metric tide: report of the independent review of the role of metrics in research assessment and management. London: SAGE/HEFCE. URL: http://sro.sussex.ac.uk/55372/.

Wilson, C., Manners, P. and Duncan, S. (2014). *Building an Engaged Future for UK Higher Education*. Bristol: National Coordinating Centre for Public Engagement. URL: https://www.publicengagement.ac.uk/sites/default/files/publication/t64422_-_engaged_futures_final_report_72.pdf.

Wimbush, E., Harper, H., Wight, D., Gruer, L., Lowther, M., Fraser, S. and Gordon, J. (2005). Evidence, policy and practice: developing collaborative approaches in Scotland. *Evidence & Policy*, 1(3), 391–407.

Wright, J.S.F., Parry, J. and Mathers, J. (2007). What to do about political context? Evidence synthesis, the New Deal for Communities and the possibilities for evidence-based policy. *Evidence & Policy*, 3(2), 253–69.

Wynne, B. (2006). Public engagement as a means of restoring public trust in science – hitting the notes, but missing the music? *Community Genetics*, 9(3), 211–20.

Yarrow, E. and Davies, J. (2018). The gendered impact agenda – how might more female academics' research be submitted as REF impact case studies? *Impact of Social Sciences Blog*, 8 March. URL: http://eprints.lse.ac.uk/89047/ (accessed 4 January 2019).

Yost, J., Dobbins, M., Traynor, R., DeCorby, K., Workentine, S. and Greco, L. (2014). Tools to support evidence-informed public health decision making. *BMC Public Health*, 14(1), 728.

Index

Note: Page numbers for figures and tables appear in italics.

2* quality 49, 185, 186
2003 Lambert Review of Business-University Collaboration 20
2004–2014 Science and Innovation Investment Framework 20

A

academia, and policy 42–3
academic advocacy 176–7
  see also advocacy
academic advocates 180
academic autonomy 41–6, 163, 167, 180
  see also autonomy
academic careers 92–4, 197
academic entrepreneurship 78
academic evidence 167–8
  see also evidence
academic incentives 168–9
  see also incentives
academic independence 90–2
  see also independence
academic publishing 154
  see also publishing
academic rigour 203
  see also rigour
academic start-up companies 78
accountability 187, 188, 192–3, 198
advice, provided by academics 98, 101, 156
advocacy 173, 176–7, 180, 200
advocacy coalition framework 164
agenda setting 177
AHRC (Arts and Humanities Research Council) 106–7, *107, 141*
'anchor institution' 201
artistry 189
arts 106–7, 111
assessors 187–92
attribution of impacts 31–3
audiences 76–8, 80, 82, *112*, 134, 136, 200
  funding for academic engagement with 140
  providing advice to 98

audit culture 132, 198
audit regimes 199, 200
Australia 15, 22, 132, 133, 166, 200
Australian Research Council (ARC) 15
autonomy 41–6, 88, 89, 132–3, 163, 167, 180, 203

B

Back, Les 57–8, 120, 122, 123, 129–30, 131, 132–3
  on digital sharing of ideas and writing 125, 136
  on impact 'superheroes' 54
  on public engagement 127, 128
'bad' impact 49–50, 60
Ball, Christopher 17, 19
Bandola-Gill, J. 8, 138, 139, 145, 150, 153
Becker, Howard 115–16
Belfiore, E. 103, 111
beneficiaries, passive 184–5
Benneworth, P. 50
bias, gender 57
bibliometric measures 36
'bid-writer' presence 189
Biotechnology and Biological Sciences Research Council (BBSRC) *141*
'blue skies' research 41, 42, 52, 178
Blunkett, David 19–20
Boswell, C. 28–9, 39
boundary organisations 16
boundary work 138, 153
Braben et al 23, 27
British Academy 100
'bullshit antenna' 191
Burawoy, Michael 43–4, 120, 128
businesses, working with researchers 24
Buxton, M. 35

C

Cairney, P. 30
Canada 16, 130–1, 132, 133–4
Canadian Institute of Health Research 16
Caplan, N. 138

careers 92–4, 165–6, 197
case studies *see* impact case studies
Centre for Management of Policy
   Studies 19
Chapman, S. 177
Chowdhury et al 64, *65*
Chubb, J. 4, 33, 35, 44, 46, 56, 63–4
   on public engagement 104, 105
citations 36
citizenship 192
coalitions of actors 164
co-creation 140
collaboration 45–6, 76, 78, 87–8, 97,
   171, 202
   easier to achieve impacts 51, 96
collective endeavour 72
Collini, S. 24
commercial impacts 103–4, 132
commercially funded research 43
communities of practice 144
community connections 129–31
community engagement 173, 176
   see also public engagement
companies, academic start-up 78
'competitive accountability' 187, 188,
   192–3, 198
competitive performativity 199
conceptual change 31
conceptual impact 74–6
co-production 30, 88–9, 91, 140, 171
costs, economic 52–3
creative adapters 173–8, 180
creative thinking 198
criticality 132–3
critical knowledge 120, 128
critical research 41, 46, 201
cross-disciplinary endeavour 72
curiosity-driven research 23, 24, 41, 52

D

Darby, S. 4
data stories 125
   see also stories
Davey Smith et al 42–3
Davies, J. 56
decision making, and evidence 171
Delivery Plans 20
Denmark 16
Derrick, G. 50, 105
disciplinary–professional practice 80

disciplines 63–98, 111–12
disinterestedness 91
division of labour 150, 151, 152
DNA 51
Donovan, C. 37–8
Duncan, S. 107, 110
Dunleavy, P. 36
Dunlop, C. 54

E

Eakin, J. 16
easy impact 82–3
economic costs 52–3
economic impact 103–4, 107
elites 39–40, 53–9, 60
eloquence 189
embellishing impact 187, 188, 189–90,
   191, 193
engagement 15, 23, 40, 80,
   99–113, 128
   absence 28
   and academic promotion 93–4
   incentives 134–5
   increased 86–8
   and innovation 203
   and research 59, 60
   stakeholder *141–2*
   see also public engagement
Engineering and Physical Sciences
   Research Council (EPSRC) *141*
enlightenment model 29–30
enthusiastic supporters 169–73, 179–80
entrepreneurs, policy 164
entrepreneurship, academic 78
equity, gender 57
ESRC (Economic and Social
   Research Council) 19, 20, 28, 47,
   54, 140, *141*
   on public engagement 101, 102
ethics 127, 203
European Union (EU) 16–17
evidence 33, 48, 110, 120, 154–5,
   160, 164
   in decision making 171
   and Kisby 181
   limited capacity to interrogate 197
   policy-based 161
   public health 163, 167–8
   and rhetoric 192, 193
   symbolic 39–40

evidence-based policy 19–20, 42–3
exaggeration 193
excellence 47–8, 55, 197, 202, 203
experiential knowledge 155
experimental work 201
expert academics 184–5
external-facing work 180
  see also outward-facing work
Eynon, R. 27

F

failures, learning from 203
Fast Track Impact 48
Fielding, M. 33
financial security, reduced 43
financial value 40, 203
'flexians' 193
Flinders, M. 150
Foucault, Michel 117
framing 177
Frie Forskningsfond 16
funding 43, 48–9, 53, 87, 94–5, 140, 178
funding applications 24

G

gender bias 57
gender equity 57
genuine impact 68, 69
Gibbons et al 43, 64, 66, 97
Gieryn, T.E. 153
global impact 202
global knowledge flows 185
Grant, J. 15
grant applications 16, 49, 202
'grimpact' 49–50

H

Habermas, J. 119
Halford, S. 120–1, 136
Halpern, D. 38
Hammersley, M. 42
Hanney, S. 35
Harkin, D. 44
health, public 97, 111, 161–81
HEFCE 22, 66
hegemonic discourse 123
hierarchies of evidence 48
history 106–7
Holmwood, John 27, 118–19, 129, 135
Hughes, A. 31

humanities 106–7, 111–12

I

ignorance, strategic role of 125,
  136, 201–2
impact case studies 33, 41, 54, 58, 61,
  70, 154, 197, 201
  2* quality 49, 185
  and change 200
  differences between
    disciplines 64, 72, 84
  economic costs 52–3
  and excellence 55
  and governmental priorities 103
  high monetary value 186–7, 203
  high-stakes financial rewards 40
  introduced in REF2014 21
  and knowledge broker
    organisations 149
  measurement 34
  mixed-methods case study
    approach 36
  and narratives 35, 37–8, 132,
    158, 199
  and NGOs 46
  and public engagement 105, 107–8,
    110, 111
  reach and significance 22
  and research 83, 85, 179, 196, 202
  and score for 13
  subjectivity of 82
  time limit 51
  and UCL 104
  and user assessors 188, 189, 190–1,
    192, 193–4
  and women 56
impact fatigue 38
impactful environments 200–1
impact industry 36–7
impact plans 15, 21, 23, 204
impact statements 21, 69, 70
  see also pathways to impact
    statements
impact summary 49, 202
'impact superstar' 202
incentives 47–8, 60, 97, 134, 150,
  151–2, 196–7
  public health 165–6, 167, 168–9, 170
independence 88, 90–2, 177, 180
Industrial Strategy Challenge Fund 24

industry 76–8
industry partners 24, 63, 98
inequalities 162–3
inequities 58, 59
informatics 78, 81
innovation 200, 203
institutionalism 39–40
institutional ownership and impact 185
institutional set-up 156
instrumental impact 74–6, 127
intellectualism, public 115–36
interactivity 100
interdisciplinary work 155
international impact 202
international inequities 58
intrinsic research 41
Irish Research Council 16

J

Jasanoff, S. 91
Jenkins Smith, H.C. 164

K

King, L. 111
Kingdon, J. 50, 164
Kisby, B. 181
knowledge 29, 39, 73, 120, 128, 155
knowledge brokers 16, 138–60, 170–1
knowledge creep 31
knowledge exchange 33, 78–9, 82,
    160, 198, 203
knowledge exchange
    organisations 137–60
knowledge synthesis 202
knowledge transfer targets 20
knowledge translation 133–4, 138, 142,
    144, 154, 155, 158, 159

L

'ladder of impact' 75–6
Ladyman, J. 24
Lamont, Michèle 121, 123–4, 132, 136
Leading the World 107
Leathwood, C. 34
Lee, C.W. 37
Leverhulme Trust 100
Lindblom, C. 50
local communities 45–6, 202
low- and middle-income (LMIC)
    setting 58

lung cancer 51

M

MacDonald, R. 17, 34
Manners, P. 107, 110
Martin, B. 31, 34
Massey, D. 202
mathematics 83
McCowan, T. 35, 46–7, 50, 51–2, 59
measurement of impact 34–8
media coverage, REF 25
Medical Research Council
    (MRC) 101, *141*
medicine 111
Meer, N. 116, 123, 124, 125, 126,
    127, 128, 129, 130, 131, 132
Merton, Robert 91
metricide 38
Meyer, M. 139
Mills, C. Wright 130
misapplication 49
misinterpretation 49
mixed-methods case study
    approach 36, 38
Mode 1 36, 43, 66, 184–5
Mode 2 43, 64, 66, 97
Modood, T. 117–18, 120, 124
monetary value 40, 186–7, 203
moral agency 191
Mroz, A. 23
'muddling through' 50
multiple publics 120–2, 124
Murji, K. 116
Murphy, T. 25
Murray, Kath 44

N

narratives 35, 37, 38, 125, 126, 158,
    187, 197, 199
    favoured by impact case studies 132
    'ghost-written' by professionals 36
National Coordinating Centre for
    Public Engagement 100
'national interest' test for grant funding
    (Australia) 15
National Science Foundation
    (USA) 16
Natural Environment Research Council
    (NERC) *142*
natural sciences 112

natural sweeteners 47
NCPPE (National Coordinating Centre for Public Engagement) 100, 107–9, 110, 111, 112, 196, 201
neoliberal reforms 43, 107, 192, 193
Netherlands 16
New Labour government 19–20
NGOs 46, 57
no-publishing penalty 154

O

Oancea, A. 64
Oliver, K. 30
Olssen, M. 53
organised scepticism 91
original research 51, 83–4, 202
'outreach' activity 105
outward-facing work 1–2, 60, 105–6, 123, 169, 200
    and pragmatic accommodators 178–9
    and women 56

P

Pain, R. 35
Pain et al 45–6
Panel on Return on Investment in Health Research 16
participatory relationships 45–6
partnership working 140, 171
passive beneficiaries, 184–5
pathways to impact 21, 23, 202
pathways to impact statements 27, 41, 159
Payback Framework 35
peer review 16, 23, 41, 49, 187, 202, 203
Penfield et al 31, 36, 38, 47, 51, 52
persuasion 31, 38, 68, 69, 105, 126, 190
Pettigrew, A.M. 31
Phillips, David 17
Phipps, Alison 121–2, 123, 125–6, 127, 128–9, 132, 135
police stop-and-search policies 44
policy 28–30, 42–3, 78, 171
policy audiences 98
    see also audiences
policy-based evidence 161
policy change 33, 158, 164
policy entrepreneurs 164

policy impact 30, 55–6, 63, 64, 81, 101, 103
    and collaborative approaches 78
    difficulty demonstrating 31
    'ladder of impact' 75
policy knowledge 120
policymakers 51, 156, 161, 165–6, 167–8
policy streams 50, 164
political science 164
politics 29, 38–9, 42, 43
portability 185
positive impact 46–50
power 29, 59
Power, M. 111
practice audiences 80
practice-based knowledge 155
practice change 158
pragmatic accommodators 178–9, 180
process, focus on, rather than outcome 157–8
productive interactions 16
professionalism 131
professional knowledge 120
promotion criteria 1, 9, 92, 93, 197
public citizenship 192
public engagement 23, 40, 99–113, 128, 173, 176
    and academic promotion 93–4
    ethics 127
    increasing public recognition 80
    unlikely to score highly in REF 196
public engagement industry 37
public events, organising 98
public good 8, 63, 119, 185, 193
public health 97, 111, 161–81
public intellectualism 115–36, 200
public interests 25, 118, 130
public knowledge 120
public policy debate 127
publics 78–80, 108–9, 118–22, 124, 136
public sphere 119, 123, 124
publishing 92, 93, 97, 152, 153, 154

Q

qualitative research 134
quality 94, 185–6, 202

quality related (QR) funding 53,
186, 187
quantitative research 134

R

RAND 15, 52
RCUK (Research Councils
UK) 100, 107
Read, B. 34
*Realising Our Potential: A Strategy for
Science, Engineering and Technology*
(White Paper) 19
recognition 80, 188, 191, 201
REF 21, 160
  cost of assessing impact 52–3
  definition of impact 85
  emphasis placed on impact should
    increase substantially 151
  and evidence 154–5
  impact as assessment criterion
    introduced 22
  and impact case studies 13, 132
  impact guidance 49–50
  impact part of wider agenda 4–5
  and institutional set-up 156
  and knowledge translation 154
  media coverage 25
  and non-portability of impact 185
  panels preferences 81–2
  and pathways to impact statements 27
  public engagement, unlikely to score
    highly 196
  and quality 185–6
REF2014 34, 57–8, 58
  2★ quality for impact case studies 49
  assessment criteria 48
  definition of impact 22
  guidance for assessing impact case
    studies 46
  and NCPPE 111
  platform for academics' public
    celebrity 55
  on public engagement 105, 107–8
  reasons impact cases studies
    introduced 15, 21
  reports from chairs 38
  and storytelling 36
  and time limits 51
  and UCL 104
  and UCU petition 23–4

  and women 56
REF2021 22–3, 46, 48, 49, 51,
  53, 185
refugee crisis 125
reifying traditional elites 53–9, 60
relational spaces 126
relationships, forging 113, 128–31
research
  commercially funded 43
  co-produced 87–8
  for external audiences 196
  and impact shaping projects 94–6
  lack of 153
  linking to impact 83–5
  original 202
  politicisation of 42
  portability 185
  public health 179
  qualitative 134
  quantitative 134
  still seen as central academic
    practice 152
Research Assessment Exercise
  (RAE) 17, 19
  see also REF; REF2014; REF2021
research councils 17, 20–1, 22, 24, 27,
  106, 142
research engagement 59, 60
  see also engagement
researchers, and policymakers 161
research evidence 33, 171
  see also evidence
research–policy relations 28–30
'Research Quality Framework'
  (Australia) 15
research translation 139, 140
resources 52–3, 60
returns on investment 106, 198
rewards 40, 48–50, 165–6, 167, 168–9,
  196–7, 200–1
rhetoric, and evidence 192, 193
rigour 185, 186, 189, 203
rituals of verification 111
Rivett, G. 111
'role distance' 70
Russell Group universities, on impact
  case studies 51

S

Sabatier, P.A. 164

Sage, D. 25
Said, Edward 44–5, 118, 131
salesperson pitch 191
Sartre, Jean-Paul 117
Savage, M. 120–1, 136
scepticism 91
science 77–8, 95–6, 101, 112,
      153, 188
Science and Innovation Investment
      Framework 21–2
Science and Technology Facilities
      Council (STFC) 142
Science Foundation Ireland 16
'science in policy' 138
science policy 138
science–policy boundary 145
Scientific and Industrial Research,
      Department of (UK) 17
scientific capital 185
'segregation for elevation' 184
self-importance 193
serendipity 72–3
Seventh Framework Programme of the
      European Union (FP7) 16
SIAMPI 16, 36
Slater, T. 45
Smith, K.E. 27, 31, 36, 38, 47–8,
      125, 136
   on 2* outputs 49
   on 'flexians' 193
   on health inequalities 163
   on institutionalisation 40
   and 'ladder of impact' 75–6
   on links between smoking and lung
      cancer 51
   on reifying traditional elites 53–4
   on research-policy relations 28–9
smoking 50, 51
social change 33
social contract 27
social contract for science 90–1
Social Exclusion Unit 19
social science, concern with academic
      independence 91–2
societal impacts 16
'soft' skills 126
'splintered logic' 150
stakeholder engagement 141–2
STAR METRICS 16
start-up companies 78

Stern Review 4, 23, 196
Stewart, E. 31, 36, 38, 47–8, 51, 53–4
   on 2* outputs 49
   and 'ladder of impact' 75–6
stories 36, 125, 126
   see also narratives
storyboarding 37
'strategic role of ignorance' 125, 201–2
superstars 202, 203
supporters, enthusiastic 169–73,
      179–80
sweeteners, natural 47
Swinnerton-Dyer, Peter 17
symbolic evidence 39–40
   see also evidence
symphonic social science 120–1
syntheses of evidence 48

T

tactical model 38
'Taking Stock: A Summary of
      ESRC's Work to Evaluate the
      Impact of Research on Policy and
      Practice' 140
target audiences 76–8, 82
targets 80–5
technology 76–8
Terama et al 104
thalidomide 47
theoretical challenge to research
      impact 28–30
theoretical work 201
'a theory of change' 188
time, and impact 31, 32
time limits 51–2
Times Higher Education 23, 25, 27, 41
tobacco companies 50
training on achieving impact 48
'transitional' knowledge 73
transparency 203
trust 171, 198
'two communities' thesis 138

U

UCL (University College
      London) 104
UCU petition 23–4
UK Research Councils 22, 24, 27
UKRI 14, 21, 22, 24, 48, 49, 202, 204
unexpected impacts 72–3

Unit of Assessment panels 22
USA 16
user assessors 187–92
UWE (University of West of
    England) 42, 56, 63

V

value, of impact and engagement 40,
    110–11, 186–7, 203

W

Warry Report 20–1
Watermeyer, R. 3, 39, 40, 42,
    53, 57, 61
  on 'army of impact administrators' 36
  on 'competitive accountability' 198
  on public engagement 54–5, 103,
    113

researching impact 'full-time
    occupation' 52
  on Warry Report 21
Weber, Max 44
Weiss, C. 31
Wellcome Trust 100, 102, 108–9
White Paper, 1993 19
Wilkinson, C. 42, 63
Williams, G. 41, 42, 45, 55–6, 57, 58
Williams, K. 15
Wilson, James Q. 120
'window dressing' 191
women, underrepresented in case
    studies 56–7

Y

Yarrow, E. 56